DATE DUE

FE 5 02			
DE 18 07			

DEMCO 38-296

SOUTH AFRICA'S DESTABILIZATION OF ZIMBABWE, 1980–89

South Africa's Destabilization of Zimbabwe, 1980–89

John Dzimba
Lecturer in International Politics
National University of Lesotho

6XS and London
the world

A catalogue record for this book is available from the British Library.

ISBN 0–333–71369–9

First published in the United States of America 1998 by
ST. MARTIN'S PRESS, INC.,
Scholarly and Reference Division,
175 Fifth Avenue, New York, N.Y. 10010

ISBN 0–312–17669–4

Library of Congress Cataloging-in-Publication Data
Dzimba, John.
South Africa's destabilization of Zimbabwe, 1980–89 / John Dzimba.
p.   cm.
Includes bibliographical references and index.
ISBN 0–312–17669–4
1. Political stability—Zimbabwe.   2. Political stability–
–Economic aspects—Zimbabwe.   3. Social stability—Zimbabwe.
4. Zimbabwe—Foreign relations—South Africa.   5. South Africa–
–Foreign relations—Zimbabwe.   I. Title.
DT2996.D95 1997
968.06—dc21
                                  97–19534
                                     CIP

This book is printed on paper suitable for recycling and made from fully managed and sustained forest sources.

10   9   8   7   6   5   4   3   2   1
07   06   05   04   03   02   01   00   99   98

Printed in Great Britain by
The Ipswich Book Company Ltd
Ipswich, Suffolk

In memory of
my father and brother

Contents

Preface

In adopting the policy of destabilization of Zimbabwe, South Africa aimed at achieving certain political and economic objectives. These included weakening SADCC's efforts to isolate South Africa, blocking Zimbabwe's policies of Socialism and reconciliation (so as to prevent it from being a multiracial state), creating a buffer against sanctions by constraining Zimbabwe publicly from supporting international sanctions against South Africa, and ensuring that there was no ANC or PAC threat. To what extent did South Africa achieve these objectives and to what degree did the policy of destabilization prove to be a success or a failure? In what way did destabilization influence political developments in Zimbabwe, notably its political unity and the ruling party's Marxist and Socialist goals? These questions are central to this book and a conclusion will be reached as to whether South Africa's destabilization of Zimbabwe was a success or a failure.

This study is an attempt to understand the development of South Africa's destabilization policy from 1980 to 1989. In particular, the study tries to identify and analyse the issues which have been reflected in the formulation and shaping of that policy.

The study examines the implications of Pretoria's policy of destabilization towards Zimbabwe, Pretoria's political intentions, and why Pretoria considered Zimbabwe's independence a threat to its economic and political interests. Zimbabwe's response to its ambivalent relationship with its aggressive and powerful neighbour is also examined.

Chapter 1 offers an analysis of South Africa's regional policy of Total Strategy. It explains how the strategy evolved, and identifies the changes that took place in the regional and domestic circumstances which acted both as the causes and result of it. The chapter critically assesses the conditions giving rise to the destabilization policy, the objectives of the policy and the application of the policy.

Chapter 2 examines the reasons why South Africa adopted this policy, its implications and political intentions. The chapter sets out the main goals South Africa hoped to achieve and explains in detail the methods used.

Chapter 3 analyses Zimbabwe's defence and security policy in the context of the South African threat. It examines the politics of Zimbabwe's defence, its internal security problems and Mugabe's response to the crisis.

Chapter 4 looks at South Africa's tactics in sabotaging the Zimbabwean economy by disrupting its transport system. It examines the political and economic leverage South Africa had over Zimbabwe and how South Africa used this leverage to neutralize Zimbabwean policies. Zimbabwe's options and response to these economic pressures are also examined. In addition this chapter seeks to draw out the positive and negative aspects of the South African destabilization of Zimbabwe.

Chapters 5 and 6 examine and interpret the economic consequences of destabilization in Zimbabwe. The impact of destabilization on Zimbabwe's internal political order and its influence upon the political development that took place are analysed. Chapter 6 critically assesses Zimbabwe's failure to implement effective economic policies.

Chapter 7 gives an evaluation of South Africa's achievements and failures with regard to its policy of destabilization of Zimbabwe. It puts forward the argument that the policy failed to achieve its main objectives, although it had some significant successes, such as the Nkomati Accord with Mozambique in 1986. The chapter will, in conclusion, address the reasons why in 1989 Pretoria abandoned the destabilization of Zimbabwe.

Acknowledgements

I would first and foremost like to thank Professor Helen O'Neil and Professor Dan Keohane, for their guidance, and endless kindness and encouragement in the working out of this book. My thanks are also due to the following: to all staff members of the Department of Politics at University College Dublin and Department of International Relations at Keele University, especially Professor Andrew Linklater and Mrs M. Groppe.

Thanks to my parents, sisters and brothers, and the Irish government for their personal and financial support. Thanks to the Brady family, Nissreena Abughannam, Tsietso Motsoane, and all my friends for their inspiration and support in times of hardship. Finally to Professor Edmund Hill for his helpful comments in the early stages of my work on the book.

I extend my gratitude to the students and the staff in the Department of Politics at the National University of Lesotho, where I taught for a year, in helping me to shape this research work. I would like to dedicate this work, however imperfect it may be, to my brother Alois Ushe Dzimba who died in the Zimbabwean struggle for independence, and who had been always supportive and encouraged me to learn.

List of Abbreviations

AFZ	Air Force of Zimbabwe
ANC	African National Congress
ARDA	Agricultural and Rural Development Authority
ARMSCOR	Armaments Development and Manufacturing Corporation
BCG	Beira Corridor Group
BCP	Basutoland Congress Party
BLEA	Bankline East Africa
BLS	Botswana, Lesotho and Swaziland
BMATT	British Military Advisory and Training Team
BNP	Basutoland National Party
BOP	Balance of Payments
BOSS	Bureau of State Security
CBI	Confederation of British Industry
CFU	Commercial Farmers' Union
CFM	Cambinos de Ferro de Mozambique
CGIC	Credit Guarantee Insurance Corporation
CIO	Central Intelligence Organization
CONSAS	Constellation of Southern African States
CP	Conservative Party
CZI	Confederation of Zimbabwe Industries
DLMA	Direct Local Market Allocation
EAD	Expressa Austral de Desenvolvimento
FLS	Frontline States
FNLA	National Front for the Liberation of Angola
FRELIMO	Front for the Liberation of Mozambique
HNP	Herstigte Nasionale Party
IDC	Industry Development Corporation
LLA	Lesotho Liberation Army
MFEPD	Ministry of Finance, Economic Planning and Development
MNC	multinational companies
MNR	Mozambique National Resistance (also called RENAMO)
MPLA	Popular Movement for the Liberation of Angola
NIS	National Intelligence Service

NP	National Party
NRZ	National Railways of Zimbabwe
OAU	Organization for African Unity
ODI	Overseas Development Institute
PAC	Pan Africanist Congress
PF	Patriotic Front
PF-ZAPU	Patriotic Front Zimbabwe African People's Union
PTA	Preferential Trade Area
RENAMO	Mozambique National Resistance (also known as MNR)
RRF	Rapid Reaction Force
SAAF	South African Air Force
SABC	South Africa Broadcasting Corporation
SACU	South African Customs Union
SADCC	Southern African Development Coordination Conference
SADF	South African Defence Force
SAMID	South African Military Intelligence Directorate
SAPEM	*Southern Africa Political and Economic Monthly*
SAS	Special Air Service
SATCC	Southern Africa Transport and Communication Commission
SATS	South African Transport Services
SDR	Social Domestic Resources
SATU	South African Trade Unions
SSC	State Security Council
SWAPO	South West Africa People's Organization
TOA	Transport Operator's Association
TRC	Tete Road Corridor
UANC	United African National Congress
UDF	United Democratic Front
UDI	Unilateral Declaration of Independence
UN	United Nations
UNITA	National Union for the Total Liberation of Angola
WBMIGA	World Bank's Multilateral Investment Guarantee Agency
ZANLA	Zimbabwe African National Liberation Army
ZANU(PF)	Zimbabwe African National Union (Patriotic Front)
ZAPU	Zimbabwe African People's Union
ZDF	Zimbabwe Defence Force
ZIFA	Zimbabwean Freedom Army

ZIMCORD	Zimbabwe Conference for Reconstruction and Development
ZIPRA	Zimbabwean People's Revolutionary Army
ZISCO	Zimbabwe Iron and Steel Company
ZNA	Zimbabwean National Army
ZPM	Zimbabwe People's Militia
ZSS	Zimbabwe Shipping Services

1 The Background of Destabilization: South Africa's Regional Policy, 1977–89

The primary purpose of this chapter is to analyse the causes that led to the development of the destabilization policy. Destabilization was the crucial element in the overall policy of 'Total Strategy' evolved prior to 1977 and was transformed into state policy after P.W. Botha became Prime Minister in 1978. Total Strategy was claimed by Pretoria to be the legitimate answer to what it saw as the Total Onslaught, that is, the threat to the South African government not from the rising ferment among its own majority black population, but from the Moscow-led communist conspiracy through regional governments, initially Angola and Mozambique and later Zimbabwe.[1] Total Strategy was Pretoria's response to a constellation of woes: developments following the uprising in Soweto in 1976, economic recession, the collapse of Portuguese colonialism, the fruitless South African invasion and débâcle in Angola during 1975–6, the collapse of its policy of detente and its growing isolation from its traditional Western allies because of their increased concern about majority rule in South Africa and their call for sanctions against it.[2]

The chapter offers an analysis of the basic system and dynamics of South Africa's regional policy of Total Strategy. It seeks to explain how the strategy evolved, the changes that took place in the regional and domestic circumstances which acted both as the cause and result of it. The objective is to reveal the interconnections between events and developments in Southern Africa and the thrust of the strategy as it changed to respond to changes in the environment. Its aim is to elucidate what the reasons were for its adoption, what its objectives were and the methods used in its implementation in the region. The chapter will argue that destabilization was a reflection in the first instance of the interests of the South African ruling class (essentially the Afrikaner group) to perpetuate the type of state it had created and accordingly to maintain the socio-economic privileges which accrued

1

from that group's control of the state. It will also illustrate the impact of the different forms of destabilization in the region: economic, military, and political. It is important to note that Total Strategy has never been a simple militarist strategy but a combination of political/diplomatic, economic, social/psychological and security.[3] The generals themselves have repeatedly stressed that the survival of South African apartheid depended primarily on the development of an adequate political response, both internally and in the region, and not mere mindless application of military might.[4]

However, in order for us to understand the context in which the destabilization policy was formulated we must know the characteristics that bound the region together. The historical, economic and political factors are the key elements that have together contributed towards the definition of the sub-region as we know it today.

1.1 DEFINING SOUTHERN AFRICA AS A REGION

Southern Africa has been defined (broadly) as South Africa plus the ten countries of the Southern African Development Coordination Conference (SADCC). These are Angola, Botswana, Lesotho, Malawi, Mozambique, Namibia, Swaziland, Tanzania, Zambia and Zimbabwe. Despite some incongruities, this definition is widely accepted as adequate for most practical purposes.[5] However, the development of the above-mentioned countries as a region was the result of a colonization process at the hands of Europeans whose main objective was that of creating white dominions in Southern Africa. From this developed the socio-economic and political structures that arose out of a capitalist system and sought to integrate the entire sub-region into the international capitalist system. To some extent, it is difficult to understand the history and development of Southern Africa except in terms of the central position of South Africa. To begin with, there is the inner core of Southern Africa that has developed and become defined around that axis in the colonization process in which South Africa is the linchpin. We refer here to the BLS countries (Botswana, Lesotho and Swaziland), Namibia which had been occupied by South Africa since 1915, and Zimbabwe which had been colonized by British settlers who came through South Africa itself. Because of the recriminations that led to serious conflict[6] – the Boer War – between Boer and Briton in South Africa towards the close of the nineteenth century, the new colony of Southern Rhodesia did not become a fifth province of the Union of South Africa that was established in 1910.

The white settlers of Southern Rhodesia voted in 1922 in a referendum to stay separate from South Africa, and thereby attained 'self-governing' colonial status in 1923. Through this colony, the British formulated the idea of the Central African Federation which included what became Malawi, Zambia and Zimbabwe. Formed as it was in 1953, at a time when African nationalism was becoming more organized in that part of the world, the Federation was doomed when the African nationalist movements in the three countries coordinated their efforts to thwart the imperialist plan by calling for the independence of Malawi, Zambia and Zimbabwe. This was to be a counterpoint to the Afrikaner-dominated South African state. In turn, the latter would reach its apex in 1948, and send a clear message to African nationalist aspirations in the three countries that the dream of a white dominion was to be kept alive. The Federation had also developed on the strength of the British imperialist interests in the area. Hence the development of the railway line at the turn of the century had linked all three countries and, in turn, gave them access to both South Africa through Botswana and to the ports of Beira and Lourenço Marques (Maputo) in Portuguese East Africa (Mozambique). Likewise, the network of roads and telecommunication links; and, subsequently, the enhanced development of the energy sector through the establishment of the Kariba Power Station on the Zambezi River in the late 1950s. All these and other developments became the obvious agency for economic and industrial developments in the Federation, facilitating the exploitation of mineral and agricultural production as major sources of the export trade to Europe and the northern hemisphere in general. Even though most Africans were opposed to the Federation of Rhodesia and Nyasaland, the ten years of its existence had considerably enhanced a process of integrating the societies of these countries, a process that had begun many centuries before colonization. Southern Rhodesia became the centre of white settler economic and political power, benefiting greatly from the material and mainly labour resources of the other two colonies, and from the neighbouring territory of Mozambique. As shall be seen shortly, this process in itself necessitated the movement of peoples between and within the countries of the Federation of Rhodesia and Nyasaland and beyond.

In the early 1960s, leading up to the declaration of the Unilateral Declaration of Independence (UDI), Rhodesia was largely ruled from Britain under the auspices of the Federation of Rhodesia and Nyasaland. After the dissolution of the Federation (1963) and UDI (1965), the white settler government found itself compelled to rely on their erstwhile opponent of yestertimes, the Afrikaner-dominated apartheid state. Before that, South African external relations were more concentrated in that configuration that expressed itself through the South African Customs Union (SACU) of which Botswana, Lesotho and Swaziland are still the other members, with the addition of independent Namibia.

The two broad strands, the SACU and Federation, in this colonization process of Southern Africa were, of course, inter-related. They account in part for much of what we hail today as projecting an integrated and unified Southern African region. Only two of the current SADCC countries fell outside the economic tentacles of either of these strands, Angola and Tanzania, but then only for historical and geographical reasons. Although a Portuguese colony, Mozambique had from the beginning of the century been an outreach of the South African economy. Maputo was an important port in the South African economic configuration, completely dependent economically on neighbouring South Africa and Southern Rhodesia, both of which countries in particular used it as a holiday and pleasure resort for the affluent white settlers. As the liberation struggle was intensified in both countries in the course of the 1960s and 1970s, the white settlers in Southern Rhodesia and Mozambique were forced to depend on South Africa, economically and militarily. In keeping with its own anti-guerrilla strategy, the South African state regarded as vital the need to develop a *cordon sanitaire* that included not only support for Rhodesia but also an alliance with the Portuguese colonialists in their war against the guerrillas in Mozambique and Angola.

But it should also be noted that South Africa contributed towards white settlement at the turn of this century in such countries as Namibia, Zimbabwe, Zambia and even Kenya. Just prior to World War I, most of the whites in the Kenyan highlands had come from South Africa,[7] with the intention of creating a 'white man's country' modelled on South Africa. Furthermore, South Africa provided almost one-half of the Europeans in Zambia during the colonial period, compared with only a quarter who came from the United Kingdom.[8] This partly explains why the Zambian mining industry developed *pari passu* with the South African economy, being largely dependent on South Africa as much for the supply of mining equipment and machinery as for skills, management and general development during most of the colonial period and even well into the post-independence period.

South Africa's economic dominance in the region originated and developed from the context of the history and development of Southern Africa as a sub-system of European colonialism. Various studies[9] have highlighted the economic tentacles that bind most Southern African countries to South Africa. The South African transport and communications system became central to most Southern African countries in their import–export trade with those outside the African continent; in particular with six of these countries landlocked, almost all were heavily dependent on South Africa's route to the sea. Most of these countries have been dependent upon South Africa for the import of manufactured goods, particularly food, industrial machinery and equipment. South Africa has considerable investments in most Southern African countries, covering the various sectors of mining, manufacturing, railways and hydro-electric construction. In addition, these dependent relationships in the field of South African investment in neighbouring territories were not confined to the formal indicators such as the equity ownership of shares. For the various informal mechanisms of economic control by way of management, sales and technical contracts and transfer pricing, though less obvious, were more important.

There is also the question of migrant labour from the neighbouring Southern African countries working in South Africa. There were about 600 000[10] such migrant labourers in South Africa by 1970; by 1985 the number had fallen to 371 008.[11] The important point to emphasize, however, is that countries such as Botswana, Lesotho and Swaziland were heavily dependent economically upon this 'export' of labour. These same countries depended heavily on their membership of the Southern African Customs Union (SACU). Thus, their economies were virtually extensions of South Africa's. In this category must also be included Namibia and Mozambique. But Zimbabwe became increasingly dependent on South Africa, particularly after UDI. One indication of that legacy of dependence that developed on the basis of the siege and vagaries of the UDI period, was the growth in the volume of Rhodesian traffic passing through South African ports, from only 10 per cent of the total exports (before the closure of the Rhodesian border with Mozambique) in 1975 to 90 per cent in 1985.[12] As already explained, prior to the UDI period, the white Rhodesian settler colonialists had endeavoured to develop independently from the Afrikaner dominated South African state. But it is a reflection of the UDI period that up to the time of Zimbabwean independence,[13] South Africa's investment in Zimbabwe was greater than in any other Southern African economy. Furthermore, five of Zimbabwe's top ten companies are either controlled by or associated with South African companies. But it is important to emphasise the other aspect with regard to this issue of South African dominance in Southern Africa. This refers to South Africa's military and external strategy in the sub-region, a strategy that developed on the strength of both South Africa's Western-backed economic might and the policy of the United States in Southern Africa.[14]

However, in the period prior to the intensification of the African Nationalist struggle in Southern Africa, the concept of a Southern African sub-system had received great attention within international politics because of its economic importance to the West. Thus, there was an evident relationship between analyses that highlighted this concept of a sub-system and those policy-makers[15] in the international arena who believed Southern Africa to be different from the rest of the African continent. The policy of the US and Britain[16] toward Southern Africa made South Africa a regional centre for the maintenance of their economic, political and strategic interests in the region. That was certainly the role in which the South African state was to be viewed in the West throughout most of the 1970s and 1980s.

The history of South Africa's external relations during this period is well known as a record of aggression and destabilization that cost its neighbours in excess of US$10 billion between 1980 and 1985.[17] This figure excludes the consequences to the region of extra defence expenditure, higher transport and energy costs, lost exports and decline in tourism, the problem of refugees, reduced production and lost economic growth.

Essentially, South Africa's objective had been to try and roll back the liberation process; to forestall for an extended period the possibility of black majority rule in South Africa by intimidating the neighbouring black states, seeking to extend its influence throughout Africa by its 'dialogue' policy of the 1970s, and attempting to impose an 'economic community' in form of the Constellation of Southern African States (CONSAS). Announced in March 1979, the CONSAS proposal sought to develop a common approach in the fields of security and political matters between South Africa, the 'homeland', members of SACU and in due course, other countries in the region. This was South Africa's version of regional cooperation, a spectre that would have pre-empted SADCC were it not for the changing balance of forces associated with the demise of the apartheid state.

1.2 THE CONCEPT OF DESTABILIZATION

The 1980–89 destabilization of Zimbabwe and other states in Southern Africa was the product of a long period of political preparation and intensive militarization in South Africa, dating back to the 1970s. This is clearly shown by Pretoria's 1975–76 invasion of Angola, when together with the US[18] they unsuccessfully tried to defeat the ruling party, the Popular Movement for the Liberation of Angola (MPLA) and ensure success for the National Union for the Total Liberation of Angola (UNITA)/National Front for the Liberation of Angola (FNLA) at the time of Angola's independence in November 1975.[19]

However, we might as well ask the question, what is destabilization? The phenomenon of destabilization is nothing new in international politics. Destabilization includes cultural, political, economic and military measures taken by one or more governments individually or collectively against another government in order to overthrow it, or to force it to do their bidding.[20] In other words it is the desire on the part of one government to actively seek to overthrow or to weaken another government and it stems from that government's intense dislike for the other's policies. South Africa's destabilization policies against countries in the region had a class and ideological basis. In this context destabilization was a weapon for the defence of the immediate interests of the Afrikaner-dominated South African ruling class in their attempts to safeguard their social privileges and property interests.

Destabilization may consist of either covert or overt acts, or combine both covert and overt acts (as we shall see in the case of South Africa) but is short of a full-scale war. A good formulation of destabilization is that given by Patel:

destabilisation is a complex of political, economic and military activities, separately and combined, short of a formal declaration of war used by South Africa against independent African states.... Thus South Africa's regional destabilisation policy is a policy of war by another name, it is an 'undeclared war' but war nevertheless, an act of state terrorism by the apartheid state against its neighbours, complemented as it is by state terrorism inside South Africa against the people of South Africa....[21]

However, looking at the conflict in the decade 1980–89, the issues at stake were clear. Pretoria was fighting to preserve apartheid's capitalist domination and imperialist hegemony in the sub-continent. Meanwhile the people of Southern Africa were fighting to extricate themselves from the exploitative system of apartheid.

1.3 CONDITIONS GIVING RISE TO THE DESTABILIZATION POLICY

(a) The Collapse of Portuguese Rule, 1974

The decision by South Africa to defend the apartheid system and turn Southern Africa into a battlefield was a direct response to developments in the region from the early 1970s into the 1980s. The collapse of Portuguese rule on 25 April 1974 led to the transformation of the political landscape in Southern Africa.[22] It transformed the internal politics of regional states. It affected the relations between states in the region. And it increased and altered the role within the region of powerful extra-regional actors. For policy-makers in Pretoria these changes in Southern Africa's political landscape were truly seismic; it meant Pretoria now faced three African-ruled states (Angola, Mozambique and Zambia) opposed to South Africa's apartheid system, and potentially a fourth (Zimbabwe or Namibia). The Soviet Union and its ally Cuba became deeply involved politically and militarily in the Southern African region. The support for the African National Congress both among South Africa's black population and by the governments of neighbouring states increased dramatically. The South African government began to mould its foreign policy to adjust to the new regional realities. Although perhaps initially only a series of *ad hoc* manoeuvres, these policy adjustments emerged by the early 1980s as a comprehensive strategy for Southern Africa.

(b) *Cordon Sanitaire* Policy in the Region as a Security Shield around South Africa

For South Africa, the Portuguese coup was little short of a disaster, especially since it caught the Pretoria government unawares. Despite the fact that there was still Rhodesia to count on, the coup introduced a breakdown of its *cordon sanitaire* (the ring of buffer states around South Africa).[23] The maintenance of the *cordon sanitaire* was a key component of South Africa's foreign policy. This was meant to safeguard South Africa's security and the preservation of white control and domination.

South African cordon policy began with Dr Malan. Malan's security policy for South Africa had three related dimensions, namely an African defence pact with the colonial governments; getting South Africa involved in a military pact with the Western powers, and resurrecting South Africa's unrelenting effort to take over the three British High Commission territories.[24] At the time the Nationalists came to power in South Africa (1948) most of Africa was still under colonial rule. There was therefore no threat to South Africa at that time. When Malan talked about a cordon policy as a key diplomatic front, what he had in mind was to talk to the neighbouring states and not to black leaders within South Africa. From this it can be deduced that the diplomatic activities he launched were intended for future security (and in this sense it was future planning) and were geared towards the British and Portuguese colonial administrators rather than at the black nationalist leaders. What Malan wanted was to develop a cooperative diplomatic relationship with colonial governments that would facilitate the process of slowing down or arresting the decolonization process which was gathering momentum and moving southwards towards the South African borders.[25] He sought to persuade the colonial governments to work with South Africa to prevent the growth and proliferation of nationalism, thereby securing a *cordon sanitaire* for South Africa. Successive Nationalist Party governments developed and refined this idea further, to the extent that there is evidence that South Africa gave military and logistical support to the Smith regime[26] and the Portuguese in Angola and Mozambique.[27]

However, apart from this, Malan tried to get the West to view South Africa as militarily important, and worth supporting. Vale observes that 'South Africa was seen as a valued, on the spot partner...to the West.'[28] This meant that South Africa could not be abandoned no matter how bad or objectionable its domestic policies were.[29] The perceived importance of South Africa to the West was underlined, as Vale notes, by a US National Security report in 1969. Vales writes:

There seems to be no underestimating the importance of [South Africa's strategic importance] in Western circles.... The clearest enunciation was...the 1969 US National Security Report (NSSM 39) which urged the...government to 'tilt' towards the Portuguese, the Rhodesian and the South African minority regimes because they represented an indefinite picture of stability.[30]

South Africa's desire to obtain land to shield itself goes back a long way. It is also a matter that occupied the attention of all South Africa's Prime Ministers until Botswana, Lesotho and Swaziland got their independence from Britain in the 1960s. Since the creation of the Union of South Africa, South Africa's objective was to build a *cordon sanitaire*, using as its core the three British High Commission territories of Botswana, Lesotho and Swaziland. Several attempts were made by almost every South African Prime Minister who came into office to incorporate these three territories into South Africa. But the British government remained resolute in its refusal to accede to South Africa's demands. Instead, they proceeded to prepare the three countries for full independence (Botswana and Lesotho got their independence in 1966, and Swaziland got its independence in 1968) with guarantees for assistance in the event of any clash with South Africa.[31] Had it succeeded in getting Britain to grant it the territories, the move would have been a major political coup. The three territories would have played a key role in South Africa's eventual Bantustan policy. The importance of these territories to South Africa were spelt out by Dr Verwoerd; talking to the Orange Free State Congress of his party in 1961, he stated simply that:

> until recently it had been assumed that the territories would one day become part of South Africa's Bantu areas, and Africans from them had therefore been accorded the same privileges as natives from South Africa's own native territories.[32]

With these territories, South Africa's policy of granting 'independence' to parts of its territory, even if racially inspired, would have been sufficiently compelling for the international community to accord it recognition. From that two things would have resulted. Firstly, it would have succeeded in creating a huge tract of Bantustan territories dispersed around South Africa. Secondly, and crucially, it would have had the 'advantage of providing a semblance of legitimacy to the entire Bantustan project by enabling the "racial" division of land in a greater South Africa to be presented as a "fair" 50:50, instead of the existing 87% white and 13% black division introduced by apartheid'.[33]

As the three territories were approaching independence, South Africa intervened in a clandestine manner. Since the South African government tried to incorporate these countries into South Africa and failed, it was determined to mould the character of their internal politics and future. It made sure that no radical or hostile political party acceded to power. In a carefully worked out plan conceived and executed by the Broederbond,[34] the Verwoerd regime supported 'safe' parties contesting elections which later formed governments in Lesotho and Swaziland. Only in Botswana did their efforts and plans founder. In Lesotho, South Africa provided financial and organizational support to the Basutoland National Party (BNP) of Chief Leabua Jonathan to prevent the Basutoland Congress Party (BCP), which it regarded as radical, from gaining power.[35] In the event, the BNP scraped home with a one-seat parliamentary majority.[36] Why was this so important? Geldenhuys' observation puts South Africa's activities into context. He points out that South Africa would do anything to preserve its security and the survival of white supremacy: '... the overriding, immutable and non-negotiable objective of national policies was the maintenance of a white nation in South Africa'.[37]

In Swaziland the Broederbond's intervention was even more revealing about the extent to which the South African government was willing to go to achieve its goal of installing compliant governments in the region. Not happy with the parties that were there, it proceeded to form from scratch a new party, the Imbokodvo National Movement [the 'King's' party]. This party subsequently went on to win the elections.[38] The overall effect of these manoeuvres was to ensure that when the three territories finally attained their independence from the British, they remained in various degrees amenable to South Africa's policy framework. In addition to these political leverages, there was and continues to exist today the all important economic dominance that South Africa exercised, through these countries' membership of the South Africa dominated economic structures of the SACU and the Rand Monetary Area.[39] These economic linkages gave South Africa enormous influence and leverage over the three countries. As Hanlon[40] has argued, these structures were never intended to benefit the three countries, despite the impression projected. Rather they were established to bring them within South Africa's control and sphere of influence. With these arrangements firmly in place, South Africa felt sufficiently secure with the immediate neighbouring states to launch a more audacious diplomatic offensive against the growing OAU membership.

John Vorster came to power in the late 1960s; in 1967 he launched a dramatic foreign policy initiative, the 'Outward Movement',[41] which was limited to the immediate neighbours. The Outward initiative had three major objectives. The first one was expansive; the second defensive, and the third aimed at getting international recognition.[42] The expansive aspect of the policy was responding to South Africa's long-held view that the defence of South Africa begins at the Zambezi river. Vorster's Zambezi river boundary represented a substantial scaling down on what some of his predecessors considered effective boundaries. The expansionist General Smuts had gone further north. He had argued that Kenya and Tanzania divided South Africa's boundaries and that '[we] cannot wait until the enemy reaches the Limpopo'.[43] This literally meant that the best defence for South Africa was forward defence (offensive strategy). The defensive objective reflected the government's hope for peaceful coexistence and good neighbourliness. The objective was based on the assumption that once a country was won over, it would cease to be a security risk. Thirdly, and no less important, the policy sought to improve South Africa's image among its immediate neighbours. The long-term view, regarding this objective, was that recognition by its antagonist neighbours, once achieved, would have a snowball effect, that is, that it would lead to immediate and unconditional international acceptance and respectability.[44]

The Outward initiative had several dimensions. These are briefly explored here to show what they were and how they fitted into South Africa's overall cordon policy.

(i) A Diplomatic Dialogue with Black States: Vorster's concern was to attempt to win recognition from his neighbours. The aim of the policy was to divide the OAU through weaning off some of its members. He sought to arrest and if possible to reverse the hostile stance taken by it in its own forums as well as at the UN. In short, he wanted to establish a *modus vivendi* with the members of the OAU.[45] But, despite some initial successes, the policy ran aground.[46] The OAU preempted South Africa's moves through its decision to adopt the 1969 Lusaka Manifesto. The manifesto, which was later adopted by the United Nations,[47] committed the OAU member countries to supporting the armed struggle in the region, and meant that they could therefore no longer engage in diplomatic intercourse with South Africa. The OAU condemned Vorster's dialogue strategy as a

stunt to confuse public opinion in Africa and to divide African states. The OAU feared that if the strategy was not countered, it would lead to the end of South Africa's isolation.

(ii) The Non-Aggression Pacts: Another way Vorster tried to secure South Africa's borders, in order to counter the 'communist threat', was to try to get neighbouring countries to sign non-aggression treaties with South Africa. This policy was launched in 1970.[48] However, the first non-aggression treaty was not signed until 1976, and only with the Transkei, one of its Bantustans.[49] None of the independent neighbouring states, for whom the policy had been intended, signed during this period until 1982 when Swaziland secretly signed a peace treaty,[50] followed by Mozambique, who signed the Nkomati agreement in 1984.[51] In fact, generally speaking, Vorster's Outward policy failed to achieve its goals. Consequently, when Portuguese rule disintegrated in 1974, it threw the whole policy of a *cordon sanitaire* into disarray.

(iii) The Regional Diplomatic Offensive: There were strong indications that with the Southern African situation rapidly approaching a crisis point, the military strategists and the Bureau of State Security (BOSS) not only sought active participation in policy decision-making but also started to demand a more pragmatic regional policy. Davies and O'Meara have credited the source of Vorster's 1974 diplomatic initiatives to BOSS.[52] Nevertheless this policy was cautious and slowly implemented. It was launched in February 1974, when Vorster announced his intentions to build a 'power bloc' of independent states in Southern Africa. Later, he introduced the concept of a 'constellation' of independent states to be bound together through economic ties, forming a united front against common enemies.[53] Besides these moves, Vorster tried to repair the *cordon sanitaire* through seeking peaceful settlements in Rhodesia and Namibia.

The initiative on Rhodesia was aimed at President Kaunda of Zambia, who was seen as a key figure in the Rhodesian problem. The idea was to resolve the Rhodesian issue between South Africa and Zambia. Regarding Namibia, Vorster arranged for the Turnhalle Constitutional Conference in September 1975 which brought together representatives of all ethnic groups for the first time, with a view to have them draw up Namibia's political future.[54] Representatives of SWAPO were excluded, and because of this, it failed to win international support. The biggest achievement by Vorster's diplomatic initiatives was the Victoria Falls Conference in August 1975 between the Smith regime and the nationalists.[55] The architects of the historic meeting were Vorster and Kaunda, and both men were present at the talks. Vorster delivered Ian Smith and Kaunda the nationalists. The former had, prior to the conference, made some minor concessions in August 1975. He had withdrawn South Africa's police units which had until then been in Rhodesia to bolster the Smith regime. The exercise was meant to show the nationalists and their supporters that they could achieve a lot more through the negotiation process than through confrontation.[56] The conference failed to resolve the Rhodesian issue. The collapse of this dialogue also signalled the end of detente. The factors responsible for the failure of this initiative were South Africa's invasion of Angola in 1975 and the brutal repression of the Soweto uprising in 1976.

(c) The Political Implications of the Portuguese Coup

The collapse of the *cordon* which had safeguarded South Africa's borders created a security crisis. The breakdown of the *cordon sanitaire* exposed South Africa's flanks to the liberation struggle. In other words, South Africa became vulnerable in a way for which it had not prepared. The South African policy-makers were aware of the seriousness of the threat posed by these developments to their security.

In general terms, the coup had three major effects on the region. Firstly, there was a 'demonstration effect' on the liberation movements in Zimbabwe, Namibia and South Africa. They concluded that if liberation movements could gain government in Angola and Mozambique, it could also be their own case in the future.[57] They believed that, by intensifying the armed struggle, they would be forcing a situation whereby the minority governments in Rhodesia and South Africa would be forced to sue for peace and agree to majority rule. They began to believe that it was possible to gain independence. The Smith regime in Rhodesia was particularly affected by the fall of Portuguese rule in Africa. Hitherto much of Rhodesia's international trade had gone through Mozambique. With Mozambique independent, it was likely that Mozambican routes and ports would be closed to it, if and when the former decided to impose economic sanctions. There was also the security angle to consider. Strategically, the coup added a further 500 km of territory to Rhodesia's already wide defence perimeter.[58] After the coup South Africa had to defend the long border with Mozambique and Angola.

Secondly, the coup had economic and military implications for South Africa. Before the coup, the situation in the region favoured the South African ruling class. South Africa was surrounded by a number of so-called 'buffer' states. To the west were the Portuguese colony of Angola and the South African occupied territory of Namibia. In the centre was the settler-ruled Rhodesia (Zimbabwe) and to the east the Portuguese colony of Mozambique. The economies of all these territories were linked and subordinated to South Africa, as suppliers of labour power, raw materials and/or services (e.g. transport), as well as being markets for South African commodities. During this period South Africa's defence, including that of Namibia, was safeguarded by the Portuguese territories. This had made the threat of liberation war seem far away. After the coup, Namibia became exposed to SWAPO attacks based in Angola. The demise of a buffer zone meant, in effect, that the liberation war had finally arrived at its doorstep. With the independence of Angola and Mozambique, with Zimbabwe's independence in the offering, Pretoria was aware that the South African liberation movements might be provided with military training, material support and territorial sanctuaries by these countries. This would intensify the ability of the liberation movements to carry out effectively acts of sabotage against symbols of governmental power, isolated white farming communities, transportation infrastructures, urban industrial and commercial targets.

The Portuguese coup gave great encouragement to the internal liberation movements against apartheid, which contributed to the Soweto uprising in 1976. The Soweto rebellion had serious international political implications; Pretoria's worry about the possibility of trade embargoes and boycotts, as well as the blocking of access to technology, capital markets, and direct foreign investment, became a reality. South Africa found that the terms of its access to international capital and technology had severely deteriorated. Apart from the international problems, internally South Africa was faced with a more serious problem of violence; in 1979 about 30 incidents[59] involving guerrilla activity had been reported. These included the bombing of property, and clashes between guerrillas and security forces. The security police estimated that there were 4000[60] black South Africans undergoing guerrilla training, which meant that recruitment for military training and insurgency had increased after the Soweto uprising. These events called into question the long-term survival of white minority rule in South Africa.

Thirdly, the coup destroyed the tripartite entente (alliance) between Portugal, Rhodesia and South Africa. The immediate impact of this was that it weakened the 'white rule front'. More importantly, it forced Western governments to reappraise their policies in the area and to seek 'ways and means of returning the territory to legality which would ensure a permanent if less privileged place for the whites in the country'.[61]

For the neighbouring black states, the coup had an equally dramatic impact. It upset, as it did for South Africa and Western governments, all their previous assumptions and strategies. The sudden collapse of Portuguese rule meant that they needed to reassess the new situation and formulate different policies and strategies. They saw opportunities, never before envisaged.[62] For one thing, they realised that the collapse of the *cordon sanitaire* on which South Africa had depended to maintain its hegemony signalled a significant change in the balance of power and the weakening of South Africa's strategic position and that of Rhodesia. There were other considerations.

For Zambia, a landlocked country, the change in the balance of power, in particular the vulnerability of Rhodesia, pointed to the possible change of government in that country. Independence in Rhodesia would have the advantage of reducing Zambia's dependence on the minority governments for its imports and exports and its burden of sanctions and resistance to the Smith regime. The end of the guerrilla war would make it possible for the government to concentrate its efforts and resources on development programmes. Zambia simply did not have the resources or the capacity to do both.

Botswana had similar considerations. A peaceful end to the conflict in Rhodesia could reduce its pervasive dependence on South Africa. It could, instead, increase its economic and political links with its neighbours to the north. It would free it from the costly responsibility of looking after refugees from Rhodesia. Similarly, Mozambique hoped for a chance to get on with the task of developing its shattered economy. After a decade of guerrilla war, the Mozambican economy was dislocated and in a state of neglect. The Frelimo government knew that they could not fully address the problems of development until the Rhodesian conflict was resolved.

South Africa's response to all these possible changes in the region was to look for a comprehensive strategy. In consequence, an attempt was made to search for such a plan. The government examined two options. Option one was backed by the then Prime Minister, Vorster, supported by General Hendrick Van den Bergh, chief of BOSS (Bureau of State Security)[63] and the Ministry of Foreign Affairs. It favoured peaceful coexistence with the emerging states with a proviso to use subtle coercive measures, principally economic, and concealed subversion to bring them into line. The second option, championed by P.W. Botha, then Minister of Defence, and General Magnus Malan, chief of staff of the South African Defence Force (SADF), argued for direct military action against Angola and Mozambique. The aim was to supplant Marxist governments and 'to promote profound political changes'[64] amenable to South Africa's point of view, thus creating a new buffer zone. In the end, the second option won, although it was never given the full range of tactical support it needed to succeed.[65] It is important here to note that although the aim of destabilization was a fundamental shift in the opponents' policies, this did not rule out the option of replacing the existing government with a regime amenable to South Africa's point of view. As D. Geldenhuys observed:

> They may or may not involve structural changes – in effect toppling the regime in power...but certainly would involve major changes in the target's behaviour....At the very least, the destabiliser demands a fundamental shift or reorientation in the target state's policy vis-a-vis the destabiliser.[66]

In South Africa's view a regime would be toppled only if a politically suitable opponent could take over and have the capacity to restore stability in the country. The most striking example of the replacement of a regime is what happened in Lesotho in 1986, when the South African government used economic blockade and supported the army to topple Dr Jonathan's government.[67]

In August 1975, South African forces from bases in Namibia invaded Angola and occupied the hydroelectric dam at Ruacana.[68] Three weeks before independence was declared by the MPLA, South Africa's forces made another push. This time it was a really large invasion with the intention of taking Luanda to prevent an MPLA government. By 11 November the independence of Angola was proclaimed and the invasion was halted.

The reasons for the halting of the invasion were diverse. Firstly, the decision to intervene in Angola proved highly divisive within the South African government.[69] The decision split the government into the two camps of the so-called 'hawks' (defence and SADF establishment) and 'doves' (BOSS and Foreign Affairs). BOSS, the architect of Vorster's detente[70] initiative, and, to a lesser degree Foreign Affairs Hilgard Muller, opposed the military option and favoured, instead, a diplomatic solution (with covert coercive diplomacy). The Defence

Ministry under P.W. Botha and the SADF wanted the military option and argued that forceful military action was the only viable strategy of deterrence. This created a serious policy dispute which resulted in what Grundy describes as 'no clear-cut policy direction'[71] with which to prosecute the war.

In the face of growing international condemnation of South Africa over the invasion, BOSS was able to convince the Prime Minister that the invasion was becoming a diplomatic liability and that it was increasingly being exploited against South Africa.[72] BOSS urged that unless the forces were withdrawn, many countries would be alienated from South Africa and would instead be sympathetic towards the MPLA government. They might even endorse the presence of the Cubans. In the end, this viewpoint prevailed.[73] The second major factor was South Africa's failure to obtain tangible Western support, particularly from the US. Prior to the invasion, South Africa had counted on US support. But this was not realized because of the indecisive American position, 'a result of the interplay among diverse branches and organs of the US government'.[74] At the same time, international pressure was mounting for South Africa to withdraw its forces.

The sending in of technical–military personnel and armaments and the provision of troops by both Cuba and the Soviets to Angola was another factor. This immediately changed the situation significantly. Against a combined force of Angolan and Cuban forces, the South African forces found it difficult to progress any further.[75] By March 1976, all South African forces had withdrawn from Angola.[76] It is important to stress here that South African forces were not defeated by the Angolan-Cuban forces. The truth was that the South African policy-making machinery on the Angola invasion was *ad hoc* and did not work well. Without clear objectives, SADF lacked the necessary political support and clear policy objectives to guide them. They could, therefore, not effectively plan the war although they had enough firepower and manpower to fight and win it.

Botha and the SADF regarded the venture as a military disaster and felt betrayed by the South African Prime Minister. The SADF had not been keen to embark on the venture but once started they wanted to do a good job but were hindered by lack of proper support. They were convinced they would have taken Luanda had they been given the necessary support and policy directives.[77] The result was a serious rift between the SADF high command and the Ministry of Defence on the one hand and the Vorster and Van den Bergh camp on the other. This

division and the Information scandal known as 'Muldergate' effectively split the National Party (NP), undermined Vorster's premiership
and led to his eventual removal from office in 1978.[78]

After the military disaster in Angola, South Africa needed time to
assess the situation and its significance in order to determine its
medium- and long-term strategies. South Africa's strategy was that
of damage limitation and it did not seek confrontation. It sought, for
example, a peaceful settlement in Rhodesia. The reasons for this were
simple and had to do with economic and strategic considerations. For
one thing, Pretoria believed that to establish good relations with the
black governments in Angola and Mozambique was a way of discouraging these states from supporting or giving bases to ANC guerrillas. South Africa's economic interaction with Mozambique was
fairly substantial. It relied on Mozambique for electricity from the
Cabora Bassa dam. It also needed the use of the Mozambican ports
for a substantial proportion of its international trade, to ease its own
congested ports. There was, in addition, the question of thousands of
migrant workers from Mozambique who provided South Africa with
cheap labour. For these reasons, South Africa felt it needed to maintain stable and friendly relations with that country to avoid the
disruption of such arrangements.

(d) The Psychological Military Implications of the Portuguese Coup

The overthrow of the fascist regime in Portugal in April 1974, followed by the independence of Mozambique and Angola, and the
humiliating end to South African intervention in Angola in 1975–6,
coupled with the advancing liberation movements in Zimbabwe and
Namibia and the Soweto uprising led South Africa to reassess its
military role in the region. South Africa began by expanding its
military capacity and developing new capabilities that would maintain
a solid military balance relative to neighbouring states and other
states in Southern Africa. The defence budget for 1974–5 was almost
50 per cent higher than that of the previous year.[79] By the next year
(1975–6) it was more than double the 1973–4 figure and by 1977–8 it
had reached R 1650 million or over three and a half times the R 472
million of a mere four years earlier.[80] Through the state-owned armaments company, ARMSCOR, a crash armaments development programme was initiated. This had the objective of producing locally
manufactured, highly mobile and long-range weaponry, suitable to
the type of aggressive military interventions experienced in Angola.

The aim was to increase the SADF's capacities as a highly mobile conventional invasion force to be used against neighbouring countries, whilst at the same time raising its capacity to fight a counter insurgency war against guerrilla forces in Namibia and South Africa itself.

Under P.W. Botha's premiership, which started in 1978, the military apparatus continued to be expanded and strengthened. Defence expenditure doubled between the last budget of the Vorster regime of 1977/8 and 1982/3 when it reached a massive R 3068 million.[81] P.W. Botha had worked out and developed the 'counter-insurgency' and intervention capabilities directed at neighbouring states. These included: (i) reconnaissance commandos, specialist units containing a high proportion of mercenaries used for hit-and-run operations such as the Matola raid[82] against ANC residences in Mozambique in 1981; (ii) ethnic battalions, units stationed near the borders of neighbouring states composed of black soldiers of the same language/cultural group as the people of the neighbouring state, ready for raids into these territories as well as to support opponent groups; (iii) opponent groups such as UNITA, the MNR, Super-ZAPU and Lesotho Liberation Army (LLA), all led and directed by SADF.

Botha reorganized the power structure of the army and created a National Security Management System which transformed the State Security Council (SSC) into the most powerful executive organ of the government. He trimmed the bureaucracy, by applying the management methods of the SADF to government. Military men became his key advisers and he appointed Magnus Malan as Minister of Defence. Malan was the former defence force chief and architect of the Total Strategy. Therefore his appointment as Minister of Defence was a clear indication that Botha wanted him to implement the exact policies of Total Strategy.

Botha set up a Cabinet Secretariat in the office of the Prime Minister which was composed of four committees; National Security, Economic, Constitutional and Social Affairs. They were all responsible to the Prime Minister. Botha himself presided over the State Security Council which embraced the above-mentioned four committees. The SSC was by far the most important and was the one that handled foreign policy issues. In practice, it was really the single most important government organ in the land, effectively a 'Cabinet' beyond the cabinet. It was the only committee with a mandate to deal with issues wider than those normally associated with the cabinet.

The meetings of the other committees were open to all government ministers whereas those of the SSC were exclusive occasions. In short the SSC was shrouded in secrecy because of the sensitivity of its agendas. Its composition comprised the very highest leaders of the ruling party, government and SADF.

The SSC made decisions on everything with security implications for the state. In this way, the SSC both formulated and coordinated the utilization of the resources of the state to achieve the various specific goals set out in the Total Strategy. It is important to note that the decisions that were made in the SSC meetings could only be revealed to the cabinet at the discretion of the president, and merely to inform it and not to solicit its counsel. Furthermore, the SSC was active even when cabinet was in recess. While this provided executive continuity, it also highlighted its superior status to that of the cabinet. South Africa had a government dominated by military influence and that administration had the objective of defending the interests of the white minority against the desires of the people for a free, unified and non-racist society.

(e) The Impact of P.W. Botha

There is certainly no denying that the Total Strategy with all its various strands (as we shall see later) emerged out of a deep political crisis that followed the Angolan débâcle, and thus brought South Africa back to a unified regional policy based on a more organized programme.

The crisis Botha inherited posed critical questions: not least, how to reorganize the ruling National Party, the state machinery, the economy and state security in order to achieve a stable economy, one in which international capital and investors would feel secure enough to conduct business. The concern of the SADF about the economy coincided with the feelings and aspirations of key business figures. The business sector had been concerned about the rapid deterioration in internal political stability and the way it was undermining confidence in the South African economy. These businesses were becoming more and more concerned about their lack of competitiveness on account of the rigid apartheid labour policies on top of the effects of the recession which had already set in by 1976. They felt that there was a need to relax some of the policies to make it possible for them to be competitive. They sought particularly the loosening of some of the controls on the mobility and training of the black labour force, if for no other reason than to give them competitive opportunities which they felt they lacked.[83] Afrikaner enterprises and large Afrikaner businesses[84] joined the campaign for the removal of some racial discriminations in certain jobs and work conditions.[85] But they quickly came into conflict with the so-called *verkramptes* (right-wing Afrikaner Nationalists) representing the white labour force who felt that their jobs and welfare were in jeopardy. This group was opposed to any change that sought to advance the black people at their expense.

The SADF establishment was increasingly getting concerned about the overall internal and external situation. Besides the growing militancy among the black population, typified by the 1976 Soweto uprising,[86] they saw a growing threat from the ANC[87] and the Soviet and Cuban presence in Angola and felt that reforms and changes were needed to transform South Africa into a secure and 'militarily defensible' state. The need to have a defensible state signalled the entrance by the military into the decision-making process.

Finally, Botha's election in 1978 to the premiership consolidated and confirmed the power of the military as a new force in the Afrikaner structures and politics. When Botha became Premier very little progress had been achieved on the Rhodesian independence question.[88] In that sense South Africa still held some sort of buffer zone. And while Rhodesia still existed, it served as a diversion and prevented world attention from focusing solely on South Africa and Namibia. But Botha was also a pragmatist. He knew too that the intensification of the Rhodesian liberation war meant that the white Smith regime could not last forever. Botha suspected[89] that the internal settlement negotiated by Ian Smith in March 1978 with three internal nationalist groups, and which resulted in the April 1979 general elections in which Bishop Abel Muzorewa became the first black Prime Minister of Zimbabwe/Rhodesia would not go far, since it had excluded Robert Mugabe's ZANU and Joshua Nkomo's ZAPU.[90] Thus the situation inherited gave him little comfort. Most of South Africa's *cordon sanitaire* had disintegrated, as a result, already noted, of the independence of Angola and Mozambique. There was an escalation of conflict in Rhodesia and Namibia, and to crown it all, South Africa also faced the threat of sanctions[91] over Namibia as the Western settlement initiative ran aground.

By the end of 1976 South Africa's domestic and regional policies had suffered severe blows, and consequently South Africa was facing a serious political crisis. The combination of internal mass unrest and the collapse of its regional policies, not least its retreat from the

Angolan war, and the worsening economic recession, created a situation which has been described as an 'organic crisis'. The crisis was so deep that it needed:

> a new balance of focus, the emerging of new elements ... new political configurations and philosophies, a profound restructuring of the state and the ideological discourse which construct the crisis and represent it as it is lived.... New programmes and policies.... Political and ideological work is required to disarticulate the old formations and to rework their elements into new configurations.[92]

It would appear that the reforms Botha introduced through his Total Strategy neatly fitted into this framework. These considerations made Botha reassess how he could best restore credibility in his economy and safeguard South Africa's embattled position in the region. For this reason, Botha's regional designs were a defensive strategy even where they appeared to be offensive in character. One of the very first policy decisions he made was to resurrect his predecessor's Constellation of Southern African States. This was a major and first component of the Total Strategy.

(f) The Total Strategy

The politics of the Total Strategy doctrine go back a long way and can be traced to the 1950s. In this sense, the strategy is a product of the East–West cold war thinking. Here we are not much interested in its historical background but in the dynamics that evolved the strategy, the changes that took place in South Africa's regional and domestic circumstances which acted both as the cause and result of it, from 1975 onwards.

In March 1975, in a Defence White Paper which Botha presented to parliament, he unveiled the defence strategy his ministry and the SADF envisaged for protecting South Africa's security. As he put it, it had to be more than just military strategy:

> It involves economy, ideology, technology, and even social matters and can therefore only be meaningful and valid if proper account is taken of these spheres.... This, in fact is the meaning of 'Total Strategy'.[93]

Botha wanted this policy to be implemented but it was halted because of divisions and inter-departmental rivalry in Vorster's government. Vorster himself did not favour the strategy and he doubted the loyalty of the Ministry of Defence. He preferred to deal with BOSS, which was run by people like Hendrik Van den Bergh, who was loyal to him. Botha never gave up about this ideal of the Total Strategy. In 1977, in a Defence White Paper he presented to parliament, Botha argued strongly for the implementation of the Total Strategy as a government policy. He finally managed to convince the cabinet. This final success and triumph over detractors was helped by a combination of factors, namely, the fall-out from the Angolan military fiasco and the 1976 Soweto uprising.

The generals and other key military leaders were worried about what they saw as Vorster's inertia and therefore felt the need for South Africa to reassert itself at the regional level and in domestic politics to curb the instability that was beginning to undermine the economy. Moreover, they saw themselves as standing alone in a hostile world. Since the Angolan invasion and the brutal suppression of the Soweto uprising, international opinion had hardened considerably. The thinking in the Ministry of Defence and the defence establishment was that South Africa faced a dangerous situation which similarly merited immediate solutions, if South Africa's security and survival were not to be compromised. The Total Strategy was seen to be the answer which would solve the security problem created by an indecisive government.[94] The White Paper accordingly listed the areas the strategy needed to encompass as follows:

> Political action, military/para-military action, economic action, psychological action, scientific and technological action, religious-cultural action, manpower services, intelligence services, security services, national supplies, resources and production services, transport and distribution services, financial services, community services and technological service.[95]

The White Paper stressed the point that national security as conceived under the Total Strategy was to be an all-encompassing concept affecting and involving all aspects of state. In other words, every aspect of human life would be called upon and used by the SADF to secure the country's security. Thus the White Paper was a watershed for the military not only for the fact that the doctrine was finally officially accepted but also for another reason. It meant the entry of the soldiers into politics and government. The ramifications of this fact were felt throughout the land as the SSC began to be revamped. Through the broadening of the concept of state security, the White Paper introduced wide-ranging changes and gave the SADF the legal and political power and platform that effectively made the SADF and the Defence Ministry the most powerful institution in the machineries of state and government, going far beyond their traditional purview.[96]

It seems that the Total Strategy was a mirror-image of Beaufre's model of modern warfare.[97] Beaufre saw modern warfare as an all-embracing conflict situation. This model stressed the importance of psychological as well as physical conflict. The Total Strategy had all these attributes. The Total Strategy's aims were:

(i) to coordinate political policy with military, social and psychological strategy; this involved the mobilization of all national resources towards set goals; this made the strategy an all-embracing programme capable of mobilizing and utilizing national resources to achieve any national goal;

(ii) to undertake careful applied research and coordinated preventive planning (the objective was to know everything about the adversary, weaknesses as well as strengths, to effectively counter the threat posed); this gave South Africa power over its enemies;

(iii) to use the information gained from (ii) above, to select counter-insurgency tactics from a wide range of options available.[98] This made the Total Strategy calculating, efficient and cost effective.

(g) The Threat Structure as Perceived by P.W. Botha

Before we look into the strategic shifts embodied in the Total Strategy, it is important to re-state its fundamental goal and historical context. From the moment the Afrikaner Nationalists won power their overriding concern has been two-fold; to maintain government control and to protect the country from domestic and external threat. Beyond that, its efforts have been geared towards achieving international acceptance; if that was not possible, at least international acquiescence. Botha's reform programme and policy framework did not deviate from this general framework, even if he introduced significant modifications in the apartheid structure.[99]

What this signifies then, in the overall structure of things, is that Botha was the first leader to draw a line between the concepts of apartheid and white supremacy. The message he tried to impress on his people, including the hardliners, was that the ideal they should be concerned with was the concept of white supremacy, of which apartheid was only one form. In his view, modifying apartheid would not necessarily impair the ideal of white supremacy. On the other hand, it would have the advantage of boosting South Africa's image immensely, and could even lead to international acceptance.[100]

The threat from liberation movements was perceived to come from five sources:

(i)   the liberation movements based in neighbouring countries;
(ii)   the conventional military threat from Frontline States (FLS) and their supporters, primarily Cuba and the Soviets;
(iii) the growing influence of churches led by Archbishop Tutu and Dr Alan Boesak;
(iv)   the growing internal violence led by ANC militants and other anti-apartheid movements, like the South African Trade Unions (SATU) and student organizations;
(v)   international sanctions.[101]

The threat from the liberation movements was perceived to be in two forms: firstly, since they were not militarily strong enough to defeat the SADF, at that time or in the foreseeable future, they were unlikely to endanger the survival of white power *per se*. But they had the capacity to effect substantial sabotage campaigns and therefore terrorize the white population, which in turn could affect morale. The second threat emanated from their influence on the black population. The government was aware that, without this influence, the rising waves of internal unrest and growing militancy among the young would not be as strong.

Similarly, the perceived threat from FLS came in two ways; the first was in the form of support (military training facilities, bases and material support) to the liberation movements. This not only made these organizations more capable of launching attacks against South Africa, but also made it quite difficult for South Africa's security forces to destroy them. The second was actual military action. Here, a distinction must be made between what FLS themselves were capable of, and what their allies or supporters could do to support the liberation struggle or in support of FLS. Realistically, direct military threat from FLS even as a combined force was highly unlikely. They did not have the resources, manpower or capability to launch an attack on South Africa.[102]

Consequently, the perceived threat was mainly of that from the Soviets and Cuba whose personnel and weaponry were already deployed in the region.[103] South Africa was anxious not to allow countries like Zimbabwe, which had a potentially powerful infrastructure, to become economically strong enough to develop a military base to rival their own. The perceived Soviet and Cuba threat was more imagined than real. The Cuban forces and Soviet military personnel in Angola were there firstly by invitation of that country's government, and secondly they were there to prevent SADF and UNITA from overthrowing the MPLA government. As such, they were in Angola in a supportive capacity rather than as a challenge to SADF. In any case, Soviet policy in the region, as elsewhere in Africa, did not involve the sending of Soviet combat troops in support of its allies. Apart from providing military advisers and hardware, there was no evidence that this policy had changed. In the context of the Soviet review of world policy, it seemed that Moscow was more concerned with putting its house in order than with giving close support to distant allies.[104]

Of all the threats considered by the ruling Nationalist Party, it was perhaps the international sanctions that posed the greatest challenge. The South African economy was heavily dependent on the world market for its exports, capital and technology, all of which were critical for its growth and development. If the world market was to be cut off from trading with South Africa as a result of international pressure, the economy would face substantial problems.[105] This fear was borne out in 1976 in the wake of security forces' brutal handling of the Soweto uprising. Under massive international pressure, many Western banks and multinational companies (MNCs) with business links in South Africa were pressured into scaling down their business and, in some cases, withdrawing altogether. The US and other Western governments banned the sale of goods embodying technologies which might have military significance.[106] These activities greatly exposed South Africa's vulnerability to a trade embargo, even though few countries would have been willing to support a total economic boycott.[107] This was one of the major problems feared by Botha's government. Botha's attempts to reform apartheid were geared towards this threat. Through such reforms, he hoped either to remove this threat or reduce it substantially. This was seen as a vital goal of the Total Strategy.[108]

The threat from the Church was a more recent phenomenon and seemed to be a backlash to Botha's unrelenting determination to eliminate any legal organizational and political activity by black opposition groups in South Africa.[109] The March 1988 government clamp-down on political activists and the banning of 18 organizations by the government appear to have convinced Church leaders that the government was not willing to tolerate any form of opposition from the majority, however peaceful or well-intentioned. Under these conditions, Church leaders felt morally and perhaps biblically bound to take up the challenge of guiding their flock in their fight for justice.[110] The following quotation may help to put this into context:

> Church services which become political rallies are not unusual in South Africa. In recent years the Church has been at the forefront of the struggle against apartheid. But last week's show of defiance was particularly significant. It happened...after the...government's draconian restrictions on 18 extra-parliamentary groups ....In a fiery speech Dr Boesak threw down the gauntlet to President P.W. Botha's government....[111]

This is not to say that the Church had been silent before. Far from it. It had always been active and sensitive to political issues as Meli demonstrated:

> Church figures have always featured strongly in the South African freedom struggle. Men such as Ambrose Reeves, Trevor Huddleston, Michael Scott, Joost de Blank, the Rvd Calata, the Rvd Mahabane, Desmond Tutu, Alan Boesak...have emerged at different times as outspoken champions of the oppressed, many of them suffering expulsion or restrictions imposed by the racist regime.[112]

What was new, and began to worry the government, was the character and the visibility of the actions that Church leaders openly used in defiance of the government policies. Archbishop Tutu captured the mood of prominent church leaders in South Africa in distinctive style. When asked about his feelings towards the government, he replied:

> 'When God says, "Love P.W. Botha," I say to him, "You can't be serious, God." He then says, "I am. The consequences of being a member of the body of Jesus Christ is that P.W. Botha is your brother." You have to work out what that theological position means. It means that I have to long for the very best for him.'[113]

Their decision to fill the gap left by the government action against the 18 organizations seemed to indicate their willingness and determination, even at the risk of their own personal freedom (and even life),[114] to function as political leaders believing themselves to be the only ones left to take up the fight. Linked to this was their apparent willingness (and this was perhaps the aspect the government feared most) to mobilize their congregations against the state.[115] It had been aware of how pervasive the effect of religions or religious figures can be. The government feared that the situation could rapidly develop into one that they would have difficulty in containing.

(h) Botha's Attempt to Counteract the Threat

Botha responded to these threats by creating a series of new initiatives and state policies, both at the internal and regional level, and these were embodied in the Total Strategy. The aims of the Total Strategy were meant to give a solution to the threat. The aims were to protect free enterprise in South Africa from the Marxist threat and the total onslaught. It involved the mobilization by the regime of the full range of economic, political, military, ideological and social-psychological resources of the South African government against its perceived enemies. It proposed a new constellation of economic, political and ideological policies; these were meant to reconstruct the basis for stable white rule in South Africa in such a way as to defuse mass struggles and incorporate specific strata of the oppressed masses into a new 'historical bloc', but within clear limits.

(i) Internal Dimension

At the internal level Botha's shift in strategy is seen in state policy towards the black working class. Botha relaxed specific controls over the vertical and horizontal mobility of black labour. (This was embodied in legislation following the 1979 Reports of two crucial Commissions of Inquiry, Wiehahn and Riekert,[116] which changed certain aspects of job reservation and the pass laws.) Some of the industrial discrimination laws were eased but in a manner which attempted to incorporate African trade unions into an industrial relations system which would isolate and contain the work-place struggles of black workers to levels and forms which did not threaten the basic structure of the apartheid system.[117] By introducing these measures the government was aiming at winning support from the burgeoning black petty bourgeoisie and stopping them from becoming more hostile not only to the structures of national oppression, but also to the apartheid system itself. Botha was also aiming at weakening the national liberation alliances by incorporating African trade unions within an industrial relations system which sought to separate economic from political struggle. In general these changes still maintained the *status quo*. Apart from these reforms, the Total Strategy also affected a far-reaching reorganization of the form of the state. This involved reorganization of the machinery of government. Botha restructured the government machinery by de-emphasizing the cabinet form of government responsible to an elected legislature, and establishing a much more executive state in which power became centralized in the leader. In specific terms, this meant the centralization of power in the hands of the prime minister and correspondingly, the erosion of the power of the cabinet and parliament. The centralization of power paved the way for the eventual transformation of the parliamentary system into an executive presidency. Hand in hand with this went the appointment of the president's council, a body of appointed Whites, Coloureds, and Indians, to advise on all matters. This was meant to achieve two objectives; firstly, to enable the ruling class to push through reform, even if against strong opposition from class forces in the previous nationalist alliances; secondly, it had the explicit purpose of dividing the nationalistic oppressed groups by incorporating some elements such as the Coloureds and Indians into emasculated representative state apparatus. This would give the appearance of conceding political rights while in reality not providing for the possibility of challenging the existing structure of power.

Militarization was one of the dimensions of the internal aspect of the Total Strategy. Under Botha's regime we began to see a huge build-up of the military and security establishment. It included a massive mobilization of the white population to join the army, and this was a radical reappraisal of the traditional conscription and recruitment policies regarding the non-whites.[118] Botha expanded both the defence and police forces and encouraged a considerable overlap of duty between the South African Police (SAP) and the military forces. As a result of this the forces used similar equipment and techniques of combat and training. A huge sum of money was channelled into the military machinery, much larger than before. Botha emphasized high standards of training and improvement in armament. Security and defence were given the highest priority. The military became not only a dominant force in the co-ordination and execution of security policy, but it also became increasingly influential in the formulation of all aspects of state policy.[119]

(2) The Regional Dimension

When it comes to the regional level, South Africa's Total Strategy had long-term and medium-term objectives. In practice, each complemented the other, leading quite often to secondary or spill-over effects with respect to one or both of the other strategic objectives. The Constellation of Southern African States was considered as a long-term objective and the destabilization policy as a medium-term object-ive.[120] The decision to resurrect the idea of constellation by Botha in 1978 meant firstly that South Africa was still committed to finding an alternative protective shield after the collapse of the *cordon sanitaire*. Secondly, it also represented the formal deployment of the Total Strategy against its neighbours. The move then represented the very first phase of the new strategy.[121] The constellation policy was promoted from 1978 to mid-1980.

The essence of the initiative was to create a formal grouping of states (to include Zaire) in the region, with South Africa being the focal point on account of its superior economic power, port facilities, communication and transport network, not to mention its military superiority. In November 1979, during the first of the several meetings between government officials and the business community, Botha invited the private sector to join with him to fund a proposed financial institution (the Southern African Development Bank) which was to be the funding agency of the constellation programme.[122] In this scheme, the key country was to be Zimbabwe. The South African strategists had drawn up plans anticipating a Muzorewa victory at the polls. The calculation was that with a government led by Bishop Muzorewa, Zimbabwe would be secured for the constellation, along with Malawi and Swaziland with whom they already had strong links. After that, Botswana, Lesotho, Angola and Mozambique would be persuaded or coerced into joining. With all these countries secured, Zambia would have been left isolated and surrounded by countries in the constellation. It would only have been a matter of time before it too would, either voluntarily or though coercion, see the sense of joining the rest in the constellation.[123] The constellation proposal had four main aims:

(i) It sought to lock its neighbours into South Africa's economic system. With that achieved, South Africa's leverage over them would have been irresistible; it would have been against their economic interest for any of them to contemplate aiding the

ANC and PAC or to campaign too strongly against South Africa in international forums.[124]

(ii) Membership of the constellation would also entail direct political and diplomatic recognition and endorsement by these countries of the Bantustans. They would have been members of the constellation with the Bantustans on an equal footing. This is why it was important that the most influential countries like Zimbabwe and Zambia should be members. Once the black states had accepted this, the major western countries could then have been persuaded into following suit. Apartheid would then become an internationally recognized reality.

(iii) The constellation would seek to split the OAU on the issue of relations with South Africa. In turn, this would undermine efforts to establish an OAU-sponsored military opposition to the Pretoria regime. And with all the potential rearguard countries on the side of South Africa, the liberation movements would find it very difficult to wage their struggle.

(iv) Achieving the above three would then have created the environment needed for the West to do business with Pretoria on its own terms without fear of international pressure.[125]

When the Constellation of Southern African States was launched, it looked secure enough. It seemed Zimbabwe was going to emerge firmly under the Muzorewa leadership, heavily dependent upon the whites to run the economy and under South Africa's stewardship. Two factors were responsible for its failure. One was the unexpected defeat of Muzorewa by Mugabe (see Chapter 2). This immediately dashed any hopes South Africa had of effecting its plans. As soon as the elections were over, Mugabe embarked on the establishment of links with the FLS alliance. The second factor was the decision by the FLS to include Zimbabwe in the newly formed Southern African Development Co-ordination Conference (SADCC), whose goals were almost diametrically opposed to those of the constellation. SADCC's goals were: to promote regional cooperation and the equitable sharing of the benefits of that cooperation; to mobilize the resources of member countries to promote national, interstate, and regional policies for economic development; to promote economic liberation and the development of a regional communications strategy and most of all, to secure international support for its strategy and aid for its projects of reducing economic dependence on Pretoria. The reduction of economic dependence on Pretoria was the major goal of SADCC.

Although SADCC was not entirely created to frustrate South Africa's regional policy, it nonetheless meant the constellation initiative could no longer be implemented along the lines South Africa had planned. Significantly, it posed a serious challenge to South Africa's immediate objective of locking the entire region into its economic hold. In addition, all the countries that it had targeted opted to join SADCC, including Malawi, Swaziland and even Lesotho, which is within South Africa's borders. In the end, Pretoria was forced to establish its own constellation with the Bantustans. The programme of creating the wider constellation was put on hold pending favourable conditions in the future or the softening up of the key states.[126]

To the South African policy-makers, the failure of the constellation policy meant that, if the neighbouring states could not be persuaded to cooperate with the Pretoria government through peaceful means, they would have to be forced. The threat became more serious from South Africa when the OAU charter (Lusaka Manifesto) specifically forbade members to have any relations with Pretoria.[127] The result was an immediate escalation in the policy and the deployment of military and economic options. The Total Strategy began to take on a new meaning as destabilization and it became the operative word of South Africa's regional policy.[128]

It is important to note that destabilization as a policy for all of southern Africa was only adopted after the independence of Zimbabwe. The foreign policy adopted by the Zimbabwean government immediately after independence had much influence on the adoption of the destabilization policy by South Africa.

The destabilization strategy was therefore intended to create the necessary conditions for recapturing the initiative for effecting the constellation policy. In reality its main objective was to hit SADCC hard, and to continue hitting them until they were ready to deal. Destabilization was implemented in two phases. The first phase involved what may be termed controlled destabilization and lasted from around mid-1980 to 1981. For strategic purposes, South Africa chose to experiment with the policy. It was a testing period, as it was used to take the temperature and reaction of the international community. The full-scale destabilization programme followed later and this time it was measured. The programme was of military attacks and economic sabotage against all the SADCC countries. It aimed to cripple their economic infrastructure and to cause political instability and thus to make these countries ungovernable.

1.4   OBJECTIVES OF THE DESTABILIZATION POLICY

The underlying objectives of Pretoria's regional policy were never overtly stated by Pretoria itself. It was also hard to find any master plan behind the many paradoxes and elements of South Africa's changing tactics and strategy towards other countries in the region. The policies pursued were opportunistic, frequently very clumsily formulated, and dependent upon the strength and position of the different countries.[129] However, it is important to state some of the key objectives as perceived by certain academics to indicate why and how the philosophy and strategy of destabilization came to dominate Pretoria's regional policies.

In early 1982 a new phase of intensified destabilization measures was initiated. Pretoria appeared to have a clearer perspective of what such destabilization was intended to achieve and what measures would be most effective against particular states. The main immediate objectives seemed to be:

(1) It sought to prevent FLS from adopting policies that might jeopardize the continued existence of white rule in South Africa.[130]

(2) It sought to discourage FLS from supporting Southern African liberation movements, by way of offering them bases, training, material support, and so on.

(3) It sought to stop FLS from launching diplomatic efforts to isolate South Africa. In short, Botha wanted FLS to be completely neutral with respect to any effort or action that might threaten the *status quo* inside South Africa. Alongside this was a parallel aim to sabotage SADCC as a regional economic unit, thereby preventing it from breaking away from its own economic stranglehold or from creating a viable rival economic unit.

The general objectives of destabilization were centred on the survival of white rule. To ensure that this did happen Pretoria had to reassert economic and political hegemony, by using pressure to bring the neighbouring states back into line. This helped to expand its exports since sales to neighbours were central to South Africa's economic growth. South Africa wanted to remain the economic focal point for the region. It hoped to be able to force the neighbouring states to reduce their links with the socialist bloc. It wished to force the neighbouring states to sign non-aggression pacts to ensure that they would refrain from actively supporting the armed struggles led by SWAPO in Namibia and the ANC in South Africa, and it obliged them to act as virtual policing agents for South Africa, by prohibiting political activity by South African and Namibian refugees in their territory. The pressure on neighbouring states was in a form of intimidation, acts of sabotage and other actions such as

(1) infiltration of the military and security organizations of the neighbouring States;
(2) encouragement of opposition to the governments of the Frontline States by giving support to dissidents, and thus generally destabilizing them politically;
(3) prevention of neighbouring countries from uniting into a common front against South Africa. It feared that they would develop a reasonable military capability and become more assertive, even provocative, in their relations with South Africa so that they would no longer be as vulnerable to South African economic and military pressure;
(4) keeping neighbouring states (especially Botswana, Lesotho and Swaziland) economically weak and dependent on South Africa, and ensuring that SADCC did not become a viable economic grouping.

Pretoria believed that if it could prevent the neighbouring states from helping the ANC then the uprisings inside South Africa would be less effective. Its tactics were to keep the liberation movements weak, divided and suppressed so as to maintain a total control over the movement of the black population. Pretoria also aimed at ensuring that 'black states' in the region would not support calls for mandatory sanctions against itself but in addition that they should shield it from any such sanctions.[131] New instruments were also developed to achieve these reformulated regional policy objectives. Military expenditure was more than doubled between 1977–8 and 1984–5 to reach R3755 million and new capabilities were developed to mount aggressive assaults against regional states.[132] At the same time considerable attention was given to ways in which economic links could be used to further the apartheid state's regional objectives. The Botha regime's strategic planners began to consider ways in which 'economic action' (mobilized through the network of structures controlled by the state security council) could be applied either in the form of 'incentive levers' to those states showing willingness to collaborate, or as 'disincentive levers' against those viewed as hostile.[133]

For P.W. Botha (who had been Defence Minister since 1966, becoming Prime Minister in 1978) to achieve these objectives, the use of military power was the only option. He tried to forge a kind of national unity government to defend white rule. Attacks on neighbouring states emerged as part of the wider strategy of his government. This strategy of attack took military, political, diplomatic and economic forms. All aspects of foreign and domestic policy were put under the purview of the military. Its decisions were sometimes referred later to the cabinet or parliament for ratification. The state security council was like a corporation board of directors or the Politburo of a Communist country. Botha was often described as an 'organization man' and the SSC acted in a technocratic and managerial way. The SSC was dominated by the military, although it also included the key political figures. This meant that the military had power to do whatever they and Botha wanted. We shall see in the next section that some of their attacks were not planned or even coordinated with the Prime Minister or Defence Minister.

1.5 APPLICATION OF THE DESTABILIZATION POLICY IN THE REGION

The regional destabilization policy was a mix of diplomatic, military and economic actions. These were applied differently from country to country, because the goals of what South Africa aimed to achieve were also different, in each state. In countries like Zimbabwe, Mozambique and Angola the idea was to pressurize for a change of government policy or if possible replace it[134] with a government that was more acceptable by South Africa. In other countries like Lesotho, Botswana, and Swaziland the aim was to seek changes in these governments' policies towards South Africa. However, as for the means of destabilization, South Africa was guided by the target state's political, economic, social and military vulnerabilities and penetrability. Such foreign policy instruments as economic and military levers were employed in most of the cases in Angola, Lesotho, Zimbabwe, Mozambique, and Botswana to a lesser degree. In the case of economic actions, these included the manipulation of food exports and other means as listed by Hanlon as:[135]

- Limiting of the use of South African railways, for example by 'manipulating the availability of railway wagons'. This was applied to Zimbabwe, Botswana, Lesotho and Zambia.
- Restrictions on migrant labour: these were applied mostly to Zimbabwe and Mozambique, and Lesotho was just threatened.
- Border closures and restrictions; this was applied to all immediate neighbours: Swaziland, Botswana, Mozambique, Zimbabwe and Lesotho. But this was used mainly on Lesotho, taking into consideration its geographic position and the fact that its economic dependence on imported supplies of food and other essential goods from South Africa made it very vulnerable. Throughout much of 1981, Pretoria used the technique of economic blockade to coerce the Lesotho government to change its policies towards South African refugees and the liberation movement. In 1984 South Africa used the same method again, which compelled Lesotho to expel the ANC refugees from Lesotho. The South African economic blockade of Lesotho in 1986 was the most serious one, which resulted in a military coup that removed Dr Leabua's government.
- Curbing imports from neighbouring states. This was done to Zimbabwe and Swaziland.
- Cutting of electricity supplies; this was applied to Mozambique and Lesotho. (The giant Cabora Bassa dam for generating electricity was a joint project dating back to colonial days of Portugal and South Africa. It was set up in such a way that Maputo would receive its power from Cabora Bassa via the South African grid.)
- Restriction of South African tourists; this was applied to Lesotho and Swaziland.
- Violation of the customs union agreement; this affected all three other members: Botswana, Lesotho and Swaziland. (The customs union is administered by South Africa which distributes the revenue and had used this as a pressure point for joint security agreements and to try to force inclusion, and thus recognition of the 'homelands'. Lesotho and Swaziland rely on the customs union for well over half of government revenue. Lesotho and Swaziland remained part of the Rand monetary zone, in which the South African reserve bank controls their monetary policy and increases their vulnerability to economic pressure.) In a way this was also applied to Zimbabwe when South Africa immediately after Zimbabwe's independence threatened to terminate the trade agreement which South Africa had previously agreed with the Rhodesian government.

On the crucial military level, destabilization had several dimensions. Before we discuss these dimensions, it is important to note that all military incursions into the neighbouring states were done with the primary objective of denying the ANC the capacity to establish a presence on its borders.[136] But these actions also carried a wider political message to the various regional governments about South Africa's capacity and willingness to project its power into the region and to defend its interests. It also had its economic aspects, as we shall see below.

In the military field, one of the dimensions used was the material support given to rebel groups in various countries, who were willing to take up arms against their governments, whether or not their objective was to overthrow the existing regime or to force it into a compromise with the opposition. The whole idea behind this method was to create political instability in these states so as to cause serious hardship to the population who would then turn their frustrations and fury on their own government and thus compel it to reconsider its (hostile) attitude towards the destabilizer. In Angola, Mozambique, Zimbabwe and Lesotho, there were already potential surrogate armies to be used by South Africa. In Angola South Africa supported UNITA in its civil war against the Angolan government; in Mozambique, it was RENAMO against the FRELIMO government; and in Zimbabwe it was Super-ZAPU; and in Lesotho it was the Lesotho Liberation Army (LLA). Their main task, with the help of South African commandos, was to target any major factory or economic installation, such as oil, electricity, post office and military bases, for instance the Inkomo Barracks and Thornhill Air base in Zimbabwe.[137]

Here are some of the activities in brief, used either directly or indirectly by surrogate armies:

- disinformation; e.g. hundreds of letters and anti-government leaflets were sent to Zimbabwe in 1983 and 1984.
- Attempted assassinations of Prime Ministers and senior government party members; e.g. the 18 December 1981 bomb attack on ZANU Headquarters in Harare.
- Assassinations, murders and kidnappings of liberation movement leaders and other personnel; e.g. in Maseru, Harare, Maputo, Lusaka, Manzini and Gaborone during 1981–3.
- Attacks on transport routes, e.g. closures of the Benguela railway in Angola, the Zimbabwe–Maputo line, the Malawi–Nacala line, the

Malawi–Beira line and the attacks on the Zimbabwe–Beira road and rail line, during 1975–87; and
- port and border inspections of cargo, harassment of transport personnel, and import licence and levy requirements, e.g. for Zimbabwe and Zambia in 1986.[138]

Some of these activities had serious economic effects on the countries; especially the closure of the routes, which resulted in the landlocked countries – Botswana, Lesotho, Malawi, Swaziland, Zambia and Zimbabwe – being denied access to routes other than those which

Table 1.1   Estimated Regional Costs (US $) of 'Destabilization', 1985

Direct war damage	1 610 000 000
Extra defence expenditure	3 060 000 000
Higher transport, energy costs	970 000 000
Smuggling	190 000 000
Refugees	660 000 000
Lost exports, tourism	230 000 000
Boycotts, embargoes	260 000 000
Loss of existing production	800 000 000
Lost economic growth	2 000 000 000
Trading arrangements	340 000 000
Total	**10 120 000 000**

Source: Reginald H. Green and Carol B. Thompson, 'Political Economy in Conflict: SADCC, South Africa and Sanctions', in David Martin and Phyllis Johnson eds, *Destructive Engagement: Southern Africa at War*, Harare, Zimbabwe Publishing House, 1986, p. 272.

traversed South Africa. This had the useful effect, from South Africa's point of view, of increasing its market power in the region, power which it had not hesitated to exploit during the UDI period. Though not initially responsible for the situation, South Africa continued to benefit from the inoperability of these routes during the destabilization era, in that it was able to exert continuous significant political and economic pressures on these countries. Towards the middle of the destabilization era South Africa began to use a policy of selective destabilization, accompanied with diplomacy. Pretoria began to categorize regional states and directed different tactics towards them. On the one hand, there were the more conservative states, such as Swaziland, Botswana and Malawi, who were seen as potential collaborators. These were offered a range of economic and other 'incentives' to encourage them to 'co operate' with South Africa. In addition to greater selectivity in identifying states, Pretoria's strategists appeared to have concentrated on trying to achieve two immediate objectives: the withdrawal of support given by regional states to the ANC and SWAPO, and thwarting attempts to reduce economic dependence on South Africa. On the other hand there were those states, like Zimbabwe, who posed a potential threat, economically and militarily, to South Africa. These were subjected to destabilization tactics on a much greater scale. We shall examine the Zimbabwe experience in detail in the next chapter.

2 Destabilization: The Zimbabwe Experience

It can be argued that the 1980–89 destabilization of Zimbabwe by South Africa had extremely adverse economic effects. On the other hand one can argue that while it crippled the economy, it also strengthened and shaped Zimbabwe's internal politics. The question is; to what extent are these statements true? Would Zimbabwe have done better economically without destabilization? To what extent did destabilization contribute to the process of political unity within Zimbabwe? How far did it contribute in diverting the ruling government from establishing its Marxist and Socialist goals? Was South Africa's destabilization of Zimbabwe a success or a failure? The latter question is the core of this book. The following four chapters will assess the economic and political damage caused by destabilization during the 1980s, and show how it imposed structural limitations on the developmental momentum and ambitions of Zimbabwe.

This chapter will examine the reasons why South Africa adopted a policy of destabilization towards Zimbabwe during 1980–89, the implications of Pretoria's policy of destabilization towards Zimbabwe and its political intentions; and why Pretoria considered Zimbabwe's independence to be a threat to its economic and political interests.

2.1 THE HISTORICAL EVENTS LEADING TO DESTABILIZATION OF ZIMBABWE

It is within the broad framework discussed in Chapter 1 that Pretoria's strategy of destabilization of Zimbabwe can best be understood. The aim was to abort Zimbabwe's independence and to ensure that Zimbabwe became a puppet state responsive to South Africa's demands and interests in the region. As time went by, this policy gradually assumed an aggressive militarist form, as we shall see.

(a) Zimbabwe–Rhodesia–South Africa Connection

We saw in Chapter 1 how important Rhodesia, colonial Angola and Mozambique had been to South Africa's security, as buffer states. But the collapse of Portuguese colonialism had meant that only rebel Rhodesia remained as a white redoubt in support of South Africa. Rebel Rhodesia increasingly became a liability to South Africa, which in pursuit of its policy of detente pressured Ian Smith to settle for majority rule, as indeed did Western powers such as the United Kingdom and the United States. However, this pressure was in no sense altruistic, but was based on the concern to ensure that the liberation armies, especially the Patriotic Front (PF), the alliance between Mugabe's ZANU(PF) and Nkomo's Zimbabwe African People's Union (ZAPU), should not win a battlefield victory. South Africa's fear was that with either Mugabe or Nkomo as Prime Minister of Zimbabwe, it would not then be possible to stop the radicalization of Zimbabwe. South Africa viewed the process towards independence, including the Lancaster House Agreement of December 1979, as an attempt to establish a moderate future Zimbabwe. The following actions were taken by South Africa to ensure that its dream of establishing a moderate government in Zimbabwe were realized.

In 1978, the South African Defence Minister was granted the power to impose a general martial law regime along all the country's borders. On the Northern border with what was then called Rhodesia, this policy manifested itself in the development of an offensive as well as defensive military infrastructure. A fifty-foot-wide barrier, mined and patrolled by units of the South African Defence Force (SADF) was erected. Military landing-strips were quickly constructed, together with the general improvement of roads for use as emergency runways. In SADF strategy, the border with Rhodesia had clearly become a 'priority region' whose importance was adequately demonstrated by the establishment of a major military base at Phalaborwa in Northern Transvaal, which was backed up by four smaller training bases specializing in counter-insurgency operations and military sabotage.[1] Many of the SADF personnel in the border area consisted of ethnic battalions, e.g. Shangaani, Ndebele and Venda, who spoke mutually intelligible languages with Zimbabweans and could therefore be infiltrated into the new Zimbabwean state as nationals. This general militarization of the border also manifested itself in the organization of the local white farmers into commando units, attached to units of the SADF.

This policy of aggressive and provocative militarism was a clear plan by the South African regime to give increasing military aid to the Ian Smith regime, in Rhodesia. But the long-term plan was to have Muzorewa (leader of the short-lived Zimbabwe-Rhodesia, 1979) succeed the Ian Smith regime and thereby prevent a possible hostile government in Harare. As Patel observed,

> when Ian Smith seemingly accepted the principle of majority rule, ... the attempt at the 'sanitization' of the revolutionary process involved the search for moderate black leadership which could be used to show that majority rule had arrived, while in practice white control could be maintained in an independent Zimbabwe, and South Africa could continue to rely upon a dependent and pliant neighbouring state.[2]

The Rhodesian internal agreement of March 1978 became the basis for the search for the creation of this dependent and pliant state. The April 1979 general election seemed to indicate some progress towards majority rule, in that the election was for the first time based on universal adult suffrage, and resulted in the appointment of the country's first black Prime Minister, Bishop Abel Muzorewa. However, Muzorewa's government was short-lived, because the internal settlement process was rejected by both Patriotic Front leaders, Mugabe and Nkomo. International recognition did not come even from a wavering United Kingdom nor from the United States. The armed struggle could only be stopped by the Patriotic Front, despite the fact that the real instruments of power still remained in white hands. The other reason why the internal settlement failed was that it could not produce conditions inside the country that would have allowed all conflicting parties to hold elections and choose a democratic government for the people by the people. Muzorewa failed to undermine the fragile unity between the parties of the Patriotic Front which was just a marriage of convenience in order to confront the internal pressure of Muzorewa and Sithole and to serve as a common front in the negotiation with Britain. The cosmetic unity of Mugabe and Nkomo before the election strengthened the liberation struggle inside by giving great hope and morale to the masses, and it also strengthened their bargaining powers in the international community as the only legitimate political organization that could bring peace in the country.

However, immediately after the internal settlement of Zimbabwe-Rhodesia, P.W. Botha proposed the creation of the Constellation of Southern African States with Pretoria as its headquarters. The Constellation of Southern African States would have included South Africa, the 'independent' Bantustans, Namibia, Zimbabwe-Rhodesia under Muzorewa, and the three majority-ruled black states that were not in the Frontline States, Malawi, Swaziland and Lesotho. Botswana and Zambia would probably have joined later through persuasion or force, in the opinion of South Africa. South Africa saw this as an explicitly anti-communist grouping, and it assumed that the neighbouring states felt that they all faced a common Marxist threat. The proposed establishment of a Constellation of States was clearly an aspect of what Prime Minister P.W. Botha saw as the key objective of the South African Total Strategy. This envisaged intense activity in four fields: the economic, the military, the political and the ideological, with the objective of ensuring the long-term survival of the exploitative and oppressive system of apartheid in South Africa. The formation of a Constellation of States was seen as a means of creating a favourable 'external environment' for South Africa. It would have provided South Africa with regional diplomatic recognition by the international community as a regional power and recognition of its nominally independent Bantustans. It would have ensured that regional independent states 'behaved themselves' by not permitting sanctuaries or transit facilities for freedom fighters. Ultimately what was being aimed at was the recognition of South African regional hegemony by neighbouring states which would realize that supporting calls for sanctions against South Africa would be at their peril. It would be therefore in their interest to moderate their political, diplomatic attacks on South Africa and to prevent the Soviet-bloc states from achieving a political and military foothold in the region. In short, regional destabilization was meant to convey to South Africa's neighbours that without proper deference to the major regional power, they would have no real possibility of political stability, economic development or military security.[3]

(b) Muzorewa's Relationship with P.W. Botha

Their friendship was based on two aspects:

(1) For P.W. Botha, Zimbabwe was important as long as it remained as a buffer state against the threat of apartheid policy. P.W. Botha needed Zimbabwe to establish a Constellation of States, since Zimbabwe was the keystone to any regional grouping, because it had the second most sophisticated economy in the region. Zimbabwe was also the 'core' of the centre of the Southern African transport system and as such had its finger on South Africa's jugular in terms of access to countries such as Zambia,

Malawi and Zaire. On the other hand, there was the stake of South African companies in Zimbabwe's economy to take into account.[4] South Africa did not want to lose these companies.

(2) Muzorewa needed South Africa for military and financial support in order to remain in power.

Of course, P.W. Botha made sure that Muzorewa got the support he needed. Mr Botha told his Parliament in 1979,

> If confusion and chaos are created for Rhodesia by outside forces, I want to warn that the South African Parliament will have to consider what steps we are going to take because we do not want and cannot afford confusion on our borders.[5]

The whole idea was to contain internal counter-insurgency operations against guerrillas of the Zimbabwe African National Liberation Army (ZANLA) and the Zimbabwean People's Revolutionary Army (ZIPRA) and to support the Rhodesian government's policy of launching major strikes into Mozambique and Zambia. In the pre-independence election in March 1980, South Africa threw its support behind Bishop Abel Muzorewa and his UANC. As Hanlon observed,

> Pretoria provided substantial amounts of money, and worked with the Rhodesian security service to organize the campaign. A high-security official, Geoffrey Price, was involved in the Muzorewa campaign. One government official told me: 'Price wrote Muzorewa's speeches; he hired the buses and helicopters, organized the rallies, and even arranged food and drinks. But it was all with South African money and according to South African instructions'.[6]

By the time of the Lancaster House Agreement, which paved the way for the 1980 independence elections, South African military involvement in the Rhodesian war had increased dramatically. Units of the SADF Special Forces and air force personnel operated jointly with the Rhodesian army and by the time of independence, the Rhodesian army had a substantial number of SADF personnel. South Africa had installed spies in the Rhodesian army. This was publicly acknowledged by South Africa's Prime Minister in early December 1979:[7] South African security forces had been operating 'for some time' inside Zimbabwe-Rhodesia to protect Pretoria's 'interests' and defend 'vital lines of communication'. At the same time it was reliably reported that one, and possibly two, SADF battalions were operating under their own command in Southern Rhodesia.[8]

Operating jointly with units of the Rhodesian Army Special Operations Division, the South African regime embarked on a programme of bombing churches in an attempt to show that ZANU(PF) was ungodly and therefore unfit to govern.[9] They forged issues of church magazines, (e.g. *Catholic Church Monthly, Moto*),[10] slandered the ZANU(PF) leadership and did their utmost to turn the churches against the liberation forces. This attempt to instil a psychology of rebellion against ZANU(PF) having largely failed, South Africa resorted to attempts at the physical elimination of the ZANU(PF) leadership, culminating in the abortive assassination attempt on Robert Mugabe in Masvingo (then Fort Victoria) Province during the electoral campaign.[11]

However, South Africa was not alone in not wanting a ZANU(PF) victory. Lord Soames, the Governor during the transition period, from December 1979 to independence in April 1980, also opposed Mugabe. In spite of South African ambitions and activities, Lord Soames' attitude and tactics, and American and British hopes that Mugabe would lose, Mugabe won the election with 57 out of the 80 black seats in the House of Assembly, Nkomo won 20 seats and Muzorewa won three seats. Mugabe's victory was a crushing blow to South African expectations. In the eyes of South Africa, Zimbabwe was now in the grip of a Marxist government, in the same way that Angola and Mozambique were. South Africa's self-conceived nightmare of a 'red corridor' from the Atlantic to the Indian Ocean seemed to be interrupted only by Zambia with its ideology of humanism. Zimbabwe's socialist policy was in sharp contrast to South Africa's defence of apartheid. Muzorewa's failure to win the election had damaged the prospects of the South African-inspired CONSAS. Mugabe's decision to join the SADCC and the Frontline States buried South Africa's hopes of the success of the CONSAS policy. But in his victory broadcast to the nation, Mugabe acknowledged the geographical and historical importance that tied the two countries. Mugabe emphasized that Zimbabwe needed South Africa as much as South Africa needed Zimbabwe. Therefore, the two countries needed to recognize their differences and try to live in mutual co-existence, but for Zimbabwe the co-existence did not mean that it would not voice its objections to apartheid.

(c) After Independence

At independence the new government called for reconciliation among all the peoples of Zimbabwe. This reconciliation offered prospects for peace, friendship and unity. As President Mugabe said, addressing the nation on the eve of independence, 'Let us deepen our sense of belonging and engender a common interest that knows no race, colour or creed. Let us truly become Zimbabweans with a single loyalty.'[12]

The historic policy of reconciliation was to be the cornerstone of ZANU(PF)'s overall policy. Reconciliation, especially between blacks and whites, was meant to heal the wounds of the past as reflected in the bitter armed struggle. This eased the worries of many whites who had expected Mugabe to seek revenge, but instead he offered the hand of friendship and trust to those who had been defeated in their long-held dreams of perpetual white rule. Nevertheless, reconciliation was also a bold stroke in magnanimity to those who had lost both the war and the election, because ZANU(PF) with its landslide victory could have governed Zimbabwe on its own. Indeed, such a policy of reconciliation was quite contrary to the fears of the whites, especially after such a long, bitter war in which thousands of people lost their lives.

To show his commitment to reconciliation, Mugabe brought Nkomo and his three other members of ZAPU into the government. He also appointed David Smith, who had been deputy prime minister in the Rhodesia Front government, minister of finance, and the head of the white Commercial Farmers' Union (CFU), Dennis Norman, minister of agriculture. More remarkably, after 30 000 people had died in the liberation war, Mugabe retained the services of the Rhodesian army commander, Lieutenant-General Peter Walls, an avowed anti-Marxist. Walls resigned a few months later when Mugabe refused to promote him to full general. In addition the new government embarked on a delicate programme of integrating ZANLA and ZIPRA with the Rhodesian army. However, this integration was not well established, because of experiences in the long war, where the anger and hatred of each group for the other had been developed and deep-rooted.

At the political level South Africa activated a programme designed to create an 'independent' military base outside the formal Rhodesian army, in conjunction with politicians like Bishop Abel Muzorewa and Reverend Ndabaningi Sithole.[13] South Africa spent large amounts of money training the auxiliary forces of the two now-discredited politicians. South Africa also funded the 1980 general election campaigns of the two black politicians in Rhodesia who were friendly to her. As observed by David Martin and Phyllis Johnson,

For the South Africans the outcome was a particularly bitter blow. They had invested US$300 million in the Rhodesian war against the nationalists and they had invested heavily in the election campaign against ZANU.[14]

All this was a campaign designed to discredit ZANU(PF). South Africa had supported the Lancaster House Agreement and the 1980 electoral process in the hope that Bishop Muzorewa would win. When he lost the 1980 general elections, South Africa, together with elements of the Rhodesian Army, attempted to launch a *coup d'état* to prevent ZANU(PF) from assuming power. The Rhodesian armed forces commander at the time, General Walls, later revealed that he had been party to a coup to prevent ZANU(PF) coming to power. The plan included a request to the British government to declare the election results invalid because of alleged ZANU(PF) intimidation.[15] It was the British refusal to cooperate, the magnitude of the ZANU(PF) electoral victory, the disunity among the Rhodesian services chiefs (particularly between the army and police chiefs), plus Robert Mugabe's conciliatory victory message, that forestalled the activation of the coup. He encouraged every Zimbabwean by saying:

As we become a new people we are called to be constructive, progressive and for ever forward-looking, for we cannot afford to be men of yesterday, backward-looking, retrogressive and destructive. Our new nation requires of every one of us to be a new man, with a new mind, a new heart and a new spirit. Our new mind must have a new vision and our heart a new love that spurns hate, and a new spirit that must unite and not divide. This to me is the human essence that must form the core of our political change and national independence. . . . If yesterday I fought you as an enemy, today you have become a friend and ally with the same national interest, loyalty, rights and duties as myself. If yesterday you hated me, today you cannot avoid the love that binds you to me and me to you. . . . The wrongs of the past must now stand forgiven and forgotten. If ever we look to the past, let us do so for the lesson the past has taught us, namely that oppression and racism are inequalities that must never find scope in our political and social system. It could never be a correct justification that because the whites oppressed us yesterday when they had power, the blacks must oppress them today because the have power. An evil remains an evil whether practised by white against black or by black against white. Our majority rule could easily turn into inhuman rule if we oppressed, persecuted or harassed those who do not look or think like the majority of us. Democracy is never mob-rule....[16]

This message was welcomed by most of the white community and had served as a continuing inspiration for Zimbabweans ever since. The reconciliatory message was ignored by South Africa in its perception of a hostile Zimbabwe. Ironically, the bold policy of reconciliation itself was a threat to South Africa because it involved black and white and black/black cooperation after a bloody armed struggle for independence and an electoral defeat. It therefore gave the lie to the argument that blacks could not govern properly, that blacks would inevitably fight amongst themselves after independence, and that whites would have neither a role nor safety under a majority-rule black government. Here was an island of potential multiracial cooperation and harmony, which stood in sharp contrast to the lie about human relations that was apartheid. Apartheid was not only a crime against humanity as declared by international law; it was also a gigantic lie.

However, if Mugabe had not announced the reconciliation policy, this would have allowed South Africa to claim vindication of its 'group policy' of apartheid as the only possible solution to human organization in a multi-racial society, while the proclamation and practice of reconciliation posed a serious alternative to apartheid. Either way, South Africa would have engaged in regional destabilization and made Zimbabwe a target state, because of the better example provided by Zimbabwe against which apartheid could be judged by the world at large. At independence, therefore, Zimbabwe was virtually a beleaguered state, constantly threatened by a powerful southern neighbour, which was singularly determined to ensure that the newly independent country remained in a state of chronic political instability and economically dependent on South Africa. The 1980s destabilization was designed precisely to ensure that this policy objective became a daunting reality.

It is important for the purpose of this book to look at some of these threats and accusations from both sides. On 9 May 1981 South Africa's Minister of Police warned Zimbabwe publicly that 'we are aware of the presence of ANC terrorists in Zimbabwe', and that South Africa would 'hit back hard' at countries harbouring guerrillas operating against the Republic.[17] Mugabe's Minister of Home Affairs, Richard Hove, responded unequivocally to South Africa's threats by

saying that Zimbabwe would defend herself with the 'utmost vigour' if
Pretoria carried out 'its long-conceived plan to invade'.[18]

In November 1980 Mugabe himself charged South Africa with
recruiting and training large numbers of guerrillas from Zimbabwe.[19]
Again on 31 January 1981, the day after South Africa's raid on the
ANC building in Mozambique, Mugabe said the attack

> is a signal, warning us not only to proceed with speed to strengthen
> our own defence forces, but also to consolidate our military alliance
> with our Mozambican brothers.[20]

These exchanges were an indication of how high tensions had became
between the two countries. South Africa was just waiting for an
opportune time to attack.

2.2 SOUTH AFRICA'S JUSTIFICATION FOR DESTABILIZING ZIMBABWE

The principal reason for the policy of destabilization of Zimbabwe
was that South Africa saw it as a threat to its own security and to its
programme for the regional economic community, CONSAS (Constellation of Southern African States). CONSAS was essentially a
strategy by South Africa to use its immense economic power and
wealth to manipulate its black member states, and to exert subtle
pressure to ensure that they 'behaved' themselves as far as the white
minority government was concerned. The whole aim of the CONSAS
was the 'total strategy' of survival of the Botha government, which
especially involved the economy as an instrument for maintaining
ultimate political power and the continuance of the basic structure
of apartheid. CONSAS policy was aimed at inducing the African
countries through economic incentives to enter into some degree of
cooperation with South Africa. This would have diminished the
potential threats, (i) of external support for its own domestic insurgents; (ii) of military attack by neighbouring states; and (iii) the threat
of international economic pressure.

However, before Zimbabwean independence the South African
government had hoped that a sympathetic government under
Bishop Abel Muzorewa would win the elections in Zimbabwe.
This could have formed a key member of a South African-dominated
regional economic community, because prior to the elections
Muzorewa had publicly hailed Botha's CONSAS idea and

committed his future government to ensure that Zimbabwe became a member.[21]

But on coming to power, Robert Mugabe prevented this from happening, with his immediate decision to form SADCC (the Southern African Development Coordination Conference) with its explicit goal of liberating their economies from their dependence on the Republic of South Africa.

SADCC is an organization formed by the nine Frontline States: Angola, Botswana, Lesotho, Malawi, Mozambique, Tanzania, Swaziland, Zambia and Zimbabwe. Zimbabwe's decision to join the FLS angered South Africa because it dashed South Africa's high hopes for her CONSAS scheme. South Africa knew that excepting itself, Zimbabwe possessed the strongest economy and transport system in Southern Africa and potentially was the hub round which any SADCC would become a reality. South Africa knew that SADCC with Zimbabwe would emerge as a strong force that would upset most of her regional plans.

Thus the collapse of CONSAS, the strengthening of the FLS by the membership of Zimbabwe and the ability of the FLS diplomatic coalition to found SADCC, represented for South Africa the most shattering regional political defeat. In addition, the CONSAS failure reinforced a creeping international perception of South Africa as a helpless giant, unable to translate her military and economic might into diplomatic supremacy despite a decade of regional schemes and initiatives.

South Africa feared that the Zimbabwean government would support the ANC and allow them to use Zimbabwe as a base to attack South Africa. South Africa's fears were justified, because after independence President Mugabe stated clearly that

> We have moral and political obligations to the people of Namibia and of South Africa. We uphold the right of Namibians to fight for their liberation, to have their land back. Similarly, we uphold the right of the people of South Africa to establish a democratic system in their country. We will assist, at international forums, in the Organisation of African Unity, the Non-aligned Movement and in the UN where we hope to play an active part in obtaining the objective of liberation in those countries.[22]

From this it was clear that South Africa was in need of an alternative means of protecting itself from the potential politico-military threat to its north. In order to counteract this threat South Africa embarked on the following objectives:

(i)   to destroy Zimbabwe's military capabilities and undermine Zimbabwe's national sovereignty;

(ii)   to destroy Zimbabwe's economy so that Zimbabwe's dependence on South Africa remained an established fact;

(iii)   to create a state of chronic political instability by supporting dissidents operating within Zimbabwe;

(iv)   to create the impression that the troubles inside South Africa were not caused by apartheid but by Marxist guerrillas infiltrating through the neighbouring states;

(v)   to create internal chaos in Zimbabwe and force her to pay more attention to her own problems and less to apartheid;

(vi)   to create a buffer against sanctions, by constraining Zimbabwe to publicly oppose international sanctions against South Africa;

(vii)   to force the Zimbabwean government to denounce its Socialist and Marxist tendencies.

With these objectives South Africa's aims were:

(i) to create poverty in Zimbabwe and use this for propaganda at home and abroad, as 'proof' that black majority rule did not work;

(ii) to make Zimbabwe ungovernable and to bring it under South African control;

(iii) to ensure that there was no ANC or PAC threat.

In summary, South Africa's overall objective of destabilizing Zimbabwe was twofold. First, it wanted life to be uncomfortable for the white population of Zimbabwe, so that they would leave and thus frustrate the efforts to create a multiracial society in Zimbabwe. Second, South Africa's destabilization was meant to slow down any development in Zimbabwe and to force the government of Zimbabwe to divert its attention from internal socioeconomic development. If this strategy had been allowed to succeed, it was likely that South Africa would have blunted Zimbabwe's determination to champion the Namibian and apartheid causes among the Frontline States. Overall, an unstable and economically crippled Zimbabwe would be no threat to South Africa.

It is also important to note that South Africa's destabilization was not solely in reaction to the independence of Zimbabwe or to its loss as a friend, but, destabilization was a pre-emptive response by South

Africa to the anticipated developments in the political system of Zimbabwe and those of Southern Africa as a whole, as a result of the independence of Zimbabwe. For South Africa the independence of Zimbabwe had certain long-term implications which would not be in the interests of South Africa's policy of apartheid. (i) South Africa feared the example of a successful multiracial society on its immediate border. (ii) South Africa detested the idea of a one-party Marxist-Leninist state in Zimbabwe as a neighbour. Potentially, that situation would have been disastrous for South Africa and its apartheid policy. South Africa was concerned that the revolutionary ideology of Marxism-Leninism could easily and quickly spill across its border to the disgruntled black majority in South Africa itself. This was possible, if not probable, because, for instance, the ANC and the Pan-Africanist Congress have both been given sanctuary in Zimbabwe. Based on the assumption that no state boundaries have ever or could ever be a barrier to ideas, it was only a matter of time before the revolutionary ideas of Zimbabwe infected the freedom-seeking South African blacks. It was this revolutionary menace of Zimbabwe whose tide South Africa was attempting to stem by destabilizing the country. How far did South Africa achieve these aims and to what extent did Zimbabwe manage to resist these pressures?

2.3 SOUTH AFRICA'S POLITICAL SUBVERSION AND MILITARY SABOTAGE

To achieve these policy objectives South Africa had to keep Zimbabwe militarily weak, politically unstable and economically dependent on South Africa. Immediately after independence, South Africa embarked on a twin programme of military sabotage and political subversion.

Certain historical factors about Zimbabwe's internal security situation helped South Africa to partially implement this programme. Firstly, by the time of independence, South Africa had an excellent knowledge of Zimbabwe's military hardware and vital strategic installations, because of its previous involvement in the Rhodesian war machinery. Secondly, while the Lancaster House Agreement made provision for the establishment of the new Zimbabwean National Army (ZNA), it made no provision for the removal of South African military elements and their mercenaries which ostensibly were integrated into the ZNA but in reality, were hostile to the new government.

However, some of these elements were in fact subsequently incorporated into the post-independence army. In particular, Zimbabwe had a special problem because it inherited the entire Central Intelligence Organization (CIO) from the Smith government. Of course a number of CIO operatives left, but a substantial proportion remained for sabotage work. These factors left Zimbabwe's security in a very dangerous position.[23]

Furthermore, these military security threats from within the newly created Zimbabwe National Army were complemented by South Africa's attempt to regroup elements of the former Rhodesian army within South Africa itself. Before its closure late in 1980, South Africa's Harare embassy was strategically placed to undertake this recruitment role. Most of those recruited were immediately assigned to operate in the security and sensitive border areas of north-eastern and northern Transvaal,[24] bordering Zimbabwe and Mozambique. These border areas had been traditionally patrolled by the 'Recces' or South Africa's Special Air Services. These were highly trained commandos and specialists in 'unconventional warfare'.

Throughout the 1980s, there were five Recce commandos, constituting the elite of the South African army. Many were former members of the Rhodesian Selous Scouts while others were hand-picked white conscripts. Falling under a separate 'Special Force' command in the SADF, the Recces were established in the mid-1970s. Since that time they periodically engaged in 'pseudo-operations'; trained anti-government rebels from Mozambique, Angola and Zimbabwe; hit at ANC targets in a series of cross-border raids and destroyed infrastructure such as oil-refineries in the Frontline States. In particular, this 'Special Force' constituted the operational arm of South African Military Intelligence. Their specific task was to run South Africa's secret war, using techniques of clandestine activity first developed by the Portuguese authorities in Angola and perfected in Rhodesia.

Some of the ex-Rhodesian soldiers operated as free-floating bands of mercenaries, available for hire to the highest bidder. For instance, during the abortive Seychelles coup in 1981, the arms for the operation were delivered to mercenary leader Colonel 'Mad' Mike Hoare from an ex-Rhodesian source in South Africa. Jack Malloch, ex-director of the then private (now nationalized) Zimbabwe air freight company Affretair (which specialised in sanctions-busting during the days of the Smith government) acted as a go-between in Zimbabwe for Mike Hoare, putting him in touch with demobilized white soldiers. Subsequently in Hoare's mercenary expedition to the Seychelles there were former members of the Rhodesian Selous Scouts and Grey Scouts.[25]

Apart from the regroupment of white elements of the former Rhodesian army, South Africa also attempted to mould Bishop Muzorewa's armed auxiliary forces into a special force for sabotage operations in Zimbabwe. At the time of the 1980 general elections between 2500 and 5000 auxiliaries of Bishop Muzorewa were reported to have deserted to South Africa.[26] Training bases were hastily set up in Northern Transvaal, commanded by former Rhodesian white army officers. One black participant claimed that at his training camp in South Africa, there were about 1600 former members of the auxiliary forces. At a High Court hearing in Bulawayo on 26 October 1989[27] a self-confessed saboteur and former member of the Rhodesian auxiliary forces, Scover Dlomo, revealed that he and several others were recruited by two white officers, a Major Van de Riet and a Major Hoare, to travel to South Africa to be trained and return to Zimbabwe to overthrow the Mugabe government and restore Bishop Muzorewa to power. However, in 1981, the entire group was formally integrated into the SADF. In the same year, elements of the group were sent to Mozambique ostensibly to destroy the railway line linking that country and Zimbabwe. But the operation was unsuccessful since the group were surprised by Zimbabwean security forces and three of their members were killed.

White civilians resident in Zimbabwe were also incorporated as agents to operate clandestinely, gathering intelligence information and sometimes carrying out spectacular acts of sabotage. The threat posed by the civilian agents of the South African government was quite substantial. At the time of independence, about 80 000 of Zimbabwe's population of about 275 000 whites were South African citizens.[28] This demographic factor provided South Africa with a significant human infrastructure for internal subversion and sabotage.

These internal and external bases for subversion and sabotage complemented each other, enabling the South African government to launch a multi-faceted programme of destabilization. The targets selected revealed that the South African government's strategy was to launch a series of attacks in quick succession which would have had the ultimate effect of weakening the security and civilian arms of the new government. Following this strategy, in August 1981 the Pretoria regime's saboteurs destroyed munitions worth Z$50 million at Inkomo Barracks, a major military base just outside Harare.[29] This act of sabotage was followed by even more spectacular acts of aggression designed to demonstrate that the regime could hit at any target inside Zimbabwe's borders. During the same month, veteran ANC leader, the movement's representative to Zimbabwe, Joe Nqabi, was assassinated.[30]

These acts were designed to demonstrate to the Zimbabwe government and the ANC that they were equally vulnerable to attack. This was further demonstrated in December 1981 when the national offices of the ZANU(PF) ruling party were destroyed by a bomb which was intended for the party leadership due to meet in the same building the same day.[31] These acts of sabotage amply demonstrated the vulnerability of the Zimbabwe government, since all the saboteurs and assassins or would-be assassins were members of the security services. The chief security officer investigating the death of Joe Nqabi, the ANC representative, used his authority to help a South African agent suspected of the murder to flee the country. The army officer suspected of carrying out the Inkomo sabotage was similarly spirited out of the country.[32] Much more seriously, evidence available since then has revealed that even the Prime Minister's security had been infiltrated. Geoffrey Price, director of security, with responsibility for the security of the Prime Minister and members of the cabinet, was identified as a spy and he evaded arrest by escaping to South Africa.

The defection of these security operatives did not result in the effective neutralization of the extensive military civilian spy network set up by Pretoria; continued acts of military sabotage and events revealed that Pretoria's infiltration of the security forces had been extensive. In July 1982, 13 military aircraft including eight Hawks bought from British Aerospace in 1981 were destroyed by saboteurs[33] at Zimbabwe's main airforce strike base near Gweru. Several white senior airforce officers were implicated in the sabotage and subsequently arrested. This act of sabotage virtually paralysed almost half of Zimbabwe's air force. Together with earlier acts of sabotage South Africa purported to demonstrate that it had the capability to strike at the nerve centres not only of civilian authority but also those of the army and air force.

At the level of security intelligence, the spy network previously coordinated by Pretoria through Geoffrey Price continued to transmit intelligence information to South Africa. For instance, in July 1983 two security operatives of the CIO, Philip Hartlebury and Colin Evans, appeared in a Harare court charged with contravening the official secrets act. The two operatives had been recruited into Pretoria's spy network by Geoffrey Price. The Director of Public Prosecutions revealed that the two had passed on to South Africa security information that they obtained in the course of their duties, including the movements of the Prime Minister and members of the cabinet.[34]

Espionage and sabotage within the formal security and military organizations was complemented by a civilian spy network largely coordinated by white civilians in key positions in the public and private sectors. Early in 1987, evidence of civilian involvement in sabotage and espionage operations became apparent. Caches of arms were discovered in Harare and at Figtree in Matebeleland, resulting in the arrest of three white civilians, two farmers and a dentist.[35] This was part of a wider network of saboteurs who were responsible for a seven-year campaign of bombing, murders and attempted assassinations until the eventual arrest of six key members of the group in 1988.[36]

These civilian operatives of the South African government were involved in the earlier sabotage operations soon after independence; that is, the Inkomo Barracks sabotage up to the 1988 bombings in Harare and Bulawayo. Radio devices seized by Zimbabwean security intelligence after the bomb explosions were similar to those captured from the Mozambican anti-government rebel group, the Mozambique National Resistance (MNR) fighting the FRELIMO government in Mozambique.[37] The equipment was highly sophisticated. It included a military transmitter-receiver called Cynical 30, manufactured by Milcom, a South African company which produces most of the military communications equipment used by the South African Defence Force.[38]

Cynical 30 is a highly sophisticated radio device normally used for covert or clandestine operations and the Zimbabwe National Army had no technical capability to intercept Cynical messages. This meant that the saboteurs could use the Cynical 30 virtually undetected. The device's communication range could be world-wide depending on atmospheric conditions, frequency and the antenna used. Other communications equipment also found included KY500, a data-transmission device also manufactured by Milcom. The device can be linked to another by telephone or could be interfaced to a miniature printer. KY500, which the Zimbabwe National Army has no capability to monitor and intercept, was probably used for secure communications with South Africa through the use of Cynical 30 radios.

Sabotage operations by civilian Zimbabwean agents of the Pretoria regime were occasionally boosted by periodic incursions from South

Africa. In August 1982, three white members of the SADF were ambushed and killed by the ZNA in the Sengwe Communal lands of Zimbabwe near the South African / Mozambique border. A group of black soldiers accompanying them fled back to South Africa. What was significant about the incident was that all three casualties were ex-Rhodesian soldiers then serving in the SADF.[39] They were members of a Special Force Unit coordinated by a special destabilization centre at the SADF headquarters that, as mentioned above, had the specific task of destabilizing neighbouring countries.[40]

2.4 THE MATEBELELAND PROBLEM EXACERBATES DESTABILIZATION

This record of destabilization was exacerbated by the internal political conflicts within Zimbabwe. Internal suspicions and tensions between the two coalition partners in the government of national unity, ZANU(PF) and PF-ZAPU, took a turn for the worse when early in 1982 government raids discovered arms caches on several farms and properties owned by PF-ZAPU.[41] Prior to this there had been many serious clashes between former ZANLA and ZIPRA guerrillas, the most serious being in November 1980 and February 1981 in Entumbane township in western Bulawayo. Fifty men were killed in the first and several hundred in the second. An investigation by Justice Dumbutshena was never published. However, in a later trial, the Director of Public Prosecutions admitted that the November 1980 clash was caused by 'the unprovoked action of ZANLA and the use by them of heavy weaponry'.[42] This led ZIPRA to cache further arms. Prime Minister Mugabe's response was to dismiss key political and military members of PF-ZAPU from the Cabinet and the ZNA. Some of them were detained. This sparked off a wave of desertions by PF-ZAPU cadres previously integrated into the Zimbabwean National Army. These deserters, together with disgruntled and demobilized ex-ZIPRA elements, launched a ruthless programme of armed banditry in the rural areas of Matabeleland.

South Africa took advantage of this internal conflict to recruit, train, arm and infiltrate dissidents into Matebeleland, as they were using UNITA in Angola, the MNR in Mozambique, and the LLA in Lesotho, and as they later were to use the 'Fathers' and 'Vigilantes' inside South Africa itself. But ZIPRA had close ties with the ANC and a strong anti-apartheid tradition, and the new dissidents refused to cooperate with the South African military. Instead, South Africa was required to create an entirely new force, under the banner of 'Super-ZAPU', to act in the shadow of, and in the name of, dissidents. Some Zimbabweans were recruited, particularly from refugee camps in Botswana, trained in South Africa, and sent back into Zimbabwe. They were well-supplied with arms, and were reported to have carried out assassinations of white farmers, and other provocative acts, which led to a crackdown by the Zimbabwe government.

This was part of a much larger military programme designed to create, within South Africa, a 'Matebele Brigade'[43] to act as a catchment group for the constant supply of dissidents for eventual infiltration into Zimbabwe. The Brigade, which was commanded by SADF officer Colonel Breytenbach, also attempted to recruit Zimbabwean migrant workers, particularly mine workers in South Africa. The heavily militarized areas of northern and eastern Transvaal served as a convenient launching pad both for SADF saboteurs and 'Super-ZAPU'/'Matebele Brigade', with four training centres, at Spencer, Phalaborwa, Madibo and Ntabeni. Some dissidents were infiltrated through the largely unpopulated and unpatrolled areas of north-western Botswana, leading to diplomatic strains and occasional military skirmishes between the armed forces of Zimbabwe and Botswana.

Dissident operations in Matebeleland were complemented by hostile propaganda from South Africa. South Africa began to beam hostile propaganda against the Zimbabwe government through Radio Truth which was launched in the studios of the South African Broadcasting Corporation (SABC) early in 1983. The programme was specifically targeted at the Ndebele-speaking population and it was broadcast in English and Ndebele.

Radio Truth accused the Zimbabwean government of corruption, incompetence, inefficiency and implementing a deliberate genocidal policy against the Ndebele. Furthermore, South Africa actively drew up plans to grant 'independence' to a fifth Bantustan – KwaNdebele, comprising a mere 200 square miles of rugged land, 45 miles northeast of Pretoria as a way of attracting Zimbabwe's Ndebele population to defect or secede to the new Bantustan.

The operations of dissidents were designed to cause maximum political and economic damage to Zimbabwe. Dissident attacks were specifically targeted on infrastructural and development projects. The backbone of the country's agricultural sector, the white commercial farmers, were singled out for attack. Rural clinics, roads, rail and other development projects were destroyed and the support staff in the health, agricultural extension, adult literacy, community development and administrative services were attacked and sometimes killed. Supporters of the ruling party ZANU(PF) in the rural areas were also attacked, together with foreign tourists. The strategy was twofold.

Firstly, it intended to demonstrate to the rural population in general that the new government was too weak to protect them; and that the only way to peace, prosperity and development was through collaboration rather than confrontation with apartheid. The aggression through the surrogate dissident attacks was a specific message designed to turn the Zimbabwean people against their government. Secondly, the attack on development and infrastructural projects was designed to disrupt post-independence reconstruction and development efforts. It gave the false impression that the new government was neglecting Matebeleland, and was therefore tribalistic and illegitimate. Finally, the kidnapping and murder of foreign tourists was intended to portray the new state internationally as chronically unstable and therefore dangerous for foreigners. In this way one of Zimbabwe's major foreign exchange-earners, tourism, would be irreparably damaged.

At the height of the dissident problem in 1985, Matebeleland resembled a region in a state of virtual civil war characterized by general militarization. For instance, between July 1985 and December 1985 the crimes committed by dissidents during that six-month period were as follows (figures for January 1985 to June 1985 in brackets): 106 murders (45), 57 rapes (37), 263 armed robberies (253).[44] Millions of dollarsworth of property was destroyed. These attacks were broadened to include the burning down of schools, clinics, hospitals and the murder of teachers.[45] Attempts to negotiate some kind of security agreement with the South African Military Intelligence Directorate (SAMID) and the civilian National Intelligence Service (NIS), did not reduce the intensity of dissident operations.[46] Instead, South Africa began to step up acts of aggression against Zimbabwe. In mid-1986 the administrative offices of the ANC and residential houses were attacked.[47]

During the same period, South Africa began to issue increasingly vocal and periodic threats to invade Zimbabwe for allegedly harbouring ANC guerrillas. Towards the end of 1985, South Africa began to build up its military strength along the common border. In addition, the South African Airforce began to violate Zimbabwean airspace frequently, with the apparent aim of gathering intelligence on Zimbabwe's troop movements. Intelligence reconnaissance on Zimbabwe was also being obtained from satellites. Pretoria used the services of the French SEP company which obtained a contract for shipping and installing a space tracking station to South Africa. At the same time, South Africa recruited about forty French pilots, engineers and technicians who had been employed by French firms making fighter aircraft and helicopter turbo engines. The information gathered was used for the deployment of the SADF's special reconnaissance and commando groups. It was also being passed to 'Super-ZAPU' dissidents. In addition, as already mentioned in this chapter, a major South African Airforce base was established about 100 kilometres from the Zimbabwe border near the northern Transvaal town of Louis Trichardt. This placed Pretoria's most advanced jet fighters within striking distance of Harare, Zimbabwe's capital city. These menacing developments were accompanied by periodic military exercises along the two countries' common border.[48]

2.5 SOUTH AFRICA'S USE OF THE MNR TO DESTABILIZE ZIMBABWE

The security problem facing Zimbabwe in the Western Province of Matebeleland was exacerbated by the opening of a second front in the Eastern Province of Manicaland, bordering Mozambique. In March 1986, a series of land-mine explosions occurred South of Chimanimani in the Eastern districts. This was an act of retaliation by the South African-backed MNR (Mozambique National Resistance) against the deployment of Zimbabwean troops guarding the Beira Corridor (road, rail and oil pipeline) in Mozambique. With a large part of Zimbabwe's army still occupied with the dissident problem in Matebeleland, the country could hardly afford a second front. Available evidence suggests that South Africa specifically ordered the MNR to open up the eastern offensive in a bid to overstretch Zimbabwe's defence capability.[49] Early in 1988 Paulo Oliveira, a former MNR representative to Western Europe, told a press conference that a Brigadier Cornelius van Niekerk of the SADF gave the green light for the MNR to begin operations in Zimbabwe.[50] These attacks, which assumed a new intensity in mid-1987, had been expected to escalate for almost a year following a series of events in Washington at the time of the 'Irangate' scandal, when profits from the sale of arms to Iran were diverted to anti-government groups elsewhere, including Nicaragua.

Although no concrete evidence has as yet emerged to trace any of the funds to Southern Africa, the timing suggests encouragement at the very least and two MNR representatives had a meeting in the White House with the Reagan Administration's Director of Communications.[51] In addition, on 17 August 1986 three representatives of the MNR and three representatives of the self-exiled Reverend Ndabaningi Sithole (leader of ZANU-Ndonga, formerly ZANU-Mwenje, one of the minority parties) met in Washington, DC, and signed a 'Friendship and Co-operation Agreement'.[52] One of Sithole's representatives, Bruce Anderson, headed a South African security company, SAPC Service (Pty) Ltd with offices in Johannesburg. Anderson left Zimbabwe to escape fraud charges.

Sithole appointed Anderson as 'his agent for Southern Africa', authorizing him to 'recruit and employ all personnel that may be necessary to carry out various duties'.[53] Sithole was to pay SAPC Services (Pty) Ltd the equivalent of Z$100 million, with the entire agreement secured by a bond of US$2.5 million. Significantly, the timing of these developments in Washington coincided with the early progress in the internal talks for political unity between ZANU(PF) and PF-ZAPU in Zimbabwe. A possible unity agreement, followed by the cessation of dissident activities in south-western Zimbabwe, would not have augured well for Pretoria's long-term strategy. It would have meant (as it subsequently did) that the South African regime lost a surrogate group of saboteurs. Thus, a new cover was required for the active destabilization of Zimbabwe. On 30 October 1986, 11 days after the plane crash that killed Mozambique's President Samora Machel, the rebel leader, Alfonso Dhlakama of the MNR, announced that he was declaring war on Zimbabwe, and incursions in the eastern front intensified.[54]

Zimbabwe's Eastern Province had been the traditional operating ground for MNR before Zimbabwe's independence. After its formation and sponsorship by the Smith regime[55] in the mid-1970s the MNR was based in the hilly areas of the Eastern Province. By 1979, a year before Zimbabwe's independence, the MNR was reporting to the CIO office in Mutare. They had two bases, one at Nyanga about 80 kilometres to the north of Mutare and another at Chisumbanje in the remote south-east of Manicaland province close to the borders of Mozambique and South Africa. Their main job then was to obtain information on ZANLA. After Zimbabwe's independence South Africa assumed the control and sponsorship of the MNR.

Several factors operated to the advantage of the MNR in Manicaland Province. In the first place, most of the MNR operatives spoke the same language as Zimbabweans along the eastern border and some of them had relatives on both sides of the border, making infiltrations quite easy. In addition, the chronic labour shortage in Zimbabwe's eastern agricultural plantations made the cheap Mozambican labourers an attractive proposition. Consequently MNR operatives were easily infiltrated as work-hungry agricultural labourers.

Secondly, having operated in the area for over ten years, the MNR had an excellent knowledge of the rugged topography of the province which was easily put to military advantage. Thirdly as mentioned above, some of the former officers and soldiers of the Rhodesian army had been periodically seconded to MNR by the SADF. A group of these officers joined an MNR contingent which sabotaged an important electricity substation on the north bank of the Zambezi river in Mozambique in 1985.[56] These officers possessed not only an excellent knowledge of the area, but were also familiar with the operational modes, battle formation and tactics of the ZNA. Finally, the area around Chipinge, south of Mutare, was the last bastion of the discredited Reverend Ndabaningi Sithole. Consequently, the Pretoria regime, through the MNR, attempted to tap the anti-government sentiments in the area by forging an operational linkage with Sithole's Zimbabwean Freedom Army (ZIFA).[57]

The areas seriously affected by the MNR insurgency were around the north-east (Mount Darwin, Rushinga and Nyamaropa); east (Nyanga); and south-east (Chipinge and Chisumbanje); all adjacent to the Mozambique border.[58] The choice of targets had been broadly similar to that of 'Super-ZAPU'. Apart from large-scale massacres, mutilations, armed robberies and rapes, the MNR concentrated on destroying developmental projects in the province. In 1987, the year which marked the onset of heightened MNR sabotage activities, several agricultural production projects of the Agricultural and Rural Development Authority (ARDA – a government parastatal body) were singled out for destruction. These ferocious bandit activities were also directed against peasants in the affected rural areas. Several incidents of brutality can be cited:[59]

(i) On 15 June 1987, a group of 100 armed men crossed the border from Mozambique and infiltrated 30 kilometres into Zimbabwe's north-eastern Rushinga district. They burnt whole villages and looted rural shops, abducted 70 villagers, wounding several others.

(ii)   On 5 July 1987, 29 of the abducted villagers, along with 10 Zimbabwean fishermen abducted in a separate incident, were found murdered inside Mozambique.

(iii)   On 2 August 1988 five MNR bandits attacked Tsovera village in Chiredzi in the Zimbabwe lowveld. The villagers fled, leaving behind children and old folk. The bandits killed the children aged between two and five years before looting food and clothing from several homesteads. The whole village was set alight.

(iv)   On 3 August 1988, five MNR bandits stole livestock from Mashamba village, Chiredzi. Twelve people were seriously assaulted.

(v)   On 16 August 1988, five MNR bandits attacked Chimbi village in Chisumbanje, killing two people, wounding several others and looting the village.

(vi)   On 2 September 1988, bandits attacked Ngera village, Rushinga, abducting several people and fatally wounding two.

(vii)   At Rukangare business centre in Chisumbanje, on 14 September 1988 about 10 MNR bandits looted several shops.

(viii) On 29 November 1988 about 30 MNR bandits raided Ndali village in Chiredzi Communal Lands. They killed a total of eight people and looted clothing and food.

(ix)   On 4 December 1988 the MNR attacked and looted Kashava village in the Mount Darwin area.

These incidents marked the beginning of an intensification of the MNR offensive across the rugged and mountainous 1200-kilometres eastern frontier. As already catalogued, with the offensive came the pattern of MNR brutality all too familiar to Mozambique – murder, mutilation, rape and arson. These brutalities have punctuated the daily lives of villagers, children, school pupils, etc. in the north-eastern border, from Rushinga down to Chiredzi. In many areas, villagers have been reduced to virtual bush-dwellers in fear of MNR attacks on homesteads. From 15 June 1987 to 16 December 1988 a total of 286 Zimbabwean villagers had been murdered by MNR bandits inside Zimbabwe.[60] Significantly, during the onset of the MNR's eastern offensive in mid-1987, 'Super-ZAPU' also intensified its operations in the Midlands and Matebeleland provinces, killing white farmers and missionaries[61] and stretching the operational capacity of the ZNA almost to the limit.

This gruesome record of destabilization by South Africa, 'Super-ZAPU' and the MNR proved to be very costly for the Zimbabwe government in particular and civil society in general. The dissident menace, coupled with the possibility of an attack from South Africa, forced Zimbabwe to maintain a disproportionately large army and police force for such a small country. In 1986, the armed forces numbered 42 000, while police and paramilitary forces numbered 18 000. After 1986, two additional brigades were added. Frequently, a semi-reserve force was periodically called up for fixed periods of service. As we shall see in the next chapter, the consequent defence spending had adverse effects on investment levels, not only in the productive sectors of the economy but in other vital service sectors of society as well.

Apart from the regular army and police, Zimbabwe had to embark on a programme of general militarization in all its provinces in an attempt to forestall the sporadic dissident and South African attacks on vital installations and developmental projects. A National Militia, numbering about 20 000, was trained and deployed in all the eight provinces. This increased level of militarization did not augur well for the democratic development of the country. It served at times to increase the power of the military–security establishment and the executive over the legislature and the judiciary. In addition, the general proliferation of arms in society through the militia programme increased the danger that violent crime would become a means of livelihood, particularly in a situation of rising unemployment and economic decline.

3 Zimbabwean Defence and Security Policy in the Context of the South African Threat

The South African strategic framework briefly summarized in Chapter 1 forced Zimbabwe to remain on the defensive during the 1980s. It was clear that South Africa had decided that life for Mugabe should not be easy. Yet in general terms, Zimbabwe had more of a posture than a policy against South Africa, which was long on rhetoric and short on coherence. This posture was increasingly isolating Zimbabwe and caused real danger for Mugabe. This chapter will examine the strength and weaknesses of the Zimbabwean government in relation to defence policies and national security during the destabilization period.

During the early 1980s the extent of Zimbabwe's security weakness has been shown by the following factors. Firstly, it was painfully evident that only a handful of Zimbabwean decision-makers had any real understanding of South African security policy in the region, moulded as it was around the philosophy of the Total National Strategy. This was a dangerous situation for Zimbabwe given that South Africa dominated the region. Secondly, Zimbabwe's own security and defence policies lacked coherence and long-term planning. Thirdly, Zimbabwe remained vulnerable to South African incursions on its borders. Fourthly, Zimbabwe had committed itself to the survival of the Front for the Liberation of Mozambique (FRELIMO) in the government of Mozambique. The Mozambican civil war showed all the signs of draining Zimbabwean resources without necessarily saving the FRELIMO government. In this sense the Mozambican commitment was without doubt the most serious obstacle to Zimbabwe's economic-growth prospects over the years that followed. Finally, Zimbabwe's unresolved security problems in Matabeleland posed a serious threat to the country's stability.

However, apart from all these dangers and threats, Mugabe remained strongly committed to fight for the end of the apartheid government. The question then was, how long could this commitment outlast South African hostility and endure in a regional atmosphere of deep insecurity?

We can begin to answer this question by analysing Zimbabwe's behaviour in the context of South Africa's policy of destabilization. We have seen in Chapter 1 factors that raised South Africa's fears about Mugabe's coming to power, such as:

(i)   Mugabe's socialist ideologies which were in sharp contrast to South Africa's defence of apartheid and capitalism;

(ii)   the fear of Zimbabwe being used by ANC as a base to attack South Africa; the fear of Mugabe preventing Zimbabwe from joining the South African-inspired CONSAS;

(iii)   the concern about Zimbabwe becoming economically strong enough to reduce its ties with South Africa and Zimbabwe's possibility of building a military strong enough not to be deterred by South Africa;

(iv)   Mugabe's bold policy of reconciliation – his commitment to a multi-racial society posed a serious alternative to apartheid;

(v)   the fear of the 'total onslaught'[1] from the Moscow-led communist conspiracy through Zimbabwe.

3.1 ZIMBABWE IN THE CONTEXT OF SOUTH AFRICA'S THREAT

Robert Mugabe's first year in power was symbolized by racial reconciliation, economic recovery, and pragmatic social and foreign policies. Mugabe had tried to allay South African fears by not seeking direct confrontation with the South African government. After independence Mugabe announced that South Africa's and Zimbabwe's future relations would be conducted on the basis of a mutual recognition of the differences that existed between the two countries. The differences were marked by their political ideologies; South Africa disliked Zimbabwe's multiracial policy and its socialist[2] rhetoric and Zimbabwe disliked the South African apartheid system. Mugabe assured South Africa that Zimbabwe would not interfere in South Africa's internal affairs and, similarly, it would expect South Africa to respect Zimbabwe's sovereignty.[3] But Zimbabwe's foreign policy was well known to be hostile towards the apartheid system. The Zimbabwean Foreign Minister Witness Magwende demonstrated this point clearly when he addressed the UN General Assembly, in New York on 11 October 1982:

> Regarding the obnoxious apartheid system in South Africa itself, Zimbabwe's position is well known. We have always said that we would like to see the total dismantling of apartheid and racist minority rule in that part of our region. We demand, instead, a democratic system of government which sees all the people of that country, regardless of race, religion, language, and sex, as equal citizens of their land.[4]

On the same note the Foreign Minister told the UN General Assembly that the government and people of Zimbabwe supported the struggle for freedom, equality and social justice being waged by the liberation movements in South Africa. He appealed to the international community, to continue and even intensify its material, moral, diplomatic and political support to the commendable efforts of South Africa to free itself from the apartheid yoke.

To the South Africans this made Mugabe in many respects more dangerous than Samora Machel, the leader of Mozambique. While Machel embraced Marxism-Leninism, Mugabe practised social democracy. While Machel accepted ANC guerrilla cadres, Mugabe rejected them. This was Mugabe's most important foreign policy, the reasons for which he stated himself at the time:

> I cannot see us organizing war against South Africa. It is not our responsibility to do so. It is the duty of the people of South Africa themselves to take up arms against the system if they feel it oppresses them.... We will not be able to assist militarily. However, not that we are against South African liberation movements fighting but the realities are that we must act in a manner conducive to the preservation and consolidation of the independence of our own country. We have just emerged from seven years of armed conflict, and we do not want to be fighting another war against South Africa. That aside, there is also the fact that South Africa is our neighbour and we have to co-exist with it. The economic ties between Zimbabwe and South Africa are a reality we have to recognize for a long time to come.[5]

This was a very important initiative because Mugabe avoided falling into South Africa's trap, which was to find a military excuse to attack

Zimbabwe. Mugabe's policies surprised some people especially when he preferred British military assistance instead of Soviet military aid in the merger of ZANLA, ZIPRA and the Rhodesian army. Internationally, Mugabe's political prestige soared and it was postulated by conservative American academics that Mugabe was a potential 'African Bismarck'.[6]

Here Mugabe was doing the unthinkable, that is, making African revolution respectable, even moderate. But little of this was welcome to Pretoria, because it was unclear about Mugabe's motives. The fact that Zimbabwe did not fit into the Afrikaner belief that the Frontline States were part of Moscow's 'total onslaught' on South Africa made it difficult to fully apply the policy of 'total strategy'. To Pretoria, Mugabe's moderation was the equivalent of Lenin's New Economic Policy: a transitional phase while the Marxist true-believers, led by the subtle Mugabe himself, entrenched themselves in power. It was not in South Africa's interests to allow a consolidation of Zimbabwean military and economic strength to fuel the concealed ideology of Afro-Marxism.

The South African government used the ethnic and radical tensions in the new Zimbabwe to achieve some of its aims of 'total strategy'. In his economic policy towards South Africa, Mugabe was quite clear that he would remain fully committed to the anti-apartheid cause; he would channel his commitment through his active role in the international community and the Frontline States. He stated,

> We will assist, . . . at international forums in the Organization of African Unity (OAU), the Non-aligned Movement and in the UN, where we will abide by the organization's decisions with regard to the situation in Namibia and South Africa and we hope to play an active part in obtaining the objective of liberation in those countries.[7]

Mugabe knew that his own government could not stand alone against South Africa's military and economic pressure without the help of the international community, and with all these moves he was trying to avoid a direct confrontation with the South African government. He wanted the apartheid problem to remain an international problem and not to be a South African–Zimbabwean problem. At the same time Mugabe was aware that Zimbabwe's stability, prosperity and freedom depended very substantially on the political changes in South Africa.

Many of Mugabe's actions on economic policy towards South Africa were initially restrained because a large proportion of Zimbabwean industry was, in whole or in part, in South African ownership. The Zimbabwean government was aware that South Africa could use this ownership as an effective lever against any serious attempts to oppose Pretoria's interests. This could have had a serious effect on the Zimbabwean national economy. As a result, Mugabe's economic and political moves both inside and outside the country needed to be weighed carefully before being implemented.

However, the military and economic power of South Africa strengthened Mugabe's government call for reconciliation and national unity[8] in the country because he knew that there was no way he could stand against South Africa's pressure if divided. Apart from national reconciliation and national unity, the government needed to build a strong army, an army committed to serve the interests of the nation and not the interests of any particular political party.

3.2   DEFENCE AND SECURITY POLICY

After independence, Zimbabwean defence and security policy had been haunted rather than shaped by the South African threat. Zimbabwe's vulnerability to the armed might of Pretoria, along with pragmatic calculations concerning economic strategy, dictated an ambiguous, indeed incoherent defence posture.

Zimbabwe's first priority was the integration of the three rival armies for purposes of internal security. The joint high command set up in April 1980 faced the staggering task of welding a regular army of some 40 000 troops from over 80 000 combatants. Aided by an outstanding British military advisory and Training Team, the new Zimbabwe National Army (ZNA) underwent an extraordinarily rapid development in the years 1980–86. Integration was completed by early 1982. This army survived the ZIPRA–ZANLA clashes at Entumbane in 1982 in which several hundred men were killed. This marked an achievement for Mugabe because everybody feared that the ZIPRA–ZANLA clash could spread into the ZNA and lead into a serious civil war.

During this period, both ZANLA and ZIPRA guerrillas stockpiled arms. Some former ZIPRA guerrillas blamed ZANLA for the clashes and also believed that ZIPRA guerrillas and commanders were being marginalized in the army integration exercise. Generally speaking, there was some discontent in Nkomo's ZAPU Party at the way Mugabe's ZANU Party shared power. Seeds for the creation of the problem had been sown at independence and before. While the majority of PF-ZAPU members accepted ZANU(PF) leadership, there was a small group which saw things differently. Though it might be true that the country was free, they could not accept that PF-ZAPU was the junior partner in the government. At this juncture, it is important to highlight some of the central issues that caused discontent among the people with the way things were going in the new government. It became clear within the government leadership that their socialist ideals were basically incompatible with the structural features of the government.

After independence, many Zimbabweans came home to join the administration; among them were those less committed to socialism, less ideological than some of the leaders in the party. This group of people were seen as 'aspiring inheritors'[9] who desired to have fine houses, good government transport and as good a standard of living as the white settlers. In January 1989, Mugabe set up a commission of inquiry,[10] known as the *Sandura Commission*, in order to root out corruption among Ministers and reduce elitism. At least five Cabinet Ministers were found to be involved in corruption and they lost their jobs.[11] These findings confirmed the serious doubts which existed about any trend towards autocratic tendencies where the party leadership was not accountable to the electorate on a regular basis.

This symbolized the conflict within the party between the reformists, who believed that structural factors must take precedence over ideological purity, and the radicals, who believed that only strong action in pursuit of the proper ideological goals could alter the structural constraints in Zimbabwe. Such conflict of ideas raised a problem as to how best to resolve this frustrating reality which lay at the heart of political dispute within the party. On one hand, the government found it difficult to meet popular demands and to cope with the initial challenges created by the war. This produced not only pockets of disaffection in the countryside but also within the leadership. To make things worse, the country was faced with the most severe droughts, and this resulted in a decline of the government's popularity. The people's hopes of the post-independence era had been dashed. There was economic decline and this caused an escalation in the cost of living. Although the minimum wage had twice been increased, the farm workers and domestic servants could not translate this into a noticeable increase in their standard of living, as transport costs, rents, many items of food, and consumer goods increased even more in price. On the other hand, while the government had made pronouncements and promises about land distribution and the creation of new jobs, not much land had been distributed, nor had new jobs been created in the numbers desired. Shortages had not been eliminated and many people were conscious that the promises of independence had not been truly fulfilled. This was particularly true with Matabeleland, where the historical division of land between the races was more disadvantageous to blacks than in Mashonaland. There was greater pressure on the land from Matabele peasants, but the problem was that there was little fertile and well-watered land available for purchase and distribution. The droughts had compounded the feeling among these peasants that independence had not brought any kind of millennium. The combination of drought and overworked communal lands had created conditions of real distress to most peasants.

Apart from these problems, there was discontent among the ZIPRA and ZANLA forces. Although ZANU and ZAPU had come together in the latter months of the guerrilla war to form the Patriotic Front, this was more due to the wishes of their patrons in Mozambique and Zambia than to the desires of their leaders. Many of the ZANU leadership, particularly those who had themselves been personally involved in the guerrilla war, believed that their efforts and the blood of their comrades had been primarily responsible for the downfall of white rule. They felt that ZIPRA forces had done less than their share of the fighting and moreover, had been deliberately kept out of the battle for use at a later date. Certain ZANU politicians believed that Nkomo had not committed them wholeheartedly to the liberation struggle, because Nkomo's long-term plan was to watch while the white settlers and the ZANLA forces fought each other and then move in with his more conventional forces to establish a victorious position over both the other armies. Even those who did not hold such views harboured doubts about Nkomo's motives and resented ZAPU'S expectation that it should enjoy political power greater than was warranted by its contribution to the war. The basic question at stake, therefore, was control of political power by PF ZAPU. This discontent was widened by Mugabe's dismissal of Nkomo and three other ZAPU ministers from the government after the discovery of arms caches on farms owned by the ZAPU company Nitram. Mugabe felt that the hidden arms were part of a plan to overthrow his government. Therefore, the dismissal of the ZAPU ministers by the government was meant to demonstrate two things; that the government was not prepared to be taken for granted and to make ZAPU's senior political leadership accountable for the activities of its structures and members even though it may not have been involved.

The expulsion of Nkomo and the continued detention of Dabengwa and Masuku[12] infuriated most of the ZAPU people. But in many ways the worst blow was the confiscation of Nitram and other properties. As a result several hundred men were thrown out of work and some evicted from their homes or farms. This was a big blow because many of them had invested some of their demobilization money in Nitram and lost what they saw as their only hope for a better settled life. Hundreds of these men returned to the bush in Matabeleland and took weapons with them and in addition there were incidents of armouries being robbed.[13] Some dissidents were able to establish bases in remote country near Lupane, which ZIPRA had controlled during the liberation war. Some turned to banditry elsewhere and some were used by the South African government. Mugabe quickly responded by sending in the army and imposing a series of curfews. A lot of killing took place. It is estimated that up to the time of the amnesty in 1988, 342 bandits had been killed, 57 wounded and 275 captured, 618 civilians were killed and 484 wounded, while 68 security forces were killed and 79 wounded.[14] However, by 1986 the ZNA was fielding five infantry brigades with a sixth brigade forming a Presidential Guard of brigade strength. In addition, the training infrastructure, based on an NCO School of Infantry, a Military Academy for junior officer training and a Staff College offering a command and staff course, made the ZNA one of the most advanced of African armies.[15] With information training taking place at a Battalion Battle School in Nyanga, the ZNA was able to provide operational support to Mozambique in addition to waging counter-insurgency in Matabeleland.

While these achievements were real, they were not without cost. South Africa tried to dislocate Zimbabwe's military development while providing the very rationale for it. This led President Mugabe to embark on a policy of building up a large and strong army. In January 1981 he stated that Zimbabwe would have to create a large army at the expense of economic growth because Pretoria 'poses a threat to our democracy'.[16] Mugabe's fears were soon underlined when the SADF infiltrated and destroyed a quarter of Zimbabwe's Air Force planes in 1983.[17] This was a devastating blow because much of the AFZ's strike and interception capability was destroyed. The pilot expertise of the AFZ was irretrievably lost and the ZNA lost its air umbrella. It was unlikely that the AFZ would for years attain the strike capability and operational effectiveness it possessed in 1982. This posed grave problems for ZDF operations in Mozambique.

It was then clear that the country's defence policy had to be immediately revised if it was to survive the South African threat. The defence policy needed to concentrate on much more careful resource planning, on threat assessment and financial budgeting. It needed to increase its army. It needed to re-equip her Air Force and replace all the planes destroyed by the South African saboteurs. At Army Headquarters both the operations and logistics branches required a proper planning organization. The ZNA had to acquire more conventional military skills when it assumed the defensive role in a newly independent Zimbabwe. The government policy of appointing the army high command according to political reliability rather than professional prowess had to change. The army needed professional leaders, people who were able to study and think carefully about South Africa's policy of 'total strategy'. The Zimbabwean government needed to tighten up its security on its borders to prevent South African incursions.

Apart from these factors, Zimbabwe's survival also depended on how it managed firstly its general geostrategic situation and secondly, how deeply Zimbabwean forces became committed to the survival of the FRELIMO government in Mozambique. In both areas, South Africa was crucial in Zimbabwe's security equation. Thirdly, how would it resolve its internal conflict between ZANU and ZAPU? In terms of its general geostrategic position, Zimbabwe remained vulnerable to South African incursions in the south, through Beitbridge, in the west along the long Botswana–Zimbabwe border, in the northwest from SADF units stationed in the Caprivi Strip and in the east from MNR guerrillas and potentially, also from ZANU–Sithole insurgents. Such strategic vulnerabilities created a serious problem for Zimbabwe which was almost insuperable.

This was not the only serious security problem that Zimbabwe faced during the 1980s. Its defence establishment lacked the mobility to create a quick-reaction force. The lack of such a force was displayed during the May 1986 SADF raid on ANC offices in Harare. With the vital air umbrella unavailable, Zimbabwe faced a serious defence problem. In practical terms, there was little the ZDF could do to prevent South African incursions from the south, west and northwest, given its minuscule defence resources. Zimbabwe's hopes rested on the achievements of its forces in Mozambique where the government had put much of its military commitment.

3.3 ZIMBABWE'S MILITARY INVOLVEMENT IN MOZAMBIQUE

The security of the Mutare–Beira oil pipeline in 1982 was not the only major reason why Zimbabwe committed itself to Mozambique. Zimbabwe could have sent its troops to Mozambique regardless of the Mutare–Beira oil pipeline, because under the terms of the 1981 Zimbabwe–Mozambique Defence Agreement it is stated: 'We have concurred that an attack against Mozambique shall be regarded as an attack against Zimbabwe...'.[18] This agreement would have required Zimbabwe to send its troops because Mozambique was an old ally[19] and its involvement in the Mozambican war could be seen as a repayment of its war debts. By ensuring that FRELIMO government remained in power Mugabe secured his own political stability because he would not tolerate Zimbabwe opposition groups operating from bases in Mozambique. The other reason why Zimbabwe would have joined in the Mozambican war regardless of the economic interests, is that, since African countries had rallied behind Zimbabwe's struggle for liberation, independent Zimbabwe was conscious of its indebtedness for that support. Zimbabwe saw itself as having an important responsibility in continuing the struggle for the total liberation of Africa, as an expression of its gratitude for the invaluable support it received from the rest of the continent.

The Zimbabwean nationalists were aware of the wholehearted support given by the Frontline States of Zambia, Mozambique, Botswana, Angola and Tanzania. In fact these states sacrificed or delayed their own development as a contribution to Zimbabwe's liberation.[20] States like Zambia and Mozambique incurred the wrath of Ian Smith, to the extent that their economic infrastructures were wrecked by the Rhodesian attacks. Zimbabwean guerrillas used the neighbouring countries as sanctuaries and as staging bases for the fight to the finish in Zimbabwe, thus exposing those countries to retaliation of the Rhodesian Air Force. The Frontline States' logical expectation was that as soon as independence for Zimbabwe was accomplished, the real task of economic development in the Frontline region would resume in earnest, with Zimbabwe playing a pivotal role. This would

be so, not only because it would be Zimbabwe's expression of gratitude for the support it received during the war, but also because, for
historical reasons, Zimbabwe had a more developed economy, which
would in turn stimulate the economies of the other states. In this
sense, Zimbabwe had an obligation to help Mozambique, as it had
sacrificed so much for the independence of Zimbabwe. Zimbabwe
took the disturbance in Mozambique seriously because South Africa
was behind the civil war in Mozambique. Mugabe perceived South
Africa as a fundamental threat not only to the survival of Zimbabwe
but to Southern Africa as a whole.

For Mugabe apartheid not only symbolized the antithesis of the
new Zimbabwean domestic order, but the policies of the South African
regime also presented an immediate threat to Zimbabwe's ability to
establish domestic stability and maintain its legitimacy. Mugabe saw
South African racism as the underlying cause of regional tensions and
instabilities, which resulted in the diversion of resources from development to defence. Apartheid was perceived as a direct threat to
Zimbabwe rather than merely a distant evil; such perceptions spurred
the government towards overt and active opposition to South Africa.
Mugabe became more convinced that his country's apparent success
in creating a prosperous non-racial society was one of the most
important reasons for South African destabilization. He considered
the costs of policies such as economic sanctions against South Africa
to be short-term necessities in the face of a fundamental threat to the
stability of the new Zimbabwe and his conviction was that the risk
was worth taking because the cause was right. Conversely, Mugabe
anticipated that elimination of apartheid would lead to the end of
destabilization, which was a precondition for any successful pursuit
of peace at home or in the region. Mugabe viewed the elimination of
apartheid as fundamental for maintaining a non-racial society at
home as well as supporting the pan-African ideal of racial equality.
The more South Africa intensified its attacks on Zimbabwe, the more
determined and convinced Zimbabwe was that the South African
regime must go, together with its policy of apartheid.

Mugabe became even more vocal both abroad and at home in
attacking the South African policy of destabilization and argued
strongly for implementation of sanctions. Zimbabwe had joined the
international system and had established itself as a voice to be
reckoned with in world councils.[21] It used its position and influence
to persuade the international community to isolate South Africa and
to support it in its effort of resisting the military and economic

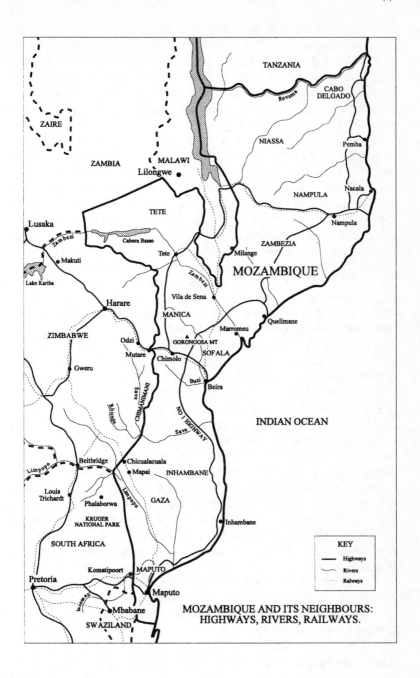

MOZAMBIQUE AND ITS NEIGHBOURS:
HIGHWAYS, RIVERS, RAILWAYS.

pressure from South Africa. Mugabe's foreign policy of reconciliation, his commitment to racial equality, his attempt to strengthen cooperation and solidarity among the other black-ruled states in Southern Africa through the promotion of Southern African regional cooperation, and his commitment to pursue opposition to apartheid boosted his image within the international community as an able and serious leader.

By adopting this dangerous policy against South Africa, Mugabe knew that he had the support of the rest of the Frontline States, the whole African continent and the rest of the progressive world. Through the Frontline States the OAU, the Non-Aligned Movement and the Commonwealth, Mugabe demanded the promotion of mandatory comprehensive international sanctions against South Africa. For Mugabe this was one of his weapons to fight against the apartheid regime. Although acknowledging that all Zimbabweans would suffer, Mugabe assured them that the country would survive. In support of Mugabe's stand, *The Herald* averred that 'to those who say the move is tantamount to suicide, we can only say that the way things are going we are being slowly strangled anyway.'[22] The *Financial Gazette* declared its support by calling for coordinated international pressures on the South African government because 'the futility of dialogue with the South African government without accompanying pressure has been demonstrated in all Commonwealth conferences. Time has been wasted and more lives lost.'[23]

These factors dictated an acceleration of Zimbabwean military involvement in Mozambique. As a consequence, the number of troops guarding the Beira Corridor went up from 7000 to 10 000 in a matter of months in 1984. On 7 August 1985 Mugabe gave an open-ended commitment to the survival of Mozambique, by stating that Zimbabwe would eventually deploy up to 30 000 troops.[24] This was clearly related to the importance of guarding the pipeline and reopening Beira for Zimbabwe's trade but a debate between those arguing for a minimal defence of the 'Beira Corridor' and those wanting a wider commitment to FRELIMO'S security seems to have been won by the latter.

The Beira Corridor was of major strategic importance for Zimbabwe in re-establishing peace in Mozambique, because if the Mozambican rail and road routes were cut, Zimbabwe would be almost entirely dependent upon South Africa for surface transport. The Zimbabwean Minister of State for Security, Emmerson Munangagwa, stated that 'It [the Beira Corridor] is so important that we will keep it open at every cost.'[25] This perception was reinforced by the airborne assault by ZNA paratroops on the Gorongosa base at Casa Banana in August 1985 and the overrunning of the MNR's territorial base on the Pungwe at Nyarunyaru in November 1985. Nevertheless Zimbabwean operations were still limited and they failed to prevent further MNR penetration into Zambezi and Tete provinces, which cut Mozambique virtually in half. In November 1986 after the death of President Machel, Mugabe told the Zimbabwean parliament that

> Survival of Mozambique is our survival. The fall of Mozambique will certainly be our fall. . . . All and one stand together. All and one fight together.[26]

The words were followed by serious political actions. Mugabe knew that it would be very difficult for him to fight the enemy alone; effective cooperation was needed from other independent African states in the region. Mugabe took the initiative in proposing the establishment of an African Defence Force for protecting the security, especially of the Southern African countries suffering under the destabilization policy. This proposal was endorsed by African chiefs of Staff in Harare at an OAU summit,[27] but nothing materialized afterwards, in terms of the implementation of the proposed idea. There were suggestions of a possible Commonwealth military force to protect the Beira Corridor, but nothing further was discussed about this proposal. It could have been difficult to agree upon a Commonwealth Defence Force, given the problems encountered already in the Commonwealth in obtaining consensus on the sanction issue. Another possibility was a Non-Aligned Movement Defence Force, which could have included land, sea and air units coupled with a Non-Aligned technical and administrative corps and Non-Aligned Movement Compensation fund.[28] Once again this idea was never explored.

However, Mugabe managed to persuade the Frontline States to stand firm with Maputo and denounce MNR's activities. This was welcomed by the Tanzanian government, which sent 2000 troops to operate in the northern part of Mozambique. Pressure was applied to Malawi to secure its border to prevent MNR's infiltration. It was agreed between Britain, Zimbabwe and Mozambique that the number of Mozambican officers being trained by British Military Advisory and Training Team (BMATT) would be doubled by mid-1987.[29]

Zimbabwe's widened commitments in the east also led to attempts to provide security in the west by convening a meeting of the Botswana–Zimbabwe joint commission on defence and security. Mugabe succeeded in getting increased Botswana aid in border surveillance against ZIPRA insurgents and managed to persuade Gaborone to declare the MNR a 'regional problem'.[30] This was an astute political move by Mugabe because it lessened the internal security burden and deepened his relationships with his neighbours. The whole idea of border cooperation was to isolate MNR and so weakened its position.

As a sign of his commitment, Mugabe increased his military and defence spending which then overtook the education vote as the largest ministry appropriations, outweighing developmental planning. Nineteen per cent of the Zimbabwean budget was appropriated to defence.[31] Yet the commitment to Mozambique was fraught with danger for Zimbabwe. The SADF's support for the MNR presented the spectre of South Africa attenuating Zimbabwe's military capability by supplying and arming the MNR. The ZDF faced the prospect of being bled to death in the Mozambican bush by Pretoria without the SADF firing a shot. Mugabe then had to face up to the economic and financial demands of two major complementary requirements: the funding of his external military commitments and the increasing cost of the country's internal security.

3.4   THE INTERNAL SECURITY PROBLEM: MUGABE'S COMMITMENT

Yet more problems loomed in the face of the 'Eastern commitment' and involved questions concerning increased reliance on the Zimbabwe People's Militia[32] (ZPM) for internal security, along with the possibility of conscription; MNR infiltration into eastern Zimbabwe to outflank the ZDF; and finally the issue of air-force rearmament.

Mugabe needed to do something; in 1982 the strength of the ZPM was aimed at 20 000. By 1985 some 9000 militia had trained but in 1986 the funds allocated to paramilitary training in the defence vote actually decreased. Paradoxically, while the ZPM role increased, the funds to meet its demands did not match the role. If conscription and national service was introduced it was quite possible that defence spending would have become ruinous.[33] Then there was the threat of MNR infiltration into eastern Zimbabwe while the ZDF remained locked in operations in central and northern Mozambique. In 1986 when the MNR declared war on Zimbabwe for supporting FRELIMO, Mugabe dismissed the challenge with the derisive comment, 'Oh, come on.'[34] In June 1987 there was an attack on a village in Rushinga by MNR. This threat did not worry Mugabe very much, and he continued to restructure the internal security network.

Mugabe was aware that unless the air force attained the strike capability and operational effectiveness it possessed in 1982, his internal security was at great risk from South Africa. In May 1986 Mugabe announced that his government was determined to re-equip the AFZ in order to defend the sovereignty of the nation.[35] In April 1987 it was alleged that Mugabe had purchased advanced jet combat interceptors, such as the 12 MiG-29 Fulcrums from the Soviet Union.[36] This deal was denied by the Zimbabwe government, but it is worth considering the reasons why it would have raised problems for Zimbabwe's security if such modern jet combat aircraft were purchased.

Firstly, the AFZ did not possess the pilots to fly such advanced combat jets as the MiG-29s and this could only imply a more active Eastern bloc role in the Zimbabwe defence effort. The spectre of MiG-29s being flown by Russian or Cuban pilots would provide South Africa with all the justification required to launch a pre-emptive strike on Zimbabwe.

Secondly, in attempting to counter South African air supremacy by tackling its own combat-fighter weakness, Zimbabwe might well be playing directly into the hands of Pretoria's military hawks who could point out that Zimbabwe was fulfilling its role in the Marxist 'total onslaught' on South Africa. The pressure for pre-emption could have well become overwhelming.

Thirdly, if Soviet jets and Eastern bloc personnel were to be stationed at the AFZ bases of Thornhill and New Sarum, Zimbabwe would have courted South African aggression. The destruction of the AFZ's new British Hawk jets in 1982 by South Africa was a clear signal that it did not want Zimbabwe to possess any aircraft that could offset Pretoria's air superiority.

In short, any potential AFZ air combat ability which offset South African air superiority, even marginally, risked a bellicose response from Pretoria. All these factors created a political and security problem for Mugabe against his enemy, South Africa. Mugabe was left with very little option. He either had to make a deal with the South African government or he had to make sure that the Matabeleland problem was solved and that there was political unity in the country. Anything apart from this unity would leave Mugabe's political position dangerously exposed. The one thing he could do was to agree to share power with ZAPU.

The South African threat to Zimbabwe's defence plus the dissidence problem forced the two political leaders Mugabe and Nkomo to accept that Zimbabwe was greater than its internal factions and that national interest superseded party interests. The time had come for both the politicians and the people of Zimbabwe to realize that the future strength and prosperity of Zimbabwe lay in the unity of its peoples under national goals and not under any party's interests. The people of Zimbabwe needed politicians who were genuinely committed to the restoration of peace, law and order as well as social and economic development.

It was apparent that national unity and the freedom and the independence of the people of Zimbabwe could only be achieved by solving the internal security problem. The reality was achieved on 22 December 1987 when the two major parties signed the national unity accord. The success of the unity accord spelled an end to all the anti-government rebels, and most of the dissidents responded positively by giving themselves up to the security forces. At least 115 dissidents were known to have come forward.[37] As a result, Matabeleland North and South and the affected areas of the Midlands all returned to normal by 1988. The peace that unity accord brought to Matabeleland contributed immensely to the consolidation of the nation's political stability.

3.5　THE POLITICS OF ZIMBABWEAN DEFENCE

Mugabe was not only Prime Minister; he was also the Minister of Defence, and maintained a keen interest in defence matters. In the early 1980s Mugabe was pragmatic and cautious over the nature of the South African threat to Zimbabwe, but after half a decade of destabilization, the Prime Minister had become almost pan-Africanist in his conviction that South African hegemony in the region had to be resisted. This was politically a wise thing for Mugabe to do because the South African military problem needed the cooperation of the whole region. Mugabe's tactics towards his enemy were changing from direct confrontation to political negotiation.

In 1986 Mugabe called for an OAU defence force to counterbalance 'the mammoth army of South Africa'. He also demanded that the West should arm and train the ANC in its war on apartheid.[38] While this was important, Mugabe required greater cohesion in his own security decision-making, and a much more balanced relationship with the United States in the future. This was important in the international political dimension because Zimbabwe would need the support of the United States on matters affecting Zimbabwe's security in relation to South Africa. To prevent this happening, Mugabe needed to cease his condemnation of America's policy of constructive engagement; its demise could only leave Zimbabwe more isolated in the region in South African eyes. The waning of American influence throughout Southern Africa generally could only strengthen the hand of South Africa's military. An improved relationship between Harare and Washington would have helped Zimbabwe to swing the United States more firmly behind the policy of the Frontline States for change in South Africa. Ultimately, sensible diplomacy would have substantially reinforced Zimbabwe's future security by making Harare Washington's regional ally.

Apart from this, it is important to note that it was within the ruling ZANU Politburo that Zimbabwe's future security and defence policies were decided. There existed in the Politburo a powerful Karanga[39] triumvirate which was influential in security matters and which was more cautious than Mugabe himself. While they accepted the need to assist their old ally Mozambique, they were impatient over what they saw as the ramshackle Mozambican military and deteriorating territorial security. Although the momentum of Zimbabwean military involvement had increased, infighting within the Politburo was to be expected if Mugabe threw the bulk of the ZDF into the fray.

Despite this the survival of Zimbabwe's future security needed the ZANU–ZAPU unity accord, because the military position in Matabeleland would have certainly improved and allowed the ZDF to concentrate on Mozambique and South Africa. Mugabe needed to move quickly into the national unity accord in order to cope with the South African threat. These converging problems and their possible resolution posed questions about the country's future security and political stability which would put Mugabe's political skills and analytical judgement to the test.

This growth of the military did not augur well for the democratic development of the country and it led to the loss of certain civil liberties in its society. From independence up to 1989, Zimbabwe maintained the State of Emergency declared by the Smith regime in 1965, which had been used to detain those struggling for freedom. All detainees were released in 1980, but by 1983, 71 people were being held in detention under security laws and 49 of them without trial. At various stages in 1982 about 1334 people were held in detention.[40]

Infringements of civil liberties were deemed necessary to neutralize Pretoria's agents. In 1981, a law was passed empowering the Minister of Home Affairs to confiscate property of anyone who by trial and conviction were held to be subversive or acting prejudicially to state security. The verdict of an appeal to a three-man tribunal might then be overturned by the Minister of Home Affairs.

This draconian legislation was followed by government moves to tighten the Criminal Procedures and Evidence Act to ensure that, in future, the government would not lose major cases on technical grounds. This served to give the government a repressive image and, although necessary, it was propagandized by the media to distort the real intentions of the government. In the areas most affected by dissident activity, the rule of law virtually collapsed and was replaced by army regulations akin to martial law. In addition, the government passed regulations protecting security forces from being sued for damages. However, the Supreme Court ruled that these regulations were in contravention of the constitution's Declaration of Human Rights and could not be given force even by a State of Emergency. This created potential conflict between the executive and legislature and the judiciary. In general, the political cost of destabilization for Zimbabwe has been minimal compared to the economic harassment and destruction that it suffered at the hands of South Africa and its surrogate armies.

4 Economic Sabotage

This chapter looks at South Africa's tactics in sabotaging the Zimbabwean economy by disrupting Zimbabwean transport. It will also show the political and economic leverage South Africa had over Zimbabwe and how South Africa used this leverage to neutralize Zimbabwean policies. Zimbabwe's options and response to these economic pressures will also be examined.

The South African destabilization of Zimbabwe had positive and negative aspects. The positive side to the process was that by destabilizing Zimbabwe, South Africa in a way encouraged Zimbabwe to be more self-reliant politically and economically. The negative political aspects of destabilization have been felt most acutely on the economic front, as will be indicated.

4.1 ECONOMIC DEPENDENCE

For a long time, Rhodesia was economically dependent on South Africa. During the time of the Unilateral Declaration of Independence (UDI, 1965–79), the Smith regime looked favourably on South Africa, firstly for a preferential market to trade goods, and secondly, because South African ports served as sympathetic trans-shipment points in the very expensive sanctions-busting operations. As a result of this the costs of dissociation for both countries increased substantially. It must be realized that South Africa's major reasons for supporting the Rhodesian regime included a combination of political and economic factors. Politically a white government in Rhodesia protected Pretoria's interests in the region and it would also be easy to deal with. As a trading partner Rhodesia was very important for South Africa in transporting its exports and import goods to other African states in the region such as Zambia, Zaire, Malawi and Botswana. Most importantly many white South Africans had businesses and families in Rhodesia and Pretoria felt it had a duty to protect the interest of its people. Furthermore, South Africa was banking on a victory for the more moderate and potentially cooperative party led by Muzorewa. It was primarily on the expectation of this outcome that Pretoria exerted such strong pressure on the government of Ian Smith to negotiate an end to the war.

4.2 SOUTH AFRICA'S POLITICAL AND ECONOMIC LEVERAGE: ZIMBABWE'S OPTIONS

Following Zimbabwean independence in 1980 and the victory of the ZANU(PF) party, it was not easy for South Africa to adjust to the existence of an avowedly Marxist and hostile government which marked out the elimination of the apartheid system and minority rule in South Africa as one of its prime political objectives. This drove South Africa to reverse its support for an African government in Rhodesia/Zimbabwe. The question which must be addressed is, how much economic power did South Africa have to influence Zimbabwe to change its hostile attitudes? The following factors played an important role in South Africa's attempt to influence Zimbabwe to change its hostile policies.

(i)   At independence South Africa supplied 30 to 40 per cent of Zimbabwe's imports and bought a not insignificant amount of Zimbabwe's exports (25 per cent). Overall about 90 per cent of Zimbabwe's trade went through South Africa.[1] It was precisely in this most vulnerable area of commercial exchanges that the Pretoria regime attempted to pressurize and blackmail Zimbabwe into granting a political accommodation with the racist regime.

(ii)   Concerning Zimbabwe's exports to South Africa, in 1981 the Pretoria regime threatened to terminate the Preferential Trade Agreement signed 15 years before by the Smith government. This would have had the automatic effect of increasing the price of Zimbabwean goods, thereby out-pricing them on the South African market. The resultant industrial over-production would not only have created industrial chaos and unemployment, but would also have increased the financial squeeze on government coffers at a time when massive social and productive expenditures were being initiated. This would have had obvious negative political consequences, primarily in the form of unfulfilled rising expections, resulting in destabilizing frustrations within Zimbabwe.

(iii) The termination of the trade agreement would have created great difficulties for Zimbabwe in trying to find alternative markets for its exports. Most of the alternative routes had been effectively closed for extended periods of time by sabotage and by other security problems arising out of the conflicts in both Mozambique and Angola.

We shall look at each of these factors in detail showing how South Africa used them as weapons to squeeze Zimbabwe economically. Before we do this, let us look at what were Zimbabwe's options and the arguments for and against each course of action.

With the formation of the Southern African Development Coordination Conference (SADCC), Zimbabwe was in a good position to ease herself away from the economic pressure from South Africa. The SADCC states (Angola, Botswana, Lesotho, Mozambique, Malawi, Swaziland, Tanzania and Zambia) provided Zimbabwe with the goods and services then obtained from South Africa. Transport was important for imports and exports which went through SADCC ports and not South African ones. The existence of SADCC was supposed to be an advantage for the industries in Zimbabwe. As the most industrialized of the majority-ruled states, Zimbabwe is an important factor in regional development; with its strong economy and good transport system it made the SADCC goal of delinking a possibility. By seeking alternative routes Zimbabwe benefited from it. With SADCC in force Zimbabwe was supposed to retain some of the regional market for South Africa. The existence of alternative Zimbabwean goods made it easier for the other SADCC countries to reduce their imports from South Africa – especially Malawi and Botswana, which in 1983 derived 40 per cent and 81 per cent respectively of their imports from South Africa.[2] SADCC's delinking of South Africa, together with international sanctions, contributed to a fall in the value of the rand, and Zimbabwe benefited through cheaper supplies from SADCC. SADCC members increased their trade with each other by their membership of the Preferential Trade Area (PTA) for Eastern Africa which accelerated their delinking from South Africa. Equally important in the long term was a PTA rule that to qualify for tariff reductions, exporting firms would be mainly locally owned and managed; this forced some South African companies to relinquish majority control of subsidiaries in the neighbouring states, particularly in Zimbabwe. Thus if SADCC was successful in reducing its members' dependence, it would sharply decrease South Africa's profits and its economic leverage and power.

In this respect, much was made of the legitimate point that the routes to Beira, Maputo and even Lobito, were much shorter than any of the South African routes, and hence were the 'natural' outlets for Zimbabwean trade. On these grounds, it was argued that, given efficient operation, the shorter routes, with their lower freight charges, would be more cost-effective. This argument was reinforced by the fact that, in the absence of alternative outlets, the South African transport system had a high degree of monopoly power, and this was reflected in the charges which were established for freight services between South Africa and Zimbabwe. The conclusion drawn by many from this argument was that most, if not all, of Zimbabwe's imports from third countries could be obtained more cheaply by importing them directly from the original suppliers instead of via South Africa. The argument was extended also to imports of South African origin. South Africa, it was argued, was a high-cost producer of manufactured goods, and substitutes could be obtained more cheaply on the world market. These arguments were flawed in several respects.

Firstly, overall freight costs are not solely determined by the distance travelled, but also by the speed, handling capacities and qualitative facilities of the transport system. For all the political objections to using it, the South African transport system did have some residual cost advantages for certain commodities. Secondly, in the presence of competing routes, South Africa's market power would have been reduced and this would undoubtedly have been reflected in lower freight charges. While this would have shifted the terms of trade in Zimbabwe's favour, it might none the less have retained the competitive advantage of the South African routes for some commodities. Thirdly, price was not the only factor which determined trade. Zimbabwe might well have been able to import spare parts for its German machines or its Japanese vehicles directly from the original suppliers, but the capacity to pick up the telephone and obtain the goods very quickly was more important to the Zimbabwean firms. Fourth, in the case of goods of South African origin, in addition to the questions of proximity, speed of delivery, local knowledge, etc., the question of their competitiveness was much more complex than suggested simply by South Africa's status as a high-cost producer.

In short, even the economic issues underlying the transport question were much more complex than many were prepared to acknowledge. The major problem posed by the alternative routes were: poor maintenance and operational inefficiencies (these rendered them less than satisfactory carriers of traffic); and most of these routes (other than Tazara) had been effectively closed for extended periods of time by sabotage and by other security problems arising out of the conflicts in both Mozambique and Angola. With these problems it was clear that heavy reliance on the South African transport system was going to be unavoidable for the foreseeable future. This pressure, together with the aggressive rhetoric which accompanied it, had unsettling effects upon the existing trade links between Zimbabwe and South Africa.

Even more important was the fact that political criteria were being put forward as the major, if not the only, basis on which to determine whether economic linkages, both general and particular, between the two countries should continue.

4.3 SOUTH AFRICA'S TACTICS FOR SABOTAGING THE ZIMBABWEAN ECONOMY

Zimbabwe's import sector was equally threatened. Immediately after independence, the South African Credit Guarantee Insurance Corporation (CGIC) placed stringent restrictions on credit insurance for exports to Zimbabwe. The scheme, which was underwritten by the South African government, was Pretoria's direct retaliation for Zimbabwe's break of diplomatic relations (in existence under the Smith regime) in 1980. Consequently, the insurance restrictions substantially reduced the amount of South African exports to Zimbabwe. The CGIC said that it was a political decision. It was noted that it was senior government officials who were on the committee that made the decision. The main purpose of this decision was to force the Zimbabwe government to make a high level request for full CGIC cover to be restored, but Zimbabwe did not respond. The target for these restrictions was the manufacturing sector. It was hoped that the resulting shortages of spare parts and other capital goods would bring that vital sector to its knees, thereby compelling the Zimbabwe government to come to some form of political understanding with Pretoria.

In 1981 the South African government gave Zimbabwe one year's notice that it would abrogate the bilateral trade agreement. This was procedurally correct, as the agreement allowed either side to terminate it after giving one year's notice. The cancellation of the agreement would have had a serious impact on the Zimbabwean economy, because about Z$54 m of goods went to South Africa under the agreement in 1980, particularly clothing, radios, steel rod and wire, as well as small quantities of cigarettes, furniture, travel goods, exhaust systems and pharmaceuticals. This would have resulted in the loss of 7000 jobs which were involved in producing these exports. This announcement was made by South Africa while the Zimbabwe government were hosting ZIMCORD (Zimbabwe Conference for

Reconstruction and Development).The purpose of this conference was to raise substantial amounts of assistance from international donors. South Africa was putting pressure on Zimbabwe to force her into ministerial contacts. The timing of the announcement by South Africa was also aimed at discouraging the donors from assisting Zimbabwe.

However, South Africa came under strong pressure from the USA, which argued that it was in South Africa's own best interests to maintain the economic power it had with the trade agreement. This was also echoed by a strong opposition group of business leaders within South Africa which disliked South Africa's policy of destabilizing the Zimbabwean economy because of their businesses in Zimbabwe. The Anglo American corporation, the head of South African Railways and others argued that the aggressive policy was harming South Africa's economic interests and pushing Zimbabwe further and further to delink herself from South Africa. In any case it made more sense to them to deal with the Mugabe government and attempt to cooperate with it. It could also have been argued that the Zimbabwe government had survived the pressure, and was, if anything, being strengthened by it. As a result of business and US pressure, South Africa relented and extended the agreement a fortnight before it was due to expire. But much of the damage had already been done; South African buyers had found other sources for many of the goods, and the uncertainty remained because Pretoria was always capable of giving notice again.

Like the other colonies in the region, Rhodesia had sent migrant labourers to South Africa. In February 1981 Zimbabwe discontinued formal recruitment of new miners in Zimbabwe by Wenela, the main South African recruitment agency. Zimbabwe did not want to continue a government-to-government recruiting agreement. Nevertheless, Zimbabwe stressed that its citizens were free to continue working in South Africa if they wished. But South Africa responded by expelling many who lacked formal contracts, and refused to renew work permits for others when their contracts were due to expire. It was only the swift moves by the Zimbabwe government to open new import lines that averted the worst effects of this commercial squeeze.

These programmes of commercial blackmail were complemented by a determined effort by South Africa to disrupt Zimbabwe's alternative routes to the sea and at the same time by stringent conditions on the use of the regime's own cargo transit facilities. Zimbabwe's geographical reality, as a landlocked state, was being turned to near cataclysmic disadvantage. A combination of factors, both internal and external, brought this situation about. South Africa began by holding up Zimbabwe cargo at its ports, causing great delays and shortages. In 1981 there were an estimated 300 000 tonnes of Zimbabwean goods stranded in South African ports.[3] Import cargo was delayed in South Africa sometimes for several weeks. On occasion South Africa claimed documents were not in order, or that their ports were congested, with the result that exports were delayed. South Africa forced much of Zimbabwean traffic through Port Elizabeth instead of Durban. This caused two problems: First, it was a longer rail trip and thus took longer and tied up wagons. Second, as there are no grain storage facilities, wheat imports had to be loaded directly on to railway wagons – thus tying up wagons and causing extra demurrage charges on ships delayed in port.

Fuel imports, especially of diesel, were increasingly subject to delay; sometimes wagons arriving from South Africa were empty. The lack of diesel in Zimbabwe disrupted the collection of the bumper maize harvest, and delayed ploughing for the coming season. The Energy Minister at that time, Simba Makoni, accused Pretoria of deliberately delaying diesel deliveries. South African Transport Minister Hendrich Schoeman implicitly admitted that South Africa was deliberately delaying Zimbabwe cargo.[4] The *Citizen*, a South African newspaper with close ties to official Pretoria, spelled out the appropriate message:

> if Zimbabwe hadn't been so hostile to South Africa, attacking it in international forums, reducing our diplomatic mission to that of a trade consulate, and announcing that it would give full political and moral support to the 'liberation' forces which intend to attack this country in growing numbers, South Africa might have been disposed to go out of its way to help Mr. Mugabe to overcome his transport crisis. . . . Indeed, what is happening in Zimbabwe is only a foretaste, on a small scale, of what might happen. . . .[5]

Schoeman insisted that the problem could only be solved if an approach was made by Zimbabwe at ministerial level, and the government in Harare must give high-level assurances that the ANC would not be allowed to operate out of Zimbabwe. Here South Africa was once again using its economic muscle to try to bludgeon Zimbabwe into political and diplomatic concessions. At the same time it was an effort to create chaos in the newly independent state, and to prevent its multiracial polices from being successful.

South African scare propaganda directed mostly at Zimbabwe's white community had resulted in the departure of a sizeable proportion of white skilled manpower, e.g. technicians, skilled artisans, who were readily absorbed into the South African economy. The manpower drainage was felt in industry in general, and most critically in the railways. The shortage of skilled artisans resulted in the decline of maintenance and repair to the point that at the beginning of 1981 there were only 120 locomotives out of the 220 needed to cope with traffic.[6] At precisely this precarious moment, South Africa delivered a crippling blow.

In May 1981, South Africa withdrew 25 locomotives originally loaned to Zimbabwe. This deliberate move to disrupt Zimbabwe's traffic flow accentuated an already critical situation, and not surprisingly, politics played a crucial role in this transport tangle. Pretoria once again came under heavy attack from Western embassies, particularly the US, for the withdrawal of the wagons and the consequent disruption of Zimbabwe's transport system. This was demonstrated by the fact that in September 1981, South Africa offered to lend Zimbabwe some locomotives if approached at a ministerial level, underlining emphatically that the price of economic help was to be some form of politico-diplomatic recognition. But the Zimbabwe government refused the offer because it resented the political strings attached. It responded almost immediately by ordering 60 new locomotives from the US and entering into contracts for foreign technicians, who did arrive in 1982.

Meanwhile 19 locomotives had to be borrowed on a contingency basis from Zambia, Botswana and Mozambique, but these could only relieve pressure slightly. Arrangements were made to shift cargo to Mozambique. The Lonrho oil pipeline was repaired and that reduced South Africa's control over Zimbabwe's fuel requirements.

The transport crisis adversely affected every sector of the economy, creating domestic shortages and blocking imports and exports. In particular, fuel procurement was hit hardest and the result was widespread shortage of diesel and petrol, which by 1981 had adversely affected all sectors of the economy.[7]

Agriculture, the backbone of the country's economy, was particularly vulnerable because of the need for diesel fuel at the beginning of the planting season. By December 1981, there were stockpiles of export commodities waiting to be transported. The country was losing between Z$4.5 million and Z$6 million per annum in lost export opportunities.[8] Naturally this also adversely affected Zimbabwe's foreign-exchange earning capacity.

Particularly badly affected was maize, which, being a bulky, low-value commodity, received low priority in rail haulage. To meet the demand from Zaire, Zimbabwe needed to dispatch 80 to 90 rail wagons a week to Kinshasa to meet an emergency demand, but it was only managing 56 wagons. Also adversely affected were the 1000 tonnes of maize due for Malawi and 75 000 tonnes for Mozambique.

This inability to transport maize exports had a regional significance. Zimbabwe's relatively developed economy, particularly the agricultural sector, offered the SADCC countries some kind of alternative to the traditional reliance on South Africa. Consequently, Pretoria attempted to demonstrate that even Zimbabwe was not immune to South Africa's blackmail.

In response to the railway crisis, the Zimbabwe government initiated a policy of allocating export quotas according to a priority based on the potential to earn foreign exchange. The chief casualty of this policy was one million tonnes of maize surplus from the exceptionally good 1981 harvest. Less than half of this surplus maize could be exported. It took well over eighteen months just to shift that proportion of the surplus.

Tobacco, which had also experienced a boom, got priority over maize because a wagon load of tobacco earned Z$522 000 compared with Z$60 000 for maize. Other commodities also suffered. For instance, the Anglo American Corporation had 100 000 tonnes of sugar, worth Z$25 million, stockpiled by the end of 1981. About 150 000 tonnes of steel billets were also stockpiled.[9]

The resultant weakened capacity to earn foreign exchange crippled many areas of economic activity. Manufacturing industry was particularly hard hit by the shortage of foreign exchange, which covered all import allocations. Foreign currency allocations for imports had been increased by 63 per cent during the 1979/80 financial year.[10] However, due to the transport and foreign exchange crises foreign currency allocations had to be slashed by 9 per cent in 1981 with further cuts in 1982.[11] Cuts of up to 100 per cent were imposed on non-essentials and chemical product quotas were chopped by 22 per cent, on top of an earlier cut of 21 per cent at the end of 1981. Tractor dealers were astounded to find quotas cut by a staggering 85 per cent. The manufacturing sector, which at the time of independence had a projected growth rate of 7 per cent per annum, could not achieve its potential for growth. In 1980 manufacturing had made a significant contribution to the economy as factories started working to full capacity when workers were released from the war.[12] Manufacturing production rose by 14.9 per cent in 1980 and a further 11.7 per cent in the first half by 1981. By the end of 1981, this growth had fallen to below 10 per cent.[13] Certain sectors such as textiles and footwear, which had worked to full capacity, began to experience little room for further expansion mainly because of raw material shortages and the need to renew equipment.

These two major problems, i.e. small import allocations and lack of raw materials, were both attributable to transport disruptions by the Pretoria regime. Transport problems increased the prices of raw materials and other essential inputs. Such problems also made exporting a highly expensive, and therefore unprofitable business. To balance its books Zimbabwe needed to export more than 2 million tonnes of goods per year, but during the 1981/82 financial year, only 250 000 tonnes actually left the country.[14] This decline in productivity also stalled the implementation of wide-ranging reforms which were designed to improve efficiency, strengthen the technological base and foster greater linkages with the mining and agricultural sectors.

The proposed reforms in the manufacturing sector were also designed to bring about greater state participation in industry, primarily through two parastatals, the Industry Development Corporation (IDC) and the Zimbabwe Iron and Steel Company (ZISCO). Local authorities and Agricultural Marketing Boards were to process commodities in downstream industries in order to generate their own income, thereby reducing the fiscal burden of state subsides. However, all these ambitious reform programmes were shelved when attention had to be concentrated on survival strategies for the manufacturing sector. The ripple effects of South African transport disruptions had the effect of delaying by many years the modernization and expansion of Zimbabwe's manufacturing sector.

4.4 THE IMPACT OF THE DISRUPTION OF ZIMBABWE'S TRANSPORT

The impact of transport disruptions was most severe on the country's mining industry. South Africa's destabilization of Zimbabwe's transport routes exacerbated the depression of the mining industry which had already set in because of the worldwide commodity slump and general recession. The value of mining production, a vital foreign-exchange earner, reached a record Z$415 million in 1980 when more than 90 per cent of the output was exported.[15] In 1981, however, the value of production fell to Z$380 million. Of course, the major problem was the fall in the price of gold and the prolonged world recession. However, routine operating costs including transport, fuel, imported equipment and supplies and skilled labour shortages showed significant increases, thereby exacerbating the spiral of decline.

The destabilization of Zimbabwe's traffic flows was not only confined to Pretoria's manipulation of South African transport facilities. Shortages of foreign exchange through lost export earnings had a constraining effect on domestic transport apart from the railways. Zimbabwe could not procure new heavy freight vehicles because of shortage of foreign exchange. Consequently, the country had to rely on expensive foreign trailer-hire operators, costing Zimbabwe about $100 million a year in foreign currency between 1980 and 1988.[16] By 1989, about 450 new heavy truck units costing millions of dollars were needed to rectify the problems caused by many years of non-procurement.[17] In a survey[18] the Zimbabwe Transport Operators' Association (TOA) showed that 42.1 per cent of the TOA members' goods, omnibus, coach and taxi fleet were out of action prior to 1980, 31 per cent in 1980/83, 5 per cent in 1984, 5.9 per cent in 1985, 5 per cent in 1986, 4 per cent in 1987, 4.2 per cent in 1988 and only 2.3 per cent in 1989.

These percentages showed the deterioration of the fleet that moved the major portion of goods and passengers by road within Zimbabwe and to the neighbouring states. The overall picture portrayed by the above percentages is quite grave. About 73.7 per cent of Zimbabwe's fleet of road haulers was over six years old in 1980 and over 42.1 per cent over nine years, creating, virtually, a museum of road-haulage power. Based on the generally accepted figure of eight years as the economic life of a heavy duty vehicle, 36.7 per cent of the goods fleet was already beyond the limit and a further 36.7 per cent would reach the limit by 1991.[19] This did not happen, because of the world recession and the decline of Zimbabwean economy as a result of drought and the political instability. Translated into figures, these percentages implied that about 1500 replacement vehicles were needed for 1990–91, with no adequate foreign currency available to meet the target. In other words, it meant a rate of delivery 7.5 times greater than the average rate of delivery achieved since 1984, which in turn gave an indication of the depths to which the road transport system had sunk. In this situation, and ignoring the natural expansion factor, the TOA estimated that Zimbabwe needed $1 billion in foreign exchange between 1989 and 1992 to rebuild its transport fleet (both road and rail) to 1980 levels.

RENAMO bandit activity had also taken its toll on Zimbabwe's haulage fleet. Direct road transport losses occurred frequently on the Tete Road Corridor (TRC) (subsequently guarded by the ZNA) through which much of Malawi's trade had flowed following the sabotage of the Nacala railway, the country's shortest route to the sea. By the end of the eighties, an estimated 30 to 40 trailer units had been destroyed or damaged or required additional spares and maintenance because of bandit attacks. The replacement cost of a trailer unit with a semi-trailer was a staggering Z$400 000 (US$120 000) an estimated total loss of between Z$12 million to Z$16 million, largely in foreign currency.[20]

The most obvious symptoms of the transport crisis were reflected in the failure by hauliers to move crops and farm inputs on time; inadequate services to commerce and industry; and very substantial payments of hard currency to foreign hauliers due to the lack of vehicles to operate on regional routes. By the end of the 1980s, the weak road haulage system was severely damaged by the railways' inability to service the domestic sector efficiently. Years of loss-making and shortage of adequate foreign currency to purchase additional locomotives reached a climax in October 1989 when the railways failed to deliver coal, Zimbabwe's vital source of energy to the manufacturing sector, agriculture and so on.[21] Industry lost millions of dollars in the form of higher operating costs and, in some cases, lost exports.

The crisis could also be attributed directly to South African mischief. Late in 1988 the South African Transport Services (SATS) informed the NRZ that it was unwilling to hire out any more locomotives to meet Zimbabwe's shortfall, offering instead to sell to Harare old steam locomotives with a life span of only three years. The plan by South Africa to sell old steam locomotives to Zimbabwe was deliberate and carefully stage-managed, and the crisis unavoidable. Major companies such as Mutare Board and Paper Mills (the country's only paper mill) and David Whitehead (the largest textile firm) reported substantial losses through lost production. The country's road transport system, already in disarray, could not cope. Domestic and industrial construction came to a virtual standstill due to shortage of vital coal burnt bricks.

Not only did the National Railways of Zimbabwe's (NRZ) problems affect the movement of coal, but more significantly delays in rail transit had a most serious impact on the efficient movement of imports and exports. In particular, the Zimbabwe Shipping Services (ZSS) reported that imports routed via Durban (South Africa) to Zimbabwe were subject to embargoes at the request of the NRZ which could not cope with the traffic. This had the effect of increasing delivery times, which forced certain importers to use expensive foreign road hauliers and incur increased storage costs, both payable in the acutely scarce foreign currency. Import containers already stuck in the backlog of the NRZ system remained at the ports for extended periods so that shipping lines experienced great difficulties in turning around containers for exports. Consequently, considerable expense was incurred in positioning empty containers from South Africa which had surplus stocks of them. Exports from Zimbabwe were seriously affected by the lack of empty containers and delays in the provision of wagons to convey cargo, resulting in lost shipments and penalties being levied on exporters who failed to meet delivery terms.

The internal transport crisis that came to a head during the late 1980s was exacerbated by the unreliability of non-South African routes to the sea. Zimbabwe's alternative routes to the coast through the Mozambican ports of Beira and Maputo came under increasing attacks from the South African-backed MNR. In October 1981, the strategic road and rail bridges linking the port of Beira to the Zimbabwe eastern border town of Mutare were sabotaged at Pungwe.[22] This was a serious blow not only for Zimbabwe but also for the United Nations World Food Programme project which was using the railway to send some of the country's maize surplus via Beira to areas in Africa desperately short of grain, including West African states such as Mali and Senegal.[23]

In November 1981 saboteurs destroyed the navigational buoys in the Beira port access channel, making the port inaccessible until repairs were carried out. On the propaganda front, during the same period Pretoria officials published figures purporting to show that Zimbabwe's combined total exports to SADCC were less than half its exports to South Africa.[24] In addition, on 2 November 1981 *The Sunday Tribune*, a South African paper, issued a report which cited figures to show how South African mines were becoming less dependent on foreign migrants to a point where they constituted less than 40 per cent of the total. This was a direct threat to Zimbabwe's migrant labourers in South Africa. Any sudden expulsion would have exacerbated the unemployment situation in the country.[25]

Thus, throughout 1981 Zimbabwe's transport situation was quite desperate, being hit simultaneously from the South African side and the Mozambican outlets. However, the Pungwe rail and road sabotage had wider strategic implications. It was timed to coincide with the movement of training equipment from North Korea destined for the training of a new army unit, the fifth brigade, in Mutare. Security 'moles' within Zimbabwe's security establishment may have facilitated the attack. The Central Intelligence Organization's (CIO) station chief for Mutare, who had not been changed since the late 1970s and was therefore coordinating MNR activities for the Smith regime, left for South Africa shortly before the sabotage.[26]

4.5 THE ATTEMPT TO ALLEVIATE THE TRANSPORT PROBLEM

To alleviate these transport problems, particularly in the railway sector, Zimbabwe had to utilize its South–South linkages. The arrival of skilled railway technicians from India and Pakistan[27] in 1982, coupled with the delivery of 35 locomotive units by US General Motors (at a cost of US$18 million)[28] temporarily reduced bottlenecks during off-peak seasons, allowing the NRZ to save on the hiring cost of locomotives during slack periods.

However, the availability of increased haulage power did not significantly blunt the economic impact of South African destabilization. As part of government attempts to reduce its economic dependency on South Africa, the Zimbabwe Oil Procurement Company announced that Zimbabwe's oil transit dependency would be transferred from South Africa to Mozambique, utilizing the Lonrho-owned pipeline from Beira to Feruka in Mutare.[29] The plan was to use the pipeline to carry diesel fuel, gasoline and aviation fuel while paraffin and other petroleum products were to be transported by rail from Mozambique. The plan was thwarted by the sabotage of the pipeline by the MNR in December 1981. South Africa was not prepared to let Zimbabwe escape so easily from its economic control.

The scheduled re-opening of the pipeline would have had two major effects. It would have made Zimbabwe independent of South Africa as a source of and transit channel for fuel and it would have eased the haulage strain on the railways, both quite unwelcome developments for South Africa. Apart from the positive political implications of cutting the South African connection, Zimbabwe stood to gain by effecting considerable cost savings. Fuel from South Africa was expensive partly because the Pretoria regime was subject to an oil boycott by most oil-producing states. As a result, the mark-up prices for re-exports of oil products to Zimbabwe were quite high. Transporting oil through the Beira–Mutare pipeline would have been considerably cheaper. At the ruling prices, it cost about Z$25 to Z$30 per tonne for pumping oil from Beira to Mutare.[30]

Transporting oil by rail during the period when the pipeline was being repaired was thwarted by the sabotage of the Beira oil-storage tanks in March 1982, by a commando unit which landed by submarine.[31] Oil stocks ran dangerously low with only two weeks' supply in storage. Industrial and agricultural sectors had to curtail production because of the shortage of fuel, with large commercial farmers experiencing up to 55 per cent cuts in their fuel allocations. Public bus services, the main form of transport for the cities' industrial workers, had to be cut by half. Fuel imports could not be effected through the Maputo–Harare system because of similar MNR sabotage operations.[32]

Throughout 1982, the Beira–Mutare pipeline operated only intermittently because of disruptions due to sabotage. On 10 October 1982, a sabotage unit comprehensively damaged the Maforga pumping station along the line. This led to a critical fuel shortage in December 1982, bringing much of Zimbabwe's road traffic to a virtual standstill, with queues of vehicles stretching several miles at petrol stations. At one point, there was only one day's supply of petrol and two days' supply of diesel in the country.[33] Pretoria proceeded to limit the flow of alternative supplies, thereby exacerbating the crisis. South Africa continued to use the fuel weapon against Zimbabwe. Supplies of base oils (lubricants) which could not be pumped through the pipeline were delayed in South Africa, forcing Zimbabwe to bring the lubricants from Beira in drums at a national cost of Z$2.5 million (US$1.3 million) up to November 1988.[34] For instance, Jet A-1 fuel for the airforce and commercial airliners had been delayed and on one occasion during the 1985 Commonwealth Summit in Nassau, the situation was saved only because the Energy Ministry had taken the precaution of ordering another shipment through Beira to coincide with one scheduled to come through Durban. The South Africans delayed the Durban shipment until they discovered that another had come through Beira and then released it.

As with other incidents of major sabotage activities, the 1982 attacks on oil installations were the result of vital security information leakages coming from inside Zimbabwe. Two of the people involved in the Beira fuel storage tanks sabotage were employees of Manica Freight Services, a company which was used to spearhead sanctions-busting for the Smith regime. Dion Hamilton, who was the Beira head of Manica, provided the information that allowed the South African Reconnaissance Commandos to raid the oil depot and the bridge. His deputy at Manica, Benjamin Fox, was identified as the man who had been taking arms and giving instructions to MNR bases near Beira.[35] Both of them were convicted and sentenced to 20 years' imprisonment. They were charged with knowing in advance about the raid and of possessing weapons and of 'acts amounting to terrorism'. The lesser charge was brought because the government was unwilling to present evidence that would have convicted Portuguese and British nationals of capital offences at a time when it was trying to improve relations with both countries.

There was strong evidence of Hamilton's role in the tanks raids; evidence of his role in the Pungwe river bridge attack was only circumstantial; after that raid he was found to have the knowledge of the structural details of the bridge and the damage done. Hamilton had worked with shipping agencies in Beira since the beginning of sanctions, and it was widely suspected that he may have been a British security agent then. This pattern of espionage was quite common throughout the entire record of South African destabilization of Zimbabwe. Vital information about the movement of Zimbabwe's trade goods was periodically passed to South African agents by disloyal senior customs officials.[36] Even some of the Mozambique railway workers were periodically compromised into transmitting sensitive information to South Africa through MNR agents.[37]

After the Beira fuel storage tanks sabotage, the Zimbabwe government was forced to sign a three-year contract with the South African state oil company, SASOL. Zimbabwe was thus forced to renew a costly dependency relationship. Annual payments for freight through South Africa amounted to Z$225 million,[38] of which about Z$85 million could have been saved by the increased use of a shorter route. Against this potential saving Zimbabwe had to meet part of the costs of the rehabilitation of the Beira Corridor and the defence of the transit routes through Mozambique costs in the order of $1 million a day. This cost is half or more of the budgeted defence spending between 1980 and 1989; roughly 10 per cent of the central government expenditure or 3 per cent of the GNP.[39] In other words, these costs of the deficit in government spending amounted to almost

50 per cent of the budgeted deficit of the 1980s. Despite Mozambican and Zimbabwean efforts to improve security along the trade routes, no guarantee existed that fuel could flow into the country unhindered. South Africa intended to bulldoze Zimbabwe into contact at ministerial level thereby granting *de facto* political recognition to the Pretoria regime.

With the cheap routes for fuel supply thus disrupted, the expensive fuel procured through South Africa had adverse effects throughout the economy. In February 1983, fuel prices in Zimbabwe had to be increased and the expensive fuel procurement costs were thus passed on to the consumer. Consequently price increases were reflected in drinks, tobacco and so on, plus a 1 per cent increase in sales tax on most retail goods. This pushed prices up by 5 per cent.[40] This price increase came on the top of the devaluation of the Zimbabwean dollar due to the world recession. As a result, a combination of higher fuel prices and indirect taxes swallowed up the benefits of the Zimbabwe dollar devaluation, which would have normally helped business.

The pattern of South African-inspired sabotage, which initially concentrated on crippling Zimbabwe's oil pipeline through Mozambique, was soon followed up by a wave of indiscriminate attacks on rail and road traffic. By 1985, the MNR's disruption of Zimbabwe's trade routes had become sufficiently serious to impel the Zimbabwe government to draft in two ZNA battalions to guard the Beira Corridor at a great cost. The improved security along the trade routes had a real potential to lure Zimbabwean importers and exporters to utilize the Beira route. Apart from the improved security situation the Beira route was far cheaper than any of the South African ports. For instance, the cost of transporting a container of tea from Mutare (close to the Mozambican border) to Beira was Z$490 compared to Z$1640 from Mutare to Durban, a saving of Z$1150.[41] Similarly, the cost of transporting a container of tobacco from Harare to Beira stood at Z$760 compared with Z$1510 from Harare to Durban.[42]

However, several factors militated against the full utilization of the newly secured Mozambican routes. As a result of periodic disruptions, shipowners regularly failed to provide a regular service for Beira because during periods of sustained sabotage the existing service capacity became seriously underutilized. This was the case particularly in periods of relative calm. To most international shippers, the route became at once unreliable and unpredictable. This was compounded by technical problems at both Beira and Maputo. Because of drought restrictions, the tonnage that could be lifted at both Beira and

Maputo was dependent upon the tide, and the figure varied between 6500 and 18 000 tonnes. The tidal variation discouraged the more regular use of the ports because of the attendant delays.

Progress on the full utilization of the Mozambique routes was retarded by the comparatively low charges, which, during periods of relative calm, the South African Transport Services offered in order to discourage Zimbabwean importers and exporters from switching over to Beira or Maputo. For instance, in 1986 the Southern African and European Container Service and the Zimbabwe tobacco industry managed to negotiate extremely low contract rates for the movements of cargo from the Zimbabwe and South African border to Durban.[43] Consequently, the periodic sabotage of the Rutenga (Zimbabwe) Maputo route was a deliberate strategy to reduce traffic at the port thereby giving unfettered advantage to South African commodities exporters. That was precisely the pattern of events in later 1987.

In early November 1987, the exporting of Zimbabwe's sugar through Maputo had to be suspended following sabotage attacks by MNR bandits on a bridge 60 kilometres west of the port. Consequently, Zimbabwe had 60 000 tonnes of exports trapped on the line between Komatipoort and Maputo and had to re-route it. It also created a shortage of rolling stock and delays on exports and foreign currency earnings, particularly since this happened during the country's peak agricultural export season (e.g. tobacco and citrus fruits).

What was particularly significant was that the MNR attacks coincided with the decision by South African exporters to increase the use of Maputo. During 1986, South African transit traffic totalled one million tonnes and South African exporters were looking at a target of something in the order of 5 million tonnes per year, anticipating the completion of improvements which were being carried out in the handling facilities.[44] As will be demonstrated below, this increased eagerness by Pretoria to use the Maputo port was a response to the heightened international campaign to impose mandatory sanctions against South Africa and the consequences for Zimbabwe were gruelling.

For Zimbabwe, then, the effects of South African destabilization during the first half of the 1980s were traumatic. In particular, the daunting transport problems became almost overwhelming. Most of the SADCC trade routes to the sea were incapable of providing a consistent, predictable, commercial service for international trade and traffic, because of the deterioration in physical infrastructure, because of the sabotage and other problems (e.g. pilfering) and sometimes because of poor management and maintenance capacity. However, during the second half of the 1980s the tempo and impact of South African destabilization changed drastically.

5 Destabilization and Economic Sanctions: The Impact on Zimbabwe

In this chapter we are going to discover that during the late 1980s the nature and impact of South Africa's destabilization of Zimbabwe's economy assumed a new dimension. Apart from heightened sabotage activities of South Africa's surrogate forces during the 1985 to 1987 period inside Zimbabwe, external events began to acquire a new significance. South Africa's sustained onslaught in other parts of the Southern African region, coupled with international responses against such activities and Pretoria's own internal problems, began to affect Zimbabwe in a negative manner.

The efforts to disrupt Zimbabwe's trade routes through Mozambique reached fever-pitch. The massive military offensive by the South African-backed MNR signalled a shift in Pretoria's strategy towards more aggressive action in the region. The MNR's military offensive in the centre and north of Mozambique began in late September 1987 and involved thousands of armed guerrillas infiltrated from Malawi into Mozambique's Tete and Zambezi provinces.[1] They seized a number of district capitals and a strategic bridge over the Zambezi River. In the previous six years, South Africa had inflicted severe damage upon the Mozambican economy. It airlifted supplies to anti-government forces and landed reinforcements by sea. But prior to the September 1987 offensive, Pretoria seemed content with a level of destabilization that disrupted the transport system, particularly the railways. This ensured the continued dependence of the region on South African trade routes with considerable benefits to the apartheid economy.

5.1 THE INTERNATIONAL SANCTIONS CAMPAIGN AND THE SHIFT IN PRETORIA'S STRATEGY

The September 1987 offensive signalled a marked shift in Pretoria's policy towards Mozambique, its neighbours and Zimbabwe in particular. The shift was caused by a combination of factors, the most

104

important being the slow but gradual tightening of the sanctions net by the international community, particularly the US Congressional vote which overturned President Reagan's sanctions veto.[2] Second, there was the role that the independent states of the region played in mobilizing support for the imposition of comprehensive mandatory sanctions against Pretoria and plans by Zimbabwe and Zambia to begin implementing sanctions of their own. A third factor was the mounting international support to secure the region's trade routes to the sea, particularly the Beira Corridor in central Mozambique. The northern and southern routes to the ports of Nacala and Maputo had been out of service intermittently for the previous three and four years respectively. The central Beira route was only operational because of the presence of some 10 000 to 12 000 Zimbabwean troops.

The specific purpose of this new offensive by Pretoria was to weaken Mozambique, and hit Zimbabwe hard through direct and indirect losses, which mounted to about US$3.5 billion annually.[3] The strategy even descended to the reprehensible practice of eliminating railway personnel. Between 1985 and 1987, 199 Mozambican and Zimbabwean railway workers were killed, with 667 wounded,[4] while trying to keep the trains rolling. The success of this strategy was spectacular. By the end of 1987, 90 per cent of the trade of Botswana and Swaziland, and least two-thirds of the combined trade of Malawi, Zambia and Zimbabwe transited South African ports. Yet for most of these countries, their shortest and cheapest routes to the sea were through Mozambique's Indian Ocean ports, which had a potential annual handling capacity of about 23 million tonnes per year. This serves to illustrate just how successful South Africa had been in maintaining the region's dependence upon its routes by bludgeoning Mozambique.

However, that success began to be threatened by the mobilization of large-scale international support to ensure that the Mozambican routes became fully functional. Up to the end of 1987, the international community had committed about US$40 million[5] to the communications infrastructure of Mozambique. Consequently, the threatened reduction in regional dependence upon South Africa and Pretoria's public anger with its neighbours over the sanctions issue did not alone explain Pretoria's changed destabilization strategy in mid-1987.

The other crucial factor was Pretoria's contingent preparations for a sanctions counter-strategy. In many ways, South Africa found sanctions-busting more difficult than was the case with Rhodesia, when the latter was ostracized in the late 1960s and 1970s for refusing to accept majority rule. Rhodesia was able to use South African ports and Portuguese-ruled Mozambican outlets before independence, to evade sanctions. But for South Africa, using its own ports, it was difficult to disguise shipping movements and the origin of goods. Consequently, with a surrogate government installed by South Africa, Mozambique would have provided the ports and the necessary cover for a massive and almost undetectable sanctions-busting operation. The two countries could have used their combined port facilities to virtually strangle SADCC states, especially Zambia, Zimbabwe and Botswana, into submitting to some form of economic and loose political confederation. South Africa's pipe-dream of a Constellation of Southern African States (CONSAS) would have been, at long last, brought to fruition. With a puppet government in Mozambique, many goods actually of South African origin could have been exported through, giving their origin as Mozambique or some other friendly country in the region such as Malawi. Mozambique would have provided an ideal cover, for example, for South African coal exports since there are massive deposits of coal in Mozambique's Tete province. If it controlled Mozambican ports, South Africa could have exported its coal, showing its origin on exporting and landing bills as Mozambique. Similarly, Pretoria could have exported such goods as steel, citrus fruit, beef and minerals showing their origin as Zimbabwe.

During the late 1980s, Southern African countries having close economic ties with Pretoria, including Lesotho, Swaziland and Mauritius, were being used as staging grounds for sanctions-busting. Many methods were used to protect South Africa from international economic isolation, for example selling goods overseas using names of non-existent companies in neighbouring countries. Swaziland, for instance, complained in late 1988 that these non-existent companies were robbing the Swaziland state of its markets. Most of Swaziland exports go via Durban. Thus, it had been very easy for South African firms to ship goods on to vessels with forged Swazi certificates of origin. Early in 1988, South African exporters substituted Swaziland's name on apples, avocados and wine shipped to Europe and Canada, although Swaziland had not exported any of these commodities. False product labels from all over the world were used for such schemes. The Pretoria regime has openly cooperated with the firms involved in the misuse of other nations' names. It was, therefore, such a range of options for sanctions-breaking that constituted an important aspect of

South Africa's shift in its strategy for destabilization, and the consequences for both Mozambique and Zimbabwe were nearly catastrophic.

While Zimbabwe paid a considerable price as a result of South Africa's destabilization, it also confronted Pretoria with a dilemma which imposed constraints on just how far to go in destabilizing the Zimbabwean economy. Zimbabwe's geographical position meant that it commanded South Africa's trade with access by land to the north, where it had significant trade with Malawi, Zaire, Zambia and Zimbabwe itself. Two railways carrying this trade ran through Zimbabwe, from Zimbabwe direct to South Africa and via Botswana, and they were vital for South Africa's northward trade as well as for the lucrative flow of the region's trade through the South African rail and port systems.

While there were few minor acts of sabotage along the railway line to Botswana in the early 1980s, it was no coincidence that the only regional railway system that was not sabotaged was the one running directly from South Africa to Zimbabwe via Beitbridge. Thus, for economic reasons, it was in South Africa's interest to destroy alternative routes in the east, to the Mozambique ports of Beira, Maputo and Nacala, and west to the Angolan port of Lobito, while leaving Zimbabwe's southern trade routes with South Africa operating smoothly.

5.2 THE BEIRA CORRIDOR : ZIMBABWE'S MISMANAGEMENT AND FAILURE TO ACT QUICKLY

Part of Zimbabwe's transport problems and failure to reduce drastically the negative impact of South Africa's machinations during the first half of the 1980s can be attributed to the absence of readily implementable contingency plans and a rapid reaction formula (RRF). This was amply demonstrated in the case of the utilization of the alternative Beira Corridor and preparations for the potentially negative effects on Zimbabwe of the imposition of mandatory international sanctions against South Africa.

Of course, very few governments in the world can contain, overnight, the type of banditry and sabotage as was perpetrated by the MNR. But that was not the only problem. Tragically the rehabilitation of the Beira Corridor did not receive the attention and seriousness of purpose that it deserved during the first half of the 1980s.

Until the end of the 1980s, when the call for anti-Pretoria sanctions somewhat abated, no Rapid Reaction Force (RRF) systems existed to cope with what were likely to be the damaging ripple-effects of international sanctions against South Africa.

Plans for the rehabilitation of the Beira Corridor started in earnest only in September 1985. The National Railways of Zimbabwe (NRZ) was to repair part of the Mutare–Beira railway line, while the Cambinos de Ferro de Mozambique (CFM, the Mozambique national railway organization) was to undertake repairs on the longer part of the line. Due to poor coordination, technical deficiencies and security problems on the Mozambique side, the CFM repair teams had operated only for a limited distance. Consequently the NRZ teams had to undertake repairs on a substantial proportion of line at considerable cost.

The repair job on the Beira line was just about the only piece of contingency planning undertaken by the Zimbabwe government until the late 1980s. Planning to curb the negative effects of the impact of international sanctions against South Africa was at best chaotic and almost non-existent. Civilian suggestions to rectify the situation were greeted with contemptuous scorn, verging on vindictiveness.

Shortly after the initiation of the rehabilitation of the Beira railway line, it became evident that any public debate over the sanctions issue was not advisable. For example, in August 1985, the Confederation of Zimbabwe Industries (CZI) commissioned a study on the implications, if mandatory sanctions were to be imposed by the international community, including Zimbabwe, and possible South African retaliatory action. In October 1985, the CZI president warned the government that the Zimbabwean economy would suffer if 90 per cent of the country's trade were cut off at the South African border.[6] Consequently, the CZI president was denounced as unpatriotic, and in sympathy with racist ideologies by the government-controlled news media. However, the Finance Minister Bernard Chidzero endorsed the CZI president's conclusions, when he said

> if the sanctions were comprehensive or total... this would automatically affect Zimbabwe in a devastating massive manner, unless the Maputo line and the Beira line were open. Equally if South Africa reacted by closing its borders... the impact would be equally sharp on Zimbabwe.[7]

While sanctions were never an electoral issue, opponents of sanctions within the ruling party were influential primarily directly within the

Cabinet policymaking process. Significant splits emerged between pan-Africanist[8] and economic nationalists within the ruling party, crucial in explaining the inconsistent nature of policy towards South Africa.[9] Mugabe was unable to develop a comprehensive nationalism which could moderate either party divisions or broader societal cleavages; the symbolism of anti-apartheid sanctions did not have an inherently unifying effect in Zimbabwe, as the narrower symbolism of UDI, and its small constituency, had in the Rhodesian period.

But in general, the sanctions issue was treated in an almost casual way. A few cabinet ministers periodically and vaguely reassured businessmen that the government had no intention of committing economic suicide by starting a sanctions war.[10] Despite concerns over the economic future of the country, the business community's opposition to sanctions was muted within the context of reconciliation; the business community remained vulnerable to accusations of undue sympathy for white-ruled South Africa. So controversial did the sanctions issue become that in 1986 and 1987, the Transport Ministry, paralysed by the scandal over Minister Ushewokunze's alleged involvement in corruption, began to lose interest in the Beira Corridor.[11] For instance, as late as April 1986, the Zimbabwean delegation to the Beira Corridor Donors' Conference was headed by a rather junior civil servant. In addition, the Treasury, lacking any political direction in according priority to the Beira Corridor rehabilitation scheme, periodically refused to allocate more money towards work on the railway line.

The real turning point in the sanctions issue came on 19 May 1986. South African agents were sent to sabotage prospects of a political settlement between Pretoria and its opponents. They raided and bombed the ANC offices together with a residential house in Harare West. This attack was designed to offset the resurgence of right-wing political activism, e.g. the Afrikaner Resistance Movement, the Herstigte Nasionale Party (HNP) and the Conservative Party (CP). Some of the senior members of the South African military establishment, the so-called hawks, supported the right-wing parties' policy of no dialogue with the ANC. Consequently, the periodic raids on ANC targets in the Frontline States including Zimbabwe, were carried out without the sanction of the Pretoria government.[12] These were designed to ensure that not even minimal grounds for dialogue could exist.

Towards the end of 1986 about 90 per cent of Zimbabwe's imports and exports arrived or left via South African ports. Apart from MNR sabotage, port inefficiencies, inadequate rail links and irregular ship arrivals were the major reasons for Zimbabwe's freight agents shunning the two main Mozambican ports which served Zimbabwe, namely Maputo and Beira. The Zimbabwe–Maputo line had been out of action for nearly two years (early 1984 to early 1986) following sabotage. In addition many of Zimbabwe's freight agents had South African principals.

In the following months after the 19 May 1986 raid, South Africa imposed a State of Emergency, and the international momentum for sanctions became much more rapid. In response, Pretoria established an interdepartmental committee not only to prepare for sanctions evasion, but also to plan economic warfare against the more vocal advocates for sanctions such as Zambia and Zimbabwe. But for Zimbabwe, there was no contingency planning either in cabinet, in the Politburo or the Central Committee of the ruling ZANU(PF). Nor was the climate suitable for real constructive debate and criticism. For instance, when at the CZI congress on July 1986, industrialists learned of planned attacks by two cabinet ministers present, accusing them of disloyalty over the sanctions issue, the CZI leadership issued a preemptive declaration of support for sanctions even though almost every member was privately opposed.[13]

It was at this very late stage that the Zimbabwe government decided in principle to set up a contingency planning committee, to work on the sanctions issue. But the committee had still not met when President Mugabe set off for the Commonwealth Conference in London in August 1986. In effect, it would not be an exaggeration to argue that Mugabe was armed with no coherent policy, only a firm determination to see the international community impose mandatory sanctions on Pretoria. While Mugabe was committing Zimbabwe to a set of wide-ranging sanctions without any clearly thought-out strategy, the Pretoria regime's equivalent planning committee announced its first economic measures against Zimbabwe. In August 1986, the South African government implemented an Import Deposit Scheme to be paid by all South African exporters to the SADCC region (except Botswana, Lesotho, and Swaziland who are members of the Southern African Customs Union, SACU). The deposit varied from 3 per cent to 100 per cent of the value of the product. This had the effect of slowing down vital imports into the Zimbabwe economy. These delays were compounded by lengthy searches of traffic at the border posts by South African customs officials.[14]

The vulnerability of Zimbabwe was clearly demonstrated during that period. While President Mugabe was advocating an uncompromising stance on the sanctions issue at the Commonwealth mini-summit,[15] it was revealed that in late July 1986 Zimbabwe and South Africa had renewed the then 22-year old agreement on preferential trade between the two countries. The renewed treaty, which gave Zimbabwe's manufactured goods preferential entry into the South African consumer market, came into effect in July 1986.[16] It was also revealed that during the previous financial year, Zimbabwe had chalked up an increasing trade deficit with South Africa, as imports exceeded exports.[17]

On the sanctions issue, therefore, South Africa had an enormous advantage over Zimbabwe, which it intended to use to devastating effect. In a state of near panic, the almost dormant Zimbabwe committee on sanctions held its first meeting on 6 August 1986.[18] This was the first time that Zimbabwean political authorities seriously considered the implications of sanctions and the need to devise counter-strategies. However, the first report produced by the Contingency Planning Committee did not discuss the specific implications of a total South African embargo. The reality was simply too perilous to countenance comfortably. The revelations of the Planning Committee impelled or persuaded the government of the importance of the Beira Corridor.

In this regard, President Mugabe's scheme, hatched at a meeting of the Frontline States in Luanda on 22 August 1986, had three components:

(i)   To persuade Zaire's President Mobutu Sese Seko to help re-open the Benguela railway line through central Angola in his own interest as well as that of the region. This would have meant Mobutu abandoning his support for UNITA, which kept the line closed.

(ii) To persuade Malawi's President Banda to similarly cease support for the MNR, and enable the re-opening of the Nacala railway line and the Blantyre to Beira railway line.

(iii) To receive military assistance from India and strengthen the defence of the Beira railway line.

None of these strategies reached implementation stage yet alone fruition. The whole situation became even more complicated by a strong MNR offensive in September 1986, threatening the Beira Corridor from the Zambezi Valley. The grand scheme seemed to wither on the vine.

By late September 1986, Zimbabwe did not seem to possess any contingency programme and Mugabe reverted to strong posturing, maintaining in New York, for instance, that Zimbabwe had less to lose than South Africa from an all-out sanctions war.[19] At a cabinet meeting on 14 October 1986 President Mugabe pushed through a decision to cut air-links with South Africa in November 1987.[20] However, this decision was never implemented because of disagreement between Presidents Masire of Botswana and Kaunda of Zambia. Four other schemes to safeguard the trade routes were considered:

(i)   The formation of an international force from the Commonwealth including contingents from Canada and Australia. Canada was lukewarm and non-committal, while Australia rejected the scheme out of hand.

(ii) The return of North Korean troops, whose presence had diminished during the previous three years, was contemplated but no active steps were taken to realize this objective.

(iii) The acquisition of new weapons, particularly combat planes for the air force. This proved too costly for the fledgling Zimbabwean economy, hit by the international recession and South African destabilization.

(iv) The training of an extra brigade for the ZNA was about the only contingency measure which was considered feasible that was implemented. Plans to regroup and reform the old Rhodesian Special Air Services (which specialized in external commando work) under some of its former officers, were considered but the rate of progress was a checkered one.

In short, the problems that confronted Zimbabwe were formidable and could have taxed even older and more established governments. The weaknesses in the formulation of contingency programmes were real enough, but they cannot be explained in terms of lack of principle and directionless vacillation as was suggested by unsympathetic observers. For instance, determined joint cooperation among SADCC countries had given rise to substantial improvements in the utilization of the Beira Corridor by June 1988.

However, despite of all these setbacks a total of 6.8 million tonnes[21] of SADCC cargo passed through SADCC ports, by the end of 1987. This represented about 63 per cent of total overseas trade for the region of 10.2 million tonnes.[22] Meanwhile major developments also took place along the Tazara line,[23] the only SADCC corridor which did not face a serious security threat. In addition, SADCC did put together a comprehensive plan for the port of Beira and this attracted the interest of donors, especially the Dutch government. At two donors' conferences that year some 90 per cent of the US$200 million for the first half of the plan was raised.[24] To facilitate private-sector involvement, two companies were formed, the Beira Corridor Group (BCG) in Harare, which represents the interests of the Zimbabwe business sector, and the Expressa Austral de Desenvolvimento (EAD) in Mozambique, presenting the Mozambique business sector. These two companies were complemented by the Southern African Transport and Communications Commission (SATCC). With its headquarters in Maputo, SATCC was the SADCC arm that sustained and coordinated the transport network in the region. The basic organizational structure of SATCC consisted of (i) a committee of ministers, (ii) a co-ordinating committee of senior officials, (iii) a technical unit.

Since 1987, the technical unit grew rapidly in relation to operational coordination, preparation of documentation for studies, projects and meetings and increasing demand for information and advice from organizations and individuals from inside and outside the region. The SATCC's operational coordination work aimed at

(i)   improvement of capabilities in the member states to operate and maintain their transport and communications systems and facilities;
(ii) elimination of institutional obstacles to the movement of traffic in the region, including the harmonization of standards, rules and regulations;
(iii) promotion of bilateral and unilateral agreements on operations;
(iv) actions relating to the routing of traffic through regional ports;
(v)   increasing the utilization of regional resources and know-how. A study by SATCC at the end of 1988 noted that attracting goods from landlocked countries through Mozambique and Tanzania was a matter of competing with an extremely efficient competitor – South Africa.

The fact that transportation through South Africa was on average more expensive than through Tanzania or Mozambique was a premium that most clients in the inland states appeared to accept in exchange for guarantees of timely delivery. Sophisticated transport equipment and techniques by SADCC states proved futile unless supported by corresponding paperwork and commercial service.[25]

This meant that parallel with the increases in the physical capacity of the ports and railways, there was an awareness that there had to be improvements in the management and support services. A lot of SATCC's attention was directed towards those two areas and according to the figures for January 1988[26] almost half the money required for SATCC operational and training projects (US$56.2 million) had been raised, with substantial amounts allocated to Mozambican ports and Dar-es-Salaam harbour. The port authorities too adopted a more businesslike and aggressive marketing approach than previously.

These improvements in the Beira Corridor became evident at the end of 1987. During that year, traffic through Beira showed a 31.7 per cent increase (over the previous year) or just under two million tonnes. About half the throughput was Zimbabwean cargo. Although oil, fertilizer and plastic imports accounted for the largest percentage of Zimbabwe's cargo traffic, cotton, tobacco, tea, and asbestos exports showed appreciable increases. These changing patterns in trade from imports to exports necessitated radical alteration in vessel scheduling and services offered by shipping lines to importers and exporters. As a result, early in 1988, the Safbank line introduced a direct service between Southern African ports, the USA east coast and the Arabian Gulf ports. In addition, they offered alternative triangular services via the Far East to the USA west coast destinations.[27]

During the last quarter of 1988 the most significant sign of rehabilitation was the completion of the new temporary container terminal at Beira Port. This led to sustained improvements in port productivity by 1989 and the port was then capable of handling 30 000 containers per annum. Work on the rehabilitation of the berths was in progress but there were delays in the construction of the roads and the rehabilitation of the Beira city infrastructure.

Bankline East Africa (BLEA) believed these developments would not have been possible had it not been for the support and encouragement of the Mozambican and Zimbabwean authorities who were jointly involved in the upgrading the Beira route, so enabling shipping lines to include the port of Beira in their schedule.[28] Although conditions fluctuated in Beira during the restructuring programme, further improvements in the quality and type of service were implemented as and when conditions permitted and cargo flows improved. By early 1989, the situation at Beira port had greatly improved. According to the Beira Corridor Group, for the first time in 15 years, total Zimbabwe traffic through South Africa would fall to below 50 per cent of all trade by the end of 1990.[29] By the end of 1988 Zimbabwe sent approximately 35 per cent of its total exports and imports through Beira. At the same time approximately 6 per cent went via the port of

Maputo. Towards the end of 1990 the route could take slightly more cargoes, particularly in the form of container traffic.

As of January 1990, the Beira Corridor was approximately 50 per cent complete, with the railway line having been fully restored and functioning normally. The pipeline was also operating well, following reconstruction work which was completed in August 1988. The rebuilding included the completion of the new pumping station at the port of Beira which was then capable of handling 20 000 tonnes of refined petroleum products per day.

The total cost of the Beira Corridor Project was then estimated at approximately Z$370 million and up to early 1990 almost Z$150 million had already been invested. Much of the proposed private sector investment, which was estimated at approximately Z$470 million,[30] was being held up by the failure of the Mozambican and Zimbabwean governments to reach agreement on the bilateral protection of investment and also by the slow bureaucratic decision-making process in both countries. It was hoped that by 1993, the bulk of Zimbabwe's trade would utilize Mozambican ports and harbours. Zimbabwe was already beginning to feel substantial benefits from the diversion of traffic back to its traditional transport routes. The transport cost was expected to reduce as more traffic was being directed to the Beira system and once the Limpopo railway line became fully operational. In addition to the reduction in transport costs, businessmen were feeling much more confident about access to international trade routes and this confidence was being reflected in improved trading conditions for many of Zimbabwe's commodities. International buyers no longer regarded landlocked SADCC states such as Zimbabwe as a risky source of raw material supplies and that was benefiting traders. Although periodic sabotage attacks were experienced, the security situation was relatively stable in 1988 and 1989. However, there were some problems such as pilfering, that reduced the attractiveness of the Beira port. Mozambique ran the risk of losing about US$5 million a year in port charges and dues because of the theft of sugar exported by Zimbabwe and Swaziland.[31] The amount of sugar stolen between 1986 and 1989 varied between 10 000 tonnes and 12 000 tonnes a year, representing about US$1.7 million (about Z$3.4 million) per annum.

In the Maputo port and rail network, sugar was one of the products most subject to robbery. These repeated robberies were already leading to a substantial reduction in the income that accrued to the Mozambican state from the transit trade. Swaziland began to channel a great deal of sugar (which should have gone via Maputo) to the port of Durban in South Africa. The average figure for the diverted sugar exports was in the region of 150 000 tonnes a year, representing a loss of income of around US$2 million.

During the 1988/89 period Maputo handled around 100 000 tonnes of sugar from Zimbabwe, less than expected. This was not because Zimbabwe sent its sugar to other ports, but because there was increased demand inside the country. However, as of 1990, it was likely that Zimbabwe, losing US$150 000[32] for every 1000 tonnes stolen would consider alternatives. If Zimbabwe switched to Durban that would mean a loss of well over US$5 million. Thus the more than 330 000 tonnes of sugar exported by the two countries via Maputo are very important for Mozambique, because the US$5 million amounted to about 5 per cent of the total income Mozambique gained from its own exports in 1988.[33] The Goba and Ressano railways meet at a junction some 10 kilometres from central Maputo. It was between that junction at Machava and the port of Maputo that most of the thefts took place.[34] In the 1988/89 period, theft on the railway accounted for more than twice the losses at the port. Mozambique railway's southern division already had a detailed picture of how the thefts occurred. The thieves included local residents, railway workers and even those who were supposed to protect the trains. For Zimbabwe, improved efficiency and reduced pilfering at the ports would greatly increase the attractiveness of the Mozambican ports and boost savings on the transport account.

By late 1989, the Beira Corridor was facing another problem: that of disinformation. The Beira Corridor Group (BCG) condemned shipping circles in Durban and Hamburg for spreading disinformation.[35] According to a report in the September 1989 issue of the *BCG Bulletin*[36] a Belgian business magazine had published misleading information portraying the Beira Corridor and Beira Port as unreliable and inefficient. The BCG pointed out that in June 1989 transit operations were almost incident-free, while during the previous month there was a derailment caused by technical faults which blocked the line for five days. Between June 1989 and September 1989, there were a few incidents affecting the railway line but the disruptions were usually rectified the same day. The BCG also reported a derailment of a unit train in the northern half of the Beira Corridor at the end of

July 1989, resulting in the line being blocked for transit traffic, and subsequently the line was sabotaged. However, the damage was quickly repaired. In addition, in early June the petroleum pipeline was blown up, but it had been repaired by mid-June 1989. Road conditions had been back to normal since late May 1989 with the road over the Pungwe Flats operating without delays. Road re-sheeting continued with expatriate assistance. The flow of goods by rail or road to Beira, however, was predominantly from Harare with many wagons and trucks returning empty. While that imbalance could have been redressed, the locomotive problem placed increasingly severe constraints on this main transport option.

Two other potential outlets for Zimbabwe, via the Limpopo railway line and the Tazara line, operated intermittently and inefficiently, respectively, while the Benguela railway line to the Angolan port of Lobito remained virtually closed because of the civil war in Angola. The Zimbabwe–Maputo railway line or the Limpopo railway line/ corridor stretches from Chicaulacuala on the Zimbabwe border along the banks of the Limpopo river to Maputo.

As of 1990, there was no road link between Zimbabwe and the port of Maputo. Viewed as a highly desirable development, such a road would add considerably to the value of the Limpopo corridor and provide a road link which does not pass through South Africa. Already SADCC had prepared the terms of reference for such a project; by 1990 funds were already being sought for a feasibility study.

Meanwhile, there had been great improvements at the Beira port as most of the rehabilitation programmes had been completed. Congestion and delays had now reduced because about eight berths out of ten were in operation. The new container-handling equipment supported by Swedish aid had been fully installed and this increased the container capacity from 15 000 tonnes per year to 60 000 tonnes. Further improvements would eventually raise this to 100 000 tonnes.[37] The channel aided by the Dutch, which began in February 1989, was deepened from 6 metres to 8.5 metres, permitting ships of up to 60 000 dwt (dead weight) to call, compared with 25 000 dwt before dredging. As for improvements to the railway in early 1990, Mozambique began negotiating with several donors for the purchase of 45 new locomotives and these arrived in mid-1990. Because of all these developments there was a major increase in capacity in 1991. The port of Beira was now able to handle 5 million tonnes per year and the railway at least 2 million tonnes per annum.

Without the Beira Corridor, Zimbabwe would have been a virtual hostage of South Africa. As the 1990s unfolded, Zimbabwe was beginning to reap economic benefits from keeping the corridor open. As already stated, the port of Beira is much closer to Harare than any of the South African ports and by late 1989 Zimbabwean shippers were already saving US$1000 for every 40 tonnes on bulk cargo and more on containerized cargo. According to the Beira Corridor Group,[38] in August 1989 when there were few sabotage incidents on the corridor it cost about US$400 less to import a 20-foot container via Beira than by the South African port of Durban. This meant that without the disruption of the railway line Zimbabwe would save a total of up to US$50 million a year. This gave a lot of encouragement to the Zimbabwean importers and exporters because when the transport was moving smoothly they gained more than the government[39] was spending on defending the corridor. The BCG estimated that the profits of some Zimbabwean companies would rise by as much as 40 per cent because of the lower shipping costs.[40]

The success of the Zimbabwe National Army in keeping the Beira Corridor open encouraged private companies to invest in the corridor. Lonrho, a private company operating in Zimbabwe, became the first major foreign company to invest in the corridor and it owned the Beira–Mutare pipeline. Other companies in Zimbabwe were also evaluating investment prospects in Beira and in the corridor. Some started investing in Mozambique's tourism industry. The Mozambican authorities required that investors provide their own security either by hiring private security guards or by feeding and clothing Mozambican soldiers. Thus, for Zimbabwe, the benefit of keeping the Beira Corridor open would seem to go beyond those of facilitating transit import/export traffic.

Unique to the Beira Corridor was the Zimbabwean private company, the Beira Corridor Group formed, as mentioned above, in 1987 and funded by 270 Zimbabwean enterprises (and a few from Malawi and Botswana) which put up US$2500 each.[41] The BCG promoted the use of transport facilities in the Corridor and represented the interests of railway and port users.[42]

In general, by early 1990 on the Beira–Zimbabwe sector security had greatly improved both because of Zimbabwean and Mozambican troop deployments and the political changes in South Africa.[43] With these developments in place there was still some fear that South Africa would step up the commercial tactics it had been using in recent years, particularly rate-cutting for contract shipments to try to keep traffic moving through South Africa rather than via Beira. In those circumstances, it was up to Mozambique to respond flexibly to such commercial pressure in order to retain the traffic already moving through Beira. Zimbabwean business circles had increasingly come to view South Africa as unreliable and willing to disrupt transport for political ends. In addition, the guerrilla experience of some of the Frontline States leaders led them to suspect that if there was no settlement in South Africa, then strikes and sabotage on South Africa's railways could make them unreliable.

5.3 SANCTIONS AND THE CONSEQUENCES FOR ZIMBABWE

During the 1985 to 1988 period, the inability of the Zimbabwe government urgently to formulate counter-strategies to blunt South Africa's likely retaliation for Harare's support for international sanctions against Pretoria raised the issue of exactly what damage Zimbabwe's economy was likely to suffer in such an eventuality. Some leading industrialists in Zimbabwe, together with the supporters of the 'Constructive Engagement' doctrine in the Western world, propagated the gospel of doom or dire consequences. They argued that Zimbabwe's participation in an all-out sanctions war against South Africa and the possible retaliation by Pretoria, would have driven the Zimbabwean economy to subsistence level.

That argument was usually reinforced with statistics showing at least 90 per cent of Zimbabwe's trade (during the period 1983 to 1985) going through South Africa because of the periodic disruption of the Mozambique routes. The logic of that argument was that were Zimbabwe to participate in the implementation of international sanctions against South Africa only 10 per cent of the country's trade would survive, reducing the country to penury. As we shall see below, such an argument was deliberately simplistic and intimidatory. Apart from these anti-sanctions arguments well-meaning loyal Zimbabwean academics and business people stayed clear of the sanctions debate, lest they came up with unpalatable statistics even in the context of a generally positive evaluation. The main reason seemed to have been that to highlight areas of hardship for the Zimbabwean economy would be tantamount to 'defeatism in the struggle against apartheid'. Indeed, commonplace statistics revealed the very high degree of inter-linkages between the economies of Harare and Pretoria but it would have been wrong to conclude that the linkages were lop-sided in favour of Pretoria, and therefore that Zimbabwe would have automatically suffered in a sanctions show-down.

During the mid-1980s the apartheid economy showed signs of disintegrating due to the internal political turmoil and the impact of limited, economic sanctions selectively applied by the Western industrialized countries. It appeared then, that in the last hour of the apartheid economy, trade with the countries of the region would have become crucial. South Africa could not have seriously maintained a regime of retaliatory pressures against its regional neighbours if full international sanctions had been implemented. According to some South African economists,[44] trade with the countries of the region was crucial to economic growth because many of South Africa's export products had become uncompetitive in the wider international market. Estimated trade with Southern African states stood around US$1.5 billion per annum in 1988.[45] Even if it came, the blockade by Pretoria was not likely to be total. The reasons were threefold. The first is based on purely trade considerations. Throughout the 1980s, South Africa remained the leading supplier of Zimbabwe's imports and the second largest market for Zimbabwe's goods after the United Kingdom. Between January and November 1985, Zimbabwe bought South African goods worth Z$252 million, mostly transport equipment, machinery, chemicals and other manufactures, and sold in return goods worth Z$172.3 million.[46] South African imports represented 18 per cent of total Zimbabwean imports of Z$1.4 billion during the eleven-month period.[47] In general, over the 1980s, Zimbabwean exports to South Africa averaged 11 per cent of the country's total exports of about Z$251.5 billion per year.[48]

Second, any serious blockade of Zimbabwe would have hit friendly countries to the north, notably Malawi and Zaire. The bulk of these two countries' trade was still shipped through Zimbabwe *en route* to South Africa. Finally a total blockade by South Africa would have been unlikely considering that country's investment and trade estimated at Z$2 billion in annual revenue from the region.[49] Certain sectors of the South African economy were specifically geared for exports to African countries and, consequently, it was likely that in the event that full sanctions were imposed by the international community, Pretoria would have, at best, prevented or disrupted exports by some SADCC countries through its territory, while leaving trade between itself and those countries intact. Zimbabwe in particular had some leverage to exert. Throughout the 1980s it paid Pretoria an average of Z$100 million per year to use the South African transport system to carry some of its 3 million tonnes of trade. Were South Africa to extend retaliatory measures to other countries of the region, the loss to Pretoria would have been approximately Z$400 million per year from that particular commercial linkage alone.[50]

However, even if South Africa took retaliatory steps, assuming the MNR's disruptive activities were controlled, then the routes through Mozambique would have constituted a safety valve for Zimbabwean commodities. This was not just mere theoretical argument or idle speculation. South Africa could not have afforded to remain pay-master-general of the MNR if international economic sanctions had been stringently applied and effectively monitored. The cumulative impact of the on-going internal revolt, coupled with the severe impact of effectively applied economic sanctions, together with heightened acts of urban guerrilla warfare would have weakened Pretoria's capacity to aid subversive elements. On the other hand, if sanctions were imposed on South Africa, leading to the non-accessibility of South African routes while the Mozambican routes were not fully secured, then Zimbabwe could have incurred serious losses in foreign exchange earnings and faced difficult choices regarding export priorities for restricted exports through the Beira Corridor. Priority could have been given to tobacco because of its high value per tonne coupled with its labour-intensiveness at the production stage (between 85 000 and 100 000 people were employed in the tobacco industry on a full-time basis throughout the 1980s, though this did not include several thousand casual labourers periodically employed during peak planting and harvesting periods). Such a choice could have been at the expense of mineral exports (gold could be airlifted). Sugar producers could have been forced to reduce cane acreages and to turn to those crops for consumption both at home and within neighbouring SADCC countries. However, the problem with this strategy would have been that the chosen production alternative would have been, in all probability, less labour-intensive than sugar. That development could have exacerbated the already large and annually growing unemployment situation. With sufficient imagination and determination on the part of the Zimbabwean government, alternative strategies could have been easily devised. For instance, during several successive years of drought since independence, Zimbabwe launched a very extensive 'food-for-work' programme. The programme involved thousands of drought-stricken rural dwellers in a massive public works programme (for example, road, bridge and dam construction) in return for a wage or grain equivalent. It was almost a miniature version of the public works programme in the United Kingdom during the Great Depression. A more expensive programme, coupled with the long-delayed National Youth Service for school-leavers could have conceivably gone a long way towards alleviating the worst aspects of the unemployment problem.

As for urban unemployment, the government could have devised ways to provide financial assistance to already existing (and help set up new) self-help cooperatives producing basic commodities for the local market and neighbouring states. For the unemployment in multi-unit firms, the government had already launched a programme of tax incentives to companies that were willing to engage and train school leavers. This too, had a potential for expansion. On a more optimistic note, it was possible or conceivable that South Africa's retaliatory actions could have induced fundamental changes in the Zimbabwean economy. It was possible that Zimbabwe's enforced reduction of foreign trade could have led to the achievement of the objective of increasing employment and the redistribution of income by concentrating more on production for domestic consumption. This observation was based on the assumption that imports of both capital and consumer goods represented lost job opportunities, e.g. the importation of a sophisticated grain mill could very well have put many small rural millers out of business with the consequent hardship and unemployment. It has to be clearly stated, however, that all these possibilities would have amounted to no more than strictly short term/ contingency strategies or determined brinkmanship pending the resolution of the South African crisis. They could not possibly have constituted the basis for a sustained long-term strategy for economic growth. Development through predominantly inward-looking strategies or in the context of autarky was simply an unavailable option for Zimbabwe. However, if Zimbabwe had carried out its stated intention of imposing the full package of Commonwealth sanctions, with specifically stated additions, there was absolutely no doubt that the Zimbabwe economy would have endured tremendous hardships. If the risk of potential South African retaliation were to be underplayed for the purposes of analytical arguments, then the measures with the greatest significance for Zimbabwe would have been

(i)   the suspension of air links;
(ii) the prohibition of purchases of iron, steel and coke from South Africa;
(iii) the abrogation of the Preferential Trade Treaty;
(iv) the suspension of financial transfers to South Africa.

Each of these measures would have had potentially serious ripple-effects throughout the Zimbabwean economy.

5.4 ZIMBABWE'S DILEMMA

(i) Air Links

The impact of Zimbabwe's suspension of air links with South Africa would not have been immediately apparent. As of late 1989 there were about 38 flights per week between Harare/Bulawayo and various points in South Africa.[51] These flights were the most profitable or the least unprofitable part of Air Zimbabwe operations.[52] If these flights had been terminated, that move would not have necessarily signalled the collapse of the airline. It was possible that there would have been an almost equivalent gain in traffic via intermediate points such as Gaborone in Botswana.

However, the management crisis and liquidity problems within Air Zimbabwe came to a head in the first half of 1988 when all eight managers either resigned or were dismissed, leaving only the general manager. Even the chairmen of the Board of Governors resigned in frustration.[53] Throughout the 1980s, Air Zimbabwe recorded rising operational losses. The subsidy bill to the already financially over-stretched Zimbabwe exchequer stood at Z$12 million in the 1985/86 Financial Year,[54] Z$45 million for the 1986/87 Financial Year and over Z$70 million 1987/88.[55]

On the brighter side, Air Zimbabwe began to benefit from the suspension of direct flights to Johannesburg by the Australian National Airline, Qantas, which began direct flights to Harare in the early 1980s. By the late 1980s other measures to improve the international air-traffic situation in Zimbabwe were becoming apparent. Until mid-1988, the Zimbabwean authorities regarded an 'open-skies' policy as a recipe for neutralizing Zimbabwe's negotiating power for royalties with other airlines. It was argued that such a policy would put the country at a strategic disadvantage. But since that period, and in line with the new economic policy announced in 1989,[56] which included making parastatals more cost-effective, an 'open-skies' policy became acceptable.

Thus, the Zimbabwean authorities finally came to acknowledge that the market had not been fully utilized. The assumption had been that other airlines coming in would result in a stiffening of competition, impelling Air Zimbabwe to become more cost-efficient. The immediate result of this policy change was the commencement of scheduled flights by three new airlines, namely Lufthansa (German Airlines), Ghana Airways and Aeroflot (Russian) while negotiation began with Air France and the Dutch Airline, KLM.[57] Another area of concern would have been aircraft maintenance. It was possible that Zimbabwe Airways could have been severely hit, if by way of retaliation, South African Airways was to withdraw servicing facilities.[58] In fact, some firms operating in Harare feared that South African maintenance engineers on private contracts might have been reluctant to come to Zimbabwe if they were to fly there by a circuitous route. However, such facilities could have been procured from a friendly airline from outside the region, although at a considerably increased cost. Significantly, throughout the 1980s, Air Zimbabwe was slowly but steadily building up its own technical reserve of personnel to boost its own technical capabilities.

It was possible that certain sectors of the chemical industry would have been adversely affected.[59] Some of the chemicals used in the production processes with a very short shelf-life and which have traditionally been procured speedily by air from South Africa, would have had to be obtained from elsewhere at a much increased cost. But, at least, despite the cost, such chemicals were readily available from sources friendly to Zimbabwe. However, both Air Zimbabwe and other SADCC airlines were still quite underdeveloped and quite expensive to operate. In particular, no SADCC airline had the capacity to handle high bulk commodities. It is also interesting to note that the combined freight of eight Southern African airports in 1985 were only a few thousand tonnes ahead of just one South African airport, Johannesburg (see Table 5.1).

As pointed out above, apart from gold, diamonds and cobalt, Zimbabwe's and indeed SADCC's exports were mostly high-bulk, low-value commodities which could not have been airlifted economically. For example, Zimbabwe's tobacco industry calculated that it needed four Boeing-747s for 365 days per year, merely to carry out the annual export tobacco crop. The practical problems of finding enough aircraft to shift the cargo in the region, let alone accommodating, maintaining and refuelling them, made air transport completely non-viable as an alternative to road and rail. For Zimbabwe, then, although the severance of direct air links to South Africa would have been initially traumatic for the fledgling airline, the damage to other sectors of the economy would not have been that devastating.

Table 5.1   Airfreight Loaded and Unloaded at Southern African Airports, 1985 (000 tonnes)

Luanda	24.4
Lilongwe	5.6
Maputo	1.8
Matsapha	0.2
Harare	36.5
Dar-es Salaam	5.4
Kinshasa	23.1
Lusaka	14.2
TOTAL	111.2
Johannesburg	88.7
For comparison	
Nairobi	35.4
Cairo	106.1
Heathrow	518.7
Gatwick	153.7

Source: Roger Martin, 'Apartheid Effect on Transport' *The Herald* 28 February 1989.

However, the fragile nature of Zimbabwe's airline system could be directly attributed to South African destabilization, leading to a forced misplacement of resources and foreign exchange losses due to exports forgone. This situation directly led to Zimbabwe's inability to maintain a viable airline. The national cargo carrier, Affretair, demonstrated the gravity of the situation. In particular, the aircargo provided by Affretair was vital to the success of one of Zimbabwe's fastest growing economic sectors, namely the horticultural industry, tapping the West European market. But severe squeezes on foreign currency allocations reduced potential exports and left Affretair with no alternative but to compete for south-bound high-yield freight to keep its operations viable. The freight flows in 1987 were as shown in Table 5.2.[60]

Table 5.2   Freight Flows, Southbound and Northbound, 1987

(a) *Southbound cargo* (general cargo)	65 per cent originated from the UK, 35 per cent originated from Europe, North America and the Far East
(b) *Northbound cargo* (Horticulture, textiles and general cargo)	80 percent of Zimbabwe's exports were destined for mainland Europe (influence of horticultural exports at play)

As Table 5.2 shows, about 65 per cent of Affretair's southbound cargo originated from Britain, with the remainder coming from mainland Europe, North America and the Far East. Zimbabwean exports, mainly horticultural produce destined for mainland Europe, constituted about 80 per cent of the carrier's northbound cargo, the remainder being destined for the UK and North America. Northbound cargo was mostly bulky, low-value freight, including flowers, hunting trophies and manufactured garments. The peak demand for exports was from November to March.

The level of southbound cargo was mainly dependent on the general macroeconomic performance of the country, including the availability of foreign currency. This lack of synchronization made the cargo carrier dependent on southbound cargo to maintain the synchronization of low-value, high-bulk exports. The whole arrangement presented the airline with the problem of coping with the peak periods and excess capacity during off-peak periods. Unfortunately the whole region was characterized by the same problem which limited potential for Affretair to exploit regional markets to compensate for Zimbabwe's own economic weakness.

During off-peak periods, the bulk of exports from Zimbabwe did not offer commercially viable airfreight rates in the context of pure freight aircraft, as opposed to cargo in the holds of passenger aircraft which is subsidized by and subject to passenger loads. This then meant that national freight aircraft looked at the horticultural products in the main as return filler loads backed on to a commercially viable load into Zimbabwe. The end result was limited airfreightable imports and the scramble for high-yield southbound freight to enable Affretair to remain viable. But again, Affretair was at a disadvantage because it faced stiff competition from wide-bodied passenger aircraft operators who looked at cargo revenue essentially as a secondary contributor to the operation of their scheduled services. In addition, passenger operators also offered greater frequency of flights. Hence, if there were no viable loads, Affretair was not able to offer rates to cater for horticultural exports. During peak seasons, Affretair periodically ran short of adequate capacity to meet demand for northbound traffic, resulting in lost exports.

(ii) Iron, Steel and Coke

As for imports of iron, steel and coke from South Africa, Zimbabwe was likely to be less adversely affected by a South African blockade. There had long been a two-way trade in steel products between the two countries, with an evident degree of specialization on both sides. In 1984, Zimbabwe imported steel products worth Z$27.3 million.[61] In spite of this, there were distinct possibilities of replacing these products either by domestic production or by imports from other sources through the Beira Corridor, but at a considerably increased cost.

However, Zimbabwe would have suffered from procurement problems both in the short to long term if it embargoed the importation of coke from South Africa, or if Pretoria withheld supplies. Zimbabwe was highly dependent on low-sulphur coke from South Africa for the production of ferro-chrome, a major foreign exchange earner. Alternative supplies would have had to be located, probably at about three times the prevailing cost – quite apart from possible transport difficulties. Zimbabwe periodically sourced its coke from South Africa such as during the late 1987 to mid-1988 period, when the Hwange furnaces closed for renovation.

(iii) The Preferential Trade Agreement

The abrogation of the Preferential Trade Agreement would have caused some hardship to Zimbabwean manufacturers, but certainly not insurmountable problems. During the Financial Year 1983/84, about 16 per cent of Zimbabwe's merchandise went to South Africa, but the proportion was down to 11 per cent (Z$80 million) in 1985.[62] Further hardship could have been encountered if the Zimbabwean government were to suspend trade assistance to Zimbabwean exporters, including the 9 per cent export incentive scheme for goods destined for the South African market. Given the high production costs in the Zimbabwean industrial sector, the country would have experienced considerable difficulties in finding alternative export markets for those goods without substantial terms-of-trade losses.

However, to the extent that during the second half of the 1980s, Zimbabwe imported more goods and services from South Africa than it exported Harare benefited from the depreciation of the South African rand. If trade sanctions against South Africa were to have been strictly enforced, they could have led to a potential reduction of South African capacity to import by up to 30 per cent and in the absence of the major adjustments to the South African economy, such a development had the potential to reduce, substantially, South Africa's Gross Domestic Product. If there were to be an equal decrease in South Africa's imports from Zimbabwe, that would have reduced Zimbabwe's merchandise earnings by about 3 to 4 per cent.[63] That reduction would not have been catastrophic in macroeconomic terms, but would have exacerbated Zimbabwe's already severely stretched foreign exchange reserves position.

(iv) Financial Transfers, Procurement and Tourism

Zimbabwe could have saved foreign exchange by suspending financial transfers such as old age pensions and company dividends to South Africa. In 1985/86 pension payments to former Rhodesian residents in South Africa amounted to about Z$63 million and dividend payments stood at Z$25 million.[64] South African financial transfers to Zimbabwe in 1984 amounted to Z$8 million.[65] Overall, Zimbabwe would have benefited from suspending financial transfers to South Africa. South African investment in Zimbabwe has been substantial. Even up to 1990, about 25 per cent of Zimbabwean capital stock was controlled by South African investors. South African investors controlled about 80 per cent of the Zimbabwean mining sector. Zimbabwe could have confiscated all these assets. In addition, Zimbabwe also owed Pretoria about Z$200 million, largely inherited from the Smith regime. The debt could have been abrogated.[66]

A ban on government procurement from South Africa would have had only comparatively minor effects. There could have been, however, substantial problems if the ban were extended to companies in Zimbabwe (notably in construction, building, chemical and pharmaceutical sectors) which supply the Zimbabwean government and buy inputs from South Africa. In addition a ban on government contracts with majority-owned South African companies would have raised difficult questions about which companies to disqualify since the majority ownership of most major companies operating in Zimbabwe was nominally South African. The tourist sector appears to be one of the few industries that would have suffered if the Harare government were to ban South African tourists from entering Zimbabwe. Throughout the 1980s about 40 per cent of tourists in Zimbabwe came from South Africa, usually on an individual, non-package basis. Their foreign currency contribution was therefore much more significant than that of the 'package deal' tourists from Western Europe and North America. The hotel-room occupancy rate which was the largest source of revenue for the hotel industry would have been drastically reduced. Overall then, the Zimbabwean economy would have experienced tremendous hardships from the imposition of international sanctions on South Africa. But it would certainly be an exaggeration to argue that the economy would have been reduced to subsistence level. The Zimbabwean economy was diversified and sufficiently resilient to the extent that a combination of reduced (input) imports, and less foreign exchange earnings could have seriously hampered growth prospects, but would not produce total disintegration. All these hypothetical arguments about the economics of sanctions are a clear indication of how difficult it was for Zimbabwe to rebuild its economic infrastructure.

6 Overall Economic and Social Impact of Destabilization

Zimbabwe's economy was devastated partly by South African proxy aggression and partly by the government's failure to implement effective economic policies. Since independence Zimbabwe was a constant target of South African destabilization and aggression (as indicated in previous chapters) through withdrawals of railway rolling stock, delays of imports, open and covert barriers to exports, border raids, commando attacks and sabotage through supply of weapons to some dissident groups in south-western Zimbabwe.

Zimbabwe suffered direct war damage from destabilization; the destruction of armaments valued at US$52.2 million at Inkomo Barracks near Harare; the destruction of the air base and five planes at Thornhill Air Base near Gweru,[1] higher transport and energy costs due to disruption, losses of production, exports and other revenue, and lost and deferred economic development. It is estimated that Zimbabwe lost about US$1400 million between 1980 and 1986.[2] This and the protection of the pipeline through Mozambique increased the burden of defence expenditure, as we shall see below. Further economic hardship was imposed through delaying petroleum supplies in late 1982, in conjunction with the sabotage of a pumping station on the pipeline through Mozambique. In addition to all these problems, Zimbabwe faced a serious drought which affected the economy heavily and on top of that the world recession exacerbated the situation.

The argument of this chapter is that the price of destabilization is not simply seen in the dead and displaced, and in the enlarged military budgets, but it is also seen in lost development and reduced living standards. Furthermore they reinforce each other. The chapter illustrates the economic damage created by destabilization directly or indirectly, on trade, social welfare, the agricultural sector, and imports and exports.

6.1 SHORTAGES CAUSED BY DEFENCE SPENDING

Part of the intended effects of the destabilization strategy and the sponsoring of dissidents has been to force the Zimbabwean govern-

130

ment to maintain extremely high levels of defence spending. As observed by Geldenhuys,

> To prevent the black states strengthening themselves economically and militarily,... South Africa can manipulate economic ties and support disaffected groups at least to the extent that a hostile regime would be compelled to concentrate its energies and resources on fighting the rebels.[3]

This had four major negative effects:

(i)   Reduction of investment in such essential areas of infrastructure as health, housing, education and socio-economic development in general;
(ii) The neutralization of the effects of the post-civil war ZIMCORD Reconstruction Project[4] by creating an atmosphere of instability inimical to foreign investment;
(iii) The projection of the image of a beleaguered state in the throes of a civil war; and
(iv) The projection of the post-independence policy of racial and political reconciliation as unworkable and therefore a total failure. This would help to reduce international pressure on South Africa itself to deracialize its own society.[5]

One imponderable question for Zimbabwe is how much money it was forced to divert from development to defence in order to protect itself from South African action, particularly against the transportation routes. Table 6.1 details the resources allocated to defence expenditure in Zimbabwe's post-independent budgets and the defence percentage of each budget. With the exception of the immediate post-independence period in 1980/81 when it was necessary to integrate two guerrilla armies with the remnants of the Rhodesian forces, after the formation of the Zimbabwe National Army (ZNA) defence expenditure began to rise. This was because of the demands on the ZNA on various fronts, the guarding of the Beira corridor and the dissidents in Matabeleland.

Both the reality and the threat of political and military destabilization by South Africa had severe economic consequences. In monetary terms the military expenditure went up in 1982/83 when there was a dramatic increase in the military activity in Matabeleland. Spending on defence, which had been expected to start to fall over the period 1984–85 with the completion of severance payments to ex-combatants and after the Nkomati Accord, continued to rise again in 1985/86 when the ZNA entered Mozambique in a combat role in three provinces.[6] The 1985–86 defence budget was the second largest spending sector after education. After that the defence spending increased each year. This highlighted the fact that the relationship with South Africa was far from being without costs, even without more effective sanctions being applied by the international community. By 1986, direct and indirect costs of destabilization to the nine SADCC member states amounted to a staggering US$10 million.[7]

Table 6.1 Zimbabwe Defence Expenditure since 1980

Year	Total expenditure National Budget Z$	Defence expenditure recurrent & capital Z$	Defence % of exp. %
1980/81	1 627 534 995	310 166 000	19.0
1981/82	2 121 722 670	329 882 000	15.5
1982/83	2 935 559 565	382 150 000	13.0
1983/84	3 052 688 909	425 636 000	14.0
1984/85	3 568 378 248	386 254 000	11.0
1985/86	3 875 298 741	519 659 000	13.5
1986/87	4 837 263 860	687 521 000	14.0
1987/88	5 390 239 626	787 291 000	14.5
1988/89	6 052 263 000	903 254 000	15.0

Total Defence Expenditure (Z$)   4 731 813 000
July 1980 to June 1989
Total Defence Expenditure (US$) 3,875,011,000 *at average annual rate of exchange*

Source: Ministry of Finance, Economic Planning and Development, June 1989, Harare.

I would argue that in a peaceful situation ZNA needed only four brigades instead of six.[8] There would have been no need to purchase MiG-21s if South Africa had not destroyed planes and all the money spent on sabotage activities could have been spent on other important areas. Table 6.2 shows some of the additional costs to Zimbabwe of destabilization. The table does not include a number of areas which cannot be quantified with any certainty; such as lost investment and tourism, increased prices of goods in Zimbabwe, less competitive exports, additional police and security costs. If these costs could be added, the total figure would be much more than that given in Table 6.2.

Table 6.2 Additional Costs to Zimbabwe of South Africa's
Destabilization since 1980

	Z$m	US$m
Additional freight costs	150 000	82 420
Locomotive hire from SATS	4 514	2 480
Truck losses/costs	1 200	660
Fuel losses/pipeline costs	1 050	611
Sabotage (quantified)	6 600	9 120
Sabotage (estimated)	4 000	3 000
Refugee maintenance	1 450	800
Additional defence costs	2 60 618	185 322
Total	429 432	284 413

Source: Johnson and Martin *Apartheid Terrorism: The Destabilisation Report*, London, The Commonwealth Secretariat in Association with James Currey, 1989, p. 76.

Shortages

Immediately after independence, army reorganization resulted in a
substantial reduction in the size of the armed forces. After the reorganization and general demobilization, the army and the air force
stood at 42 000; the police and paramilitary numbered 18 000, with an
additional 20 000 in the militia.[9] However, even then the armed forces
were still too large for such a small state as Zimbabwe. In 1982, the
defence allocation, which was already consuming one-fifth of the
national budget, was boosted by another 11 per cent to account for
well over the total national spending. Consequently, apart from education and health, which received drastically reduced allocations, the
government was forced to virtually freeze spending on some of
the most vital areas of social welfare intended to improve the conditions of the hitherto deprived black majority. For instance, the government could not pay for the several human investment programmes
such as pensions for workers, social security, free libraries in the
countryside to boost adult literacy programmes, increased health
subsidies and the introduction of comprehensive compulsory free
education. Production spending in the economic sectors was also
frozen.[10]

The Housing Ministry had its budget for high-density, low-income
housing schemes cut by more than 67 per cent to Z$195 million.[11]

Apart from recurrent defence costs, by the late 1980s various defence projects were adversely affecting other areas of society. For instance, by January 1989[12] local supplies of building cement deteriorated to an all-time low as supplies were channelled to a Z$280 million underground military bunker project. The project, which was undertaken at the country's most secret and closely guarded airfield, starved the building industry of cement. It caused severe disruptions to the economy because of the huge demand it made on cement supplies. Commercial building development throughout the country was hindered because of cement shortages. The underground bunkers were intended to house MiG-31 jet fighters, whose delivery to Zimbabwe had been stopped three years earlier because of Western objections. By 1989, Zimbabwe had finalized plans to procure an air defence system, aircraft and missiles from the People's Republic of China. About Z$207 million (US$105 million) had to be borrowed for that purpose and the missiles and aircraft arrived in October 1989.[13] The spending on the air defence system included the cost of training 200 people for a period of 10 months. The procurement of the Z$183 million (US$92 million) for the air defence radar system, was the biggest loan by China to Zimbabwe since independence. About US$8 million was for the aircraft and $4 million for missiles.[14]

The building of other state projects contributing to the severe shortage of cement, included the ostentatious new ZANU(PF) headquarters building and, ironically, new offices for the Ministry of National Housing and Construction. The shortage reached crisis levels after a breakdown in Circle Cement's (a major producer) clinker mill in March 1989 with spares not available until June 1989. There was need to utilize the scarce foreign exchange reserves to import clinker, which was normally produced locally. Portland Holdings, the other cement producer, claimed that it was not able to begin a Z$57 million expansion programme because price controls had reduced its profitability to such an extent that financing could not be obtained. There were also general shortages in other areas of the economy. For example, Payen-Zimbabwe, the main producer of gaskets, had to close for the whole of March 1989 because of a lack of materials, causing a major shortage on the market. A shortage of foam-rubber threatened to close the furniture industry; while small dairy producers were threatened with the shortage of milk storage facilities. The shortage of packaging material in May 1989 was so serious that about a quarter of COLCOM's (Pig Industry Cooperative) range of meat products were off supermarket shelves. However, the worst-affected area was that of civilian housing, with its massive backlog in construction. A government study released in September 1989,[15] revealed that Z$18 billion was needed to build a total of 1.9 million housing units in both rural and urban areas if Zimbabwe's critical accommodation shortage was to be alleviated by the turn of the century. That means an average annual production of 172 181 units would be required. Since 1985 a total of 56 000 units had been built by both the public and private sectors, or an average annual output of 18 667 units, which fell far short of the targeted figure of 172 181 units. Increased activity in the construction industry had resulted in a high demand for such building materials as bricks, cement, doors, window frames and roofing sheets, all of which were readily available.

Apart from the diversion of resources into the defence effort another major reason for these enormous shortages was the lack of foreign currency (partly attributed to South African destabilization) for the replacement of inputs. Land, resettlement, agriculture and rural development grants were also drastically slashed and so were the funds for land purchases designed to alleviate overcrowding and land hunger in the communal areas. Other important planks of government policy deserving more generous budgetary allocations were equally scaled down. Funds intended to expand state participation in the private sector were cut down. The government's contribution to the state economic and service sector programme was reduced, with statutory bodies such as parastatals and local authorities required to provide the immense figure of Z$511 million (1985). In practice, however, the programme had to be shelved because of the general lack of funds. Foreign aid donors appeared unwilling to invest in what seemed to be an unstable state.

Leftist critics of the government pointed to the failure of post-independence policies to achieve a significant shift towards the creation of a more egalitarian society and a narrowing of income differentials. On the contrary there was a loss in real earnings, negligible employment gains and little structural change, particularly in the area of land distribution. But, in addition, market-supportive critics argued that instead of providing sufficient incentives to the private sector, there had been expansion in social service expenditure and subsidies financed increasingly by borrowing.[16] The need to service the resultant debt increased foreign exchange shortages, leading to dangerously low investment levels, low growth rates and fewer resources available to promote a more egalitarian society.

There was an element of truth in these arguments. By 1986, the budget deficit had risen progressively from Z$330 million[17] in the first year after independence to Z$940 million (US$602 million) accounting for 10.8 per cent of the GDP.[18] Total subsidy payments, including those rolled over from 1985, stood at Z$500 million, double the figure two years before. Investment had fallen to only 17 per cent of the GDP between 1980 and 1984, with 46 per cent being financed from abroad, mostly through foreign borrowings, contributing to a Z$2000 million rise in foreign debt.[19] The fall of investment was mainly due to the uncertainty of the civil war in Matebeleland. In addition the bad relationship between Zimbabwe and South Africa deterred many foreign investors from investing in Zimbabwe, since 80 per cent of Zimbabwe's external trade used the South African port and railway system.

Unemployment rose, the number of those without access to land, and real wages for industrial workers were all lower than they were in July 1980. The government faced difficult decisions in its attempt to maintain and even expand growth and initiate structural change in accordance with re-distributive goals. One major improvement was in the balance of payments where the current account deficit fell from Z$533 million[20] in 1982 to Z$101 million in 1984 and recording a positive surplus by 1987.

Table 6.3 Balance of Payments, 1980–87 (Z$ million)

	1980	1981	1982	1983	1984	1985	1986	1987
Exports	929	1002	998	1174	1484	1855	2212	2400
Imports	861	1059	1114	1087	1237	1555	1686	1800
Trade balance	68	−57	−116	87	247	300	526	600
Service earnings	91	83	116	131	157	160	237	260
Outflows	242	346	309	393	401	491	496	520
Investments								
Income	83	75	83	93	101	112	111	115
Payments	119	171	245	314	257	286	404	500
Transfers	−40	−23	−62	−59	52	59	53	55
Current Account balance	−157	−439	−533	−455	−101	−146	+27	+10
Net Capital Account	−44	134	343	286	233	244	60	200
Uncredited flows		120	86	66	10	34	106	−15 N.A
Overall balance	−81	−219	−124	−159	+166	+204	+72	−190

Source: Central Statistical Office, Harare, 1987.

This marked improvement, however, was achieved largely at the cost of severely reduced imports by volume coupled with increased export prices. As a result, considerable import demand built up at a time when prospects for import expansion were less optimistic. With inflation rising, stimulating domestic demand led to the economy overheating; while efforts to stimulate export expansion and to switch import use more towards investment goods had an adverse impact upon immediate growth prospects and upon the government's redistribution objectives.

However, political developments starting in late 1986 somewhat assisted the government's economic strategy. On the one hand, there were visible signs that the forceful and sometimes brutal methods adopted by elements of the ruling party membership, local leaders and particularly the youth wing, were being dealt with harshly, both through tighter internal party discipline and, more importantly, by bringing serious cases to the courts. On the other hand, there was a real prospect of unity talks between ZANU(PF) and PF-ZAPU reaching a successful conclusion. There was, therefore, real hope that the deep wounds of regional and factional conflict could begin to be healed. But even these hopeful signs of greater internal political cohesion were under threat from South Africa. As pointed out in the previous chapters, Pretoria had already fanned the flames of division in Matebeleland by providing support for dissident activity. With up to one-quarter of the Zimbabwean army already deployed across the border in Mozambique to defend transport and fuel links against attack by the South African-backed rebels, Pretoria attempted to maintain or even intensify its activities in Matebeleland to encourage the deployment of Zimbabwe's armed forces on two large and distant fronts.[21]

6.2 DESTABILIZATION'S IMPACT ON TRADE

Over and above these factors, South Africa's control over Zimbabwe's trade remained all-pervasive. Until the second half of the 1980s, some 20 per cent of Zimbabwe's visible trade was with South Africa. Zimbabwe also ran an invisible deficit averaging Z$150 million with South Africa, with which its tourists, hotel and insurance industries are intricately linked. Throughout the first half of the 1980s, about 80 per cent of Zimbabwe's external trade used the South African port and railway system. These statistics of linkage and dependence formed a major plank in the propaganda debate warning Zimbabwe of the dangers of supporting the call for sanctions against South Africa. Yet the reality of the economic cost of the prevailing destabilization formed an essential part of any objective assessment of the situation. What all the different factors illustrated was that not only had South Africa the power to discount any optimistic forecasts made of Zimbabwe's economic prospects, but Pretoria's existing influence was already considerable. Thus, Zimbabwe's choice of supporting increased sanctions against South Africa did not represent a decision between hypothetical potential economic costs if reprisals were forthcoming against no costs if reprisals were not carried out. Rather, Zimbabwe's choice came from weighing increased and immediate costs against the hope that long-term peace and economic stability were more quickly restored. The country's shaky economic performance was exacerbated by spiralling defence costs and the general shortage of funds for productive investment. By the 1986/87 Financial Year, this situation had reached crisis proportions, resulting in a huge budget deficit, which stood at Z$1.05 billion, representing 11 per cent of the GDP.[22] This deficit, which had reached, for the first time, the billion-dollar mark, constituted a 52 per cent increase over the 1985/86 actual budget deficit of Z$691.6 million. The high levels of spending continued into the 1987/88 Financial Year when vital ministries such as Agriculture and Transport experienced negative investment levels. A major reason for increased defence spending was a newly launched weapons and general defence equipment procurement programme for the Zimbabwe National Army. In addition, Zimbabwe had to form an additional military Brigade, the Sixth Brigade and the Presidential Guard.

6.3   IMPACT ON SOCIAL WELFARE

At the level of society in general, the high defence spending had potentially explosive political repercussions. Drastic cuts in social spending necessitated by increased defence expenditure led to the removal of food subsidies by the middle of 1983. In September 1983, the price of milk went up by 50 per cent, bread by 25 per cent; maize meal (the staple food of the majority of the people) went up by 40 per cent. These spiralling prices were exacerbated by the devaluation of the Zimbabwe dollar during the same period, adding an additional 7 per cent to the already high prices. The mini-budget,

Table 6.4 Zimbabwe's Main Trading Partners
(% of Total)

	1983	1984	1985	1986	1987	1988	1989
Imports							
SA	24.5	19.3	18.9	21.4	20.8	20.1	22.3
UK	11.5	11.9	10.4	10.9	11.5	12.2	12.8
W. Germany	7.4	6.9	6.9	9.9	8.7	10.1	12.2
USA	9.5	9.3	10.1	8.3	9.4	8.5	10.2
Japan	4.7	5.3	3.9	4.3	3.9	6.1	5.2
Italy	1.8	3.0	3.0	4.3	3.0	N.A.	N.A.
Exports							
SA	18.7	18.2	10.8	12.4	9.8	8.6	10.2
UK	11.6	12.8	13.0	12.3	12.9	14.5	10.1
W. Germany	7.7	8.6	9.9	8.6	10.2	11.0	9.8
USA	6.7	6.2	8.1	5.7	6.8	7.8	8.4
Japan	6.2	5.2	4.6	4.6	5.0	3.8	7.0
Italy	5.2	5.1	5.9	5.9	4.4	6.4	5.5

Source: Central Statistical Office, *Quarterly Digest of Statistics*, 1989, p. 12.

which accompanied the devaluation, raised prices by another 4 per cent. There were also two attendant problems: (i) the serious budgetary deficit situation; (ii) the surge in inflation.

Inflation stood at 14.5 per cent in 1982 and by 1985, it had reached 18 per cent shooting up to over 20 per cent by the end of 1987. The increased food costs and the rising inflation led to the demand for unaffordable wage increases, and created a potential for food riots. There was certainly an atmosphere of civil antagonism towards the government. The situation also considerably hampered job creation programmes. Throughout the 1980s, between 80 000 and 90 000 school leavers entered the Zimbabwe job market every year, finding few jobs in an economy which grew by an average of 3 per cent per annum between 1982 and 1987, while the population grew by almost 4 per cent per annum.

Real economic growth fell by 3 per cent in 1983 after a marginal growth of 2 per cent in 1982. The scanty rainfall leading to drought, the world recession and the restrictive policies needed to make devaluation work, led to the first fall in output since independence. The 1982 Balance of Payments (BOP) deficit stood at Z$533 million – 13 per cent more than in 1981. This resource gap was too large to be sustained and the situation necessitated the first devaluation of the

Zimbabwe dollar since independence. In fact, the value of the Zimbabwe dollar had been declining since 1980 against the major Western currencies, by an average of one per cent per month. As a result, the real value of each dollar earned in 1980 fell 74 cents after tax to 17 cents by 1989.[23] Because of the fall in value, an average person in 1989 earned a money income equal to four times the amount earned in 1980, which represented a significant decline in real income terms. Higher-income earners were worse off because of the progressive nature of Zimbabwe's taxation system. To have compensated employees well for the rising cost of living since 1980, pay increases would have had to average about 15 per cent per year and on that basis, Z$350 as a minimum monthly wage would be required to purchase a basket of consumer goods that cost Z$100 in 1980. In addition to the rising costs which, according to official figures,[24] reduced the purchasing power of the 1980 dollar to 36 cents by October 1988, taxation more than doubled, absorbing 65 to 75 per cent of the income of higher earners.

Apart from defence costs, successive years of drought brought additional strains to the exchequer. Maize production was severely affected, with the result that in 1983, the Grain Marketing Board collected one million tonnes of grain, compared to 1.4 million tonnes in 1982.[25] To meet the shortfall the government had to resort to external borrowing. Consequently, foreign borrowing quadrupled from Z$350 million in 1980 to Z$1.5 billion at the end of 1982. The country's debt service rose from 3 per cent to 16 per cent over the same period. By 1984 the public debt had increased sixfold and the debt service ratio increased to about 30 per cent of the export earnings.[26]

The strained Balance of Payments situation had adverse effects on the implementation of the Transitional National Development Plan, which was supposed to lay the basis for the transformation of the economy and society. The government's ambitious development target, of 8 per cent growth a year of GNP compared with the 1982/83 period proved well beyond reach. The 1983/84 budget had been austere due to the IMF's insistence that public expenditure be reduced, as part of a standby facility of SDR 356 million. However, the February 1984 mini-budget reversed public expenditure curbs, increasing government spending by Z$304 million, resulting in a 59 per cent increase in the budget deficit (Z$717 million or 16 per cent of the GDP). The government had committed itself to reducing the overall budgetary deficit by 5.5 per cent of the GDP in the Financial

Year 1983/84. However, political pressures for high levels of spending in education and health proved too strong and the government had to relent. The abolition of food subsidies and the shelving of the land redistribution programme were politically unpopular measures. At the May Day rallies of 1984, no announcement of wage and salary increases were made, because of the need to control spending in order to reduce inflation and curb the increasing deficit.

By 1988, eight years after independence, Zimbabwe seemed still to be seeking a viable economic strategy. Satisfactory growth had been achieved in only three of the eight years. And, as pointed out above, real per capita income by the late 1980s was only marginally higher than in 1980; worse, average real wages had fallen and unemployment was conservatively estimated at 16 per cent of the labour force.[27] This unsatisfactory performance was partly attributable to circumstances outside the government's control including four years of drought, world recessions, depressed commodity prices and South African destabilization but there was also a real need for change in the domestic economic policy. Such a policy, had it been speedily implemented, would have addressed the three most crucial problem areas, namely shortage of foreign exchange, depressed investment and escalating unemployment. However, as the 1980s drew to a close, there was no consensus on the strategic policies to be adopted. Planners and interventionists, rather than liberal marketers, appeared to dominate the scene, contrary to trends elsewhere in the Third World. Examples of their influence included the establishment of a state trading corporation, the maintenance of tight price controls while easing the wage freeze and the authorities' general conviction that increased government participation in industry was needed to create employment. There were also large grey areas. The government appeared to accept the principle of trade liberalization and set up a committee to investigate the mechanics of reduced controls over foreign trade, promising a new and more liberal investment code. In spite of this however, the overriding impression was of an administration that had yet to finalize its economic priorities. It appeared to know where it wanted to go but was less sure of how to get there. This observation is supported by the economic drift of the period 1986/87. During that period no major policy initiatives were undertaken apart from the 1987 decision to limit dividend and profit remittances by foreign-owned companies. The three budgets of 1985/86, 1986/87, 1987/88 had been largely neutral in character, while the budget deficit was allowed to grow to unsustainable levels. *Ad hoc* measures, such as the curb on foreign dividends and the pay and price freeze, have predominated.

Real growth in the economy was officially put at 2 per cent for 1986/87,[28] although private sector estimates put the figure nearer zero. Most of whatever growth was registered was in the public service sector, notably in education and public administration, while manufacturing expanded at less than 1 per cent between 1981 and 1987. Net investment in recent years has been minimal. This helps to explain the tiny growth in employment, estimated during 1988 at fewer than 10 000 new jobs a year. Set against the 150 000 secondary school leavers entering the job market in 1988 and the projected 300 000 job-seekers in 1990, the gravity of the situation became all too clear.

6.4   THE IMPACT OF DESTABILIZATION ON THE AGRICULTURAL SECTOR

Another vital aspect of Zimbabwe's economy, the agricultural sector, was adversely affected by a combination of dissident activity in the rural areas in the Western and Eastern parts of the country, deliberate transport disruptions by South Africa and successive years of drought. Agriculture was one of the country's three leading export sectors, after mining and manufacturing, contributing about Z$300 million to Z$400 million on average throughout the 1980s.[29]

Undermining Zimbabwe's agricultural productivity not only had the effect of increasing dependence on South Africa, but since Zimbabwe was responsible for food security within SADCC, such a move automatically undermined SADCC's food security reserve system. More seriously, disruption of agricultural production created even higher levels of unemployment since agro-business and farming in general occupied a considerable number of the wage-earning population.

Commercial cattle farming in Matebeleland, grain production in the Midlands area and tea, coffee, timber and citrus fruit production in the Eastern districts were all seriously affected by the activities of 'Super-ZAPU' dissidents and MNR rebels respectively. In particular, beef production in Matebeleland was seriously affected. A number of farmers were killed by dissidents and had their stock stolen; others abandoned their farms. Fence-cutting by dissidents seeking popularity with land-hungry peasants seeking land to squat on became rampant.[30] A lot of the machinery was set on fire, e.g. tractors, irrigation equipment, pumps, motors and engines. These activities were devastating for the commercial farmers and it had a serious effect on the production of commercial agricultural products.

The government's tremendous success in stimulating peasant farmers, in areas which were not affected by the dissidents, to grow more food had created a massive grain surplus.[31] But the conditions of overcrowding and poor production remained in the communal areas. This was because the general insecurity there and the shortage of funds disrupted the government's land redistribution and resettlement programme for peasant farmers. The inept policies and general government indecisiveness compounded the problems. The government aimed to move about 162 000 families by 1985 on land previously owned by white farmers who were to sell their land to the state on a 'willing-buyer, willing-seller' basis.[32]

At independence, commercial farming occupied 42 per cent of the land, which included foreign-owned land, abandoned farms, and the multinational corporations and their agro-industries such as the Mazoe Estates (citrus) just outside Harare, and the vast sugar plantations in the Zimbabwe lowveld. The legal instrument or mechanism to enable the government to acquire land was relatively simple. Any commercial farmer who wishes to sell land has to offer it to the government first. However, because of the high levels of defence spending and the frequent disruption of Zimbabwe's income-generating exports by destabilization, the implementation of some of those programmes has not been possible because of shortage of funds.

6.5 THE UNITY ACCORD

However, if economic prospects looked less than encouraging during the 1980s, towards the end of the decade peace prospects brightened. The immediate success of the unity agreement between ZANU(PF) and PF-ZAPU was indicated by an apparent end to incidents involving dissidents when the December 1987 negotiations between ZANU (PF) and PF-ZAPU culminated in a Unity Accord. A general amnesty for dissidents operating in the Matebeleland and Midlands provinces was declared in April–May 1988. The eradication of the bandit menace that had plagued Matebeleland since 1982 was one of the main aims of the accord. The leader of PF-ZAPU, Joshua Nkomo, who clearly believed his credibility and reputation were at stake, put much energy into selling the agreement to his supporters when the agreement was signed in December 1987. However, rhetoric and a few cabinet posts were unlikely to placate PF-ZAPU supporters, who could hardly wait to condemn the accord, especially if it became clear, as they have always claimed, that the accord represented a ZANU(PF) takeover rather than a genuine merger. In the long run, therefore, Mugabe had to ensure there was a genuine, 'trickle-down' effect from unity for the broad masses of PF-ZAPU supporters. Considering the state of the economy at the close of the 1980s, material rewards on an expanded national scale were out of the question.

What Mugabe had managed to do was to increase the number of those in the leadership who received his patronage. Some key PF-ZAPU leaders and cadres received secure and important posts in the civil and diplomatic services and the parastatals. Mugabe also attempted, somewhat successfully, to ensure that the united (ZANU (PF) and PF-ZAPU) party's structures of control have become pervasive at grassroots level. Indeed, since independence, one of Mugabe's most successful projects has been to centralize and conso-lidate power, culminating in the introduction of the executive presi-dency in 1988. As of 1990, Mugabe's strategy of power centralization and consolidation consisted of a persistent, somewhat irrational, advocacy of a one-party state. The one-party state was seen as a means of countering or containing tribal and regional loyalties. But economically it was a great setback because foreign investors were nervous of the one-party idea.[33] Some foreign businessmen were uncertain about which direction the political situation in Zimbabwe was taking. It has also been argued that a broad political coalition in the context of a one-party state system had the distinct potential of allowing for faction-building and the development of special-interest lobbies rather than tribal/ethnic secret deals.

However, what has been conveniently ignored in these rationaliza-tions of the one-party state was the fact that such a system plays down policy issues, fostering the politics of personality and dominant tribal group hegemony, with the result that wider and more serious debate is overshadowed. Significantly, because of Mugabe's need to distribute largesse in the form of jobs in order to win political compliance, the post-merger government with its 52 ministers (out of a Lower House of 100: ministers, rather than back-benchers were in the majority in the House) attracted sharp criticism at home and abroad. This pattern of an unusually large number of ministerial posts has been an endur-ing characteristic of the Mugabe administration. Hence, the post-merger government must not be viewed as just the first round in a delicate coalition-building process, which by its very nature, precluded hasty moves. Rather, cabinet posts have become job sponges for ensuring the loyalty of nationalist veterans potentially unemployable elsewhere in the public and private sectors. On the strictly political level, these tactics served Mugabe well throughout the 1980s. But in one very important sense, time was no longer on Mugabe's side. In particular, the massive expansion of secondary and tertiary education, and the pressure on the land, reflected in the squatter problem, highlighted the nature of the Mugabe regime as it tottered into the 1990s. If the growing unemployment crisis was to be defused, Zimbabwe needed decisive – even aggressive – economic expansionist policies and strategies. In particular the decision-making process needed to be speeded up and public-sector management revolutionized. Above all, tough political decisions on taxes, subsidies, industrial policy, wages, prices and investment could not be postponed.

6.6 IMPACT ON IMPORTS AND EXPORTS

Zimbabwe in the 1980s faced a decline in investment in the manufacturing sector; a downturn that threatened to usher in a gradual shrinking of the country's industrial base. In terms of the expectations set out in the Transitional Development Plan[34] released in 1983, the sector needed an annual investment of Z$251.7 billion per annum as a necessary condition to achieve the desired 8 per cent per year growth rate.

However, by 1988 neither the first nor the second targets had been achieved. Foreign investment in the sector since independence had been minimal, mainly because of the atmosphere of instability in the country caused by destabilization; to some extent the government's policy of socialism also scared foreign investors. On the other hand domestic investment could not fill the gap, because of foreign currency shortages. Unfortunately, these problems confronted a sector which has the potential to constitute the stimulus to Zimbabwe-based economy because of the largely localized nature of its ownership, particularly during the late 1980s. A combination of equity sales by European companies and South African disinvestment increased the share of local ownership.[35]

In theory, increased local ownership and increased reinvestment levels should have led to the development of a vibrant manufacturing sector, creating more jobs. That has not been the case. According to a CZI survey,[36] investment in the manufacturing sector in 1981 was 40 per cent higher than envisaged, but partly because of increased defence spending, destabilization and the consequent reluctance of foreign investors, drought and the general international recession, the level of investment by 1982 stood at only Z$178 million, about 33 per cent below target.[37]

Simply to maintain manufacturing at the 1980 level between 1981 and 1984 needed an estimated Z$316 million per year to replace worn-out and redundant equipment. Out of that figure, at least 60 per cent or Z$190 million would have had to be in foreign currency. With a current account deficit averaging about Z$490 million during 1982/83 Zimbabwe's foreign exchange reserves were too low to cover investment needs in the sector. For instance, in 1984, food imports of about 600 000 tonnes (because of the drought) had to be paid for by taking over equity held by residents in exchange for local currency; further funds were raised through the suspension of international payments of dividends and rents. While this exercise helped to pay for food, it did so partly at the expense of Zimbabwe's image with foreign investors.

In the 1980s there was a great uneasiness in import and export circles caused by the political turmoil in South Africa, and by South Africa's restriction of Zimbabwean transit trade. This resulted in reduced exports, since South Africa had been for a long time Zimbabwe's largest export market. The political conflict in South Africa, the subsequent downturn in the South African economy and the fall of the rand had adverse effects on the Zimbabwe manufacturing sector. The fact that the two countries were pursuing extremely different government policies made their situation worse. For many years their economic structure had been that of cooperation rather than of confrontation.

In 1984, Zimbabwe exported goods worth Z$232.2 million to South Africa or 18 per cent of merchandise exports. Imports from South Africa amounted to Z$231.8 million. Zimbabwe's exports were mostly manufactures. However, during the second half of the 1980s the United Kingdom overtook Pretoria as Zimbabwe's largest export market. This was attributed to the fall in the rand against major Western currencies, the general economic depression in South Africa and possible diversification to other markets by Zimbabwean business interests. But the most worrying trend was that while the UK had overtaken South Africa as the largest export market, the bulk of export commodities to the UK were raw materials such as sugar, meat, and tobacco. Clothing exports to the UK increased but, in the long run, could not be maintained because of the constant availability of more competitively produced goods. Zimbabwe's exports to other countries of the region have been periodically threatened or actually disrupted by South Africa. Great potential has always existed for increased exports of manufactures to other countries of the Southern Africa Development Coordination Conference (SADCC) and the Preferential Trade Area for East and Southern Africa (PTA), but lack of viable transport links, the fragility of most of the economies, lack of competitiveness, payment difficulties and the need to protect domestic industries and so on have hampered larger volumes of trade to the region. In addition, South Africa's practice of heavily subsidizing its manufacturers had the effect of out-competing Zimbabwe entrepreneurs.

As discussed in the previous chapters, South Africa's manipulation of Zimbabwe's access to the seaports adversely affected the potential of the country's export of manufactured goods. Because Zimbabwe was periodically denied access to the shortest routes to the ports, the country's manufacturers became much more expensive on the international market when shipped through South Africa. Because of the added freight bill, Zimbabwe's manufactured products became less competitive than South African exports of the same type of manufactured goods. In addition, transport delays in the importation of essential commodities for the manufacturing sector occasionally caused bottlenecks in production, leading to delays in meeting export orders and the consequent loss of export markets.

Overall, then, throughout the 1980s Zimbabwe's manufacturing sector was caught in a tight grip. The sector had to export in order to raise foreign currency to maintain the supply of imported inputs necessary to sustain production. At the same time, the general shortage of the initial foreign currency allocation from the government militated against increased and expanded production. Zimbabwe's official export figures have usually masked this grim picture. For instance, in 1986, official government export figures purported to show a record visible trade surplus of Z$636 million up 82 per cent on 1985's Z$349 million.[38] In reality, however, once the depreciation of the Zimbabwe dollar had been taken into account, export earnings up to 1986 at best remained stagnant, in local terms, at 1983 levels. Hard currency earnings showed an even bleaker picture, falling about 16 per cent in SDR terms after 1981.[39] By 1985 they were some 13 per cent below the 1980 level, reflecting deteriorating terms of trade for the mineral and agricultural exports which provide some 70 per cent of total earnings.[40]

This situation had an almost devastating effect on industry in general and the manufacturing sector in particular. Because of the general shortage of foreign exchange for the sector, hard currency export earnings declined substantially, but real values were even harder-hit. In nominal Zimbabwean dollar terms, imports rose 85 per cent (1980–85) but fell 17 per cent in social domestic resources (SDR) – and by 1985 were almost a third below their 1981 peak. The following year, 1986, saw the position deteriorate even further. Official government figures showed that imports grew by 3 per cent to Z$1500 million, underlining the extent to which, in the face of falling export earnings and rising invisible payments, Zimbabwe's positive trade and current account balances had been maintained by sacrificing imported inputs. Industry bore the brunt of this sacrifice. For many companies, in 1986 their direct local market allocation (DLMA) of foreign exchange under the twice-yearly quota system was equivalent to only 35 per cent of the 1981 levels in real terms. The situation remained largely the same throughout the remainder of the 1980s. For instance, in 1989 most companies received the same DLMA as in 1988, with the value of the allocation being less than 30 per cent of the purchasing power of the early 1980s.[41] Thus, in practice Zimbabwean industrialists had not received an increase for a period of 18 months. During that period of unchanged DLMA, the Zimbabwean dollar had depreciated by approximately 14 per cent against the US dollar, and 12 per cent against the pound sterling, making the Zimbabwean dollar allocation much less. Although the Zimbabwean dollar appreciated by 8 per cent against the South African rand during that period, few Zimbabwean industries were, at that time, sourcing their inputs from South Africa and were therefore less able to take advantage of this favourable exchange rate movement.

This had profound effects on productivity. Precisely because the Zimbabwean manufacturing sector is one of the least import-dependent in Africa, with the percentage of imports to output estimated at 8 to 9 per cent, the remaining imports were crucial. The cut-backs had a larger knock-on effect, exaggerated by the highly integrated nature of Zimbabwean manufacturing.

The acute shortage of foreign currency and the critical implications were amply demonstrated in the steel shortages of 1989, which threatened many enterprises with closure.[42] The local company, the Zimbabwe Iron and Steel Company (ZISCO), could not cope with demand.[43] Importing materials from overseas also presented a number of problems. In particular, overseas steel mills planned their production on a long-term basis from firm estimated requirements supplied by regular customers. As a result, they would not accept the *ad hoc* orders Zimbabwean importers could place when *ad hoc* foreign currency allocations were issued. Zimbabwean importers were also unable to supply firm forecasts as they did not know how much foreign currency they would receive during the next twelve months.

Here are some of the indirect after-effects of South Africa's economic squeeze on Zimbabwe. The disruption of transport affected the local market particularly in the area of domestic goods. People began experiencing shortages of electric goods, certain fabrics, vehicle spares, and so on, and the situation had been quite difficult. Because of the need to maintain export levels in order to obtain foreign currency to procure essential imported inputs to remain viable, manufacturers had not been able to satisfy local demand in some domestic products. As a result, Zimbabwean shoppers had been taking shopping trips to South Africa and Botswana, particularly during the second half of the 1980s. For instance, in 1988 shoppers spent Z$63.2 million in South Africa and Botswana, compared to $36.4 million in 1987.[44] About 140 008 Zimbabweans (72 per cent of them women) in 1988 received holiday allowances of about Z$450 each, compared with 80 807 people (60 per cent women) in 1987, to purchase household goods in South Africa and Botswana. Some of these goods were for resale in Zimbabwe at artificially inflated prices of not less than 180 per cent. For many, cross-border shopping sprees constituted the only source of income.

It was in the context of these generally gloomy economic facts that Zimbabwe in the late 1980s sought to alleviate some of the problems through measures designed to liberalize the economy.[45] The government hoped that the liberalization of the economy would provide a panacea for such economic ills as unemployment, low productivity, shortage of foreign exchange and ageing industrial plant. The long-awaited revised Investment Code designed to liberalize the economy was finally unveiled in Harare a few days before the joint CBI (Confederation of British Industry)/CZI conference ('Zimbabwe: The Opportunities for Trade and Investment') held in London on 12 May 1989.[46] The three main changes in the code, which is entitled 'The Promotion of Investment Policy and Regulations,'[47] are:

(i)   A foreign investor is defined as a company with 25 per cent or more of its shares owned by non-Zimbabweans (previously the figure was 15 per cent).

(ii) An Investment Centre is to be established, initially in the Ministry of Finance, Economic Planning and Development (MFEPD), providing 'one-stop' facilities relating to all investment, employment etc., harmonizing or bringing under one roof regulations that are at present dispersed over several industries; the centre will itself approve projects worth up to million (US$52.3 million), but will consult with economic ministries above that sum; approval will be notified within 90 days.

(iii) Zimbabwe will sign the World Bank's Multilateral Investment Guarantee Agency (MIGA) and will consider negotiating bilateral investment treaties.[48] (Previously these had been opposed on the grounds that the Zimbabwean constitution provided adequate guarantees already).

It is, however, generally agreed that significant liberalization could only be made to stick if either there were massive commitments to concessional finance, if not grant aid on the part of the international community or, alternatively, if the budget deficit could be halved to between 5 per cent and 6 per cent of the GDP. The former looks most unlikely and the latter nearly impossible as almost half of the total budget expenditure is for education, health, defence and debt servicing, all of which are nearly untouchable. This would imply 12 per cent cuts in expenditure across the board elsewhere including industry, agriculture, transport, the police, energy and water development, national housing and investment, all of which are areas in which the World Bank and other aid agencies are contributing and expecting counterpart funds from Zimbabwe. In the circumstances prevailing during 1989/90, involving the costs of maintaining the Beira Corridor and defence against destabilization, even a budget deficit as low as 8 per cent would represent an inappropriate squeeze on an economy that otherwise would be growing fast. The prospects for a significant inflow of private foreign capital are, in any case, poor no matter what concessions Zimbabwe makes and whether or not it liberalizes, as can be seen by looking at flows elsewhere in the world. Even such aid flows as might eventually occur, would do little to create employment for the 150 000-plus new job entrants every year, unless it were associated with labour-intensive technology creating jobs at less than US$10 000, each an unprecedented and unrealistic requirement.

Overall then, South Africa's destabilization of Zimbabwe has been extremely costly. However, the political developments in the past years within Zimbabwe have helped a great deal towards easing the problem of huge defence expenditures. The 22 December 1987 Unity Accord between ZANU(PF) and PF-ZAPU led to a positive reduction in political tension and conflict. More significantly the April–May 1988 amnesty extended to 'Super-ZAPU' and other dissidents deprived South Africa of a surrogate army for the destabilization of Zimbabwe. Military operations have since been concentrated against the MNR in the east and the defence of the Beira and Limpopo corridors. Above all the political changes in South Africa marked a great sense of hope for peace in the whole region. Zimbabwe welcomed President De Klerk's reforms and supported his initiatives for peace in South Africa and in the region as a whole, while the tension that existed between Zimbabwe and South Africa began to ease. South Africa withdrew its support for RENAMO and the Mozambican government came to the negotiating table. All these settlements and developments in the region gave rise to a less strained atmosphere. These developments brought great hope and encouragement to the businessmen in Zimbabwe.

7 South Africa's Destabilization of Zimbabwe: Success or Failure?

The main purpose of this chapter is to evaluate the achievements and failures of South Africa's policy of destabilization of Zimbabwe. Chapter 1 has established that destabilization of Zimbabwe was intended to create the necessary conditions for recapturing the initiative for effecting the constellation policy. In reality one of its objectives was to hit SADCC hard, and prevent it from delinking itself from South Africa. Zimbabwe became one of South Africa's biggest threats because it was at the centre of the region, both politically and geographically. It was the key element in the success of SADCC because it was the hub of regional transport and was central in redirecting traffic away from South Africa. As the most developed state in the region, apart from Sourth Africa, Zimbabwe raised the prospect of industrial development independent of South Africa. Therefore by destabilizing Zimbabwe, South Africa intended to weaken SADCC's efforts to isolate it.

It is important to note that the main target of destabilization in Mozambique has really been Zimbabwean rail traffic. As a result of this, this chapter will also assess the achievements and failures of South Africa's policy of destabilization in Mozambique.

Apart from weakening SADCC, South Africa had other objectives, such as blocking Zimbabwe's policies of socialism and reconciliation and thus combating the threat of a prosperous multiracial state which was contrary to the apartheid system. In order to achieve these objectives South Africa embarked on the following strategies:

(i)   To undermine Zimbabwe's military capabilities.
(ii) To destroy Zimbabwe's economy so that Zimbabwe's dependence on South Africa was maintained.
(iii) To create a state of chronic political instability by supporting dissidents operating within Zimbabwe.

(iv) To create the impression that the troubles inside South Africa were not caused by apartheid but by Marxist guerrillas infiltrating through the neighbouring states.

(v) To create internal chaos in Zimbabwe and force her to pay more attention to her own problems and less to apartheid.

(vi) To create a buffer against sanctions, by constraining Zimbabwe publicly from supporting international sanctions against South Africa.

(vii) To force the Zimbabwean government to denounce its Socialist and Marxist tendencies.

(viii) To exacerbate poverty in the country and use this for propaganda at home and abroad, as 'proof' that black majority rule did not work.

(ix) To make Zimbabwe ungovernable and to ensure that there was no ANC or PAC threat from bases in that country.

The major concern of this chapter is to demonstrate the extent to which South Africa achieved its objectives, and to state the reasons behind the success or failure of its policy. The chapter will also address the question of the reasons behind the abandoning of the destabilization policy, in 1989, by Pretoria.

7.1 FAILURES OF SOUTH AFRICA'S POLICY OF DESTABILIZATION OF ZIMBABWE

(a) A Constellation of States

We have seen how the reactive and *ad hoc* approach of the last years of the Vorster regime gave way to a reformulation and reorganization of South African regional policy after P.W. Botha took over as Prime Minister. Guided by the doctrine of 'Total National Strategy' developed by the top military commanders, the ultimate objective of regional policy was defined as bringing into existence a new regional alliance, known as a 'Constellation of Southern African States'. The idea of achieving this and other shorter-term objectives of Pretoria's policy towards other regional states (namely, a withholding by regional states of support for liberation movements; a maintenance and deepening of their economic ties with South Africa; the non-establishment of relations, particularly in the military field, with socialist countries; and a 'moderation' of criticisms of apartheid by regional states) was seen as necessitating the application of a 'sophisticated' mix of economic, political and military measures.

It is important to note that the premises upon which a constellation was originally based had a distinctive ring of determinism about the above objectives. A constellation was portrayed by South African policy-making not merely as desirable but indeed as inevitable. The policy-makers' assumption was that the centripetal forces at work in Southern Africa, particularly economic – but political and security as well – were inexorably steering the countries in the region toward ever closer and more formal relationships, the idea being that the centrifugal elements would in the end submit to these forces. The South African government placed reliance on the primacy of economic forces and anticipated that cooperation in this field would spill over into the political and military areas. Closely related to this brand of economic determinism was a tendency to assume shared perceptions among prospective constellation partners, particularly with regard to the nature of external threats and the need for a common military and political response.

It seems that South Africa's idea of wanting the countries in Southern Africa to develop a common approach in the security field, and in the economic and political fields, was attractive and a sensible idea for the region. But why did it fail? It is not surprising that the hoped-for Constellation of States failed to materialize. The basic reason for the failure was that the political and ideological divisions between South Africa and black African states had developed to such an extent that the latter were unwilling to formalize relations with the Republic. In addition, internationally recognized black states, who were members of the OAU, would not consider joining a formal association in which internationally unrecognized former 'Bantustans', Rhodesia (prior to 1980), and South African-controlled Namibia, would be their equal partners. In other words, the divisions militated against the notion of a spillover factor and against the assumption of shared perceptions regarding the nature of external threats and the need for a common military and political response. Botswana, Lesotho and Swaziland indicated that they would not consider joining a constellation as long as South Africa adhered to its racial policies. A more important setback to South Africa's constellation plan was the emergence in 1980 of an independent Zimbabwe under the premiership of Robert Mugabe. Mugabe not only made it plain that Zimbabwe had no intention of playing the key role South Africa had reserved for it in a constellation, but he quickly demonstrated his political distance from the Republic by joining forces with the Frontline States in their attempt to form a new economic grouping, SADCC. This aimed at reducing black states' dependence on the South African economy, by reducing their dependence on South Africa for transportation and communication links. Lesotho and Swaziland joined the SADCC, which reflected the black states' opposition to South Africa's proposed constellation.

Mugabe's foreign policy towards South Africa's domestic policies blocked any hopes of the constellation's survival. Mugabe's anti-apartheid policies were demonstrated by his immediate replacement of the diplomatic ties between Harare and Pretoria with trade representation only.[1] Mugabe became increasingly outspoken in support of the 'liberation struggle' against South Africa and in condemnation of South Africa's domestic political order. In short, Zimbabwe became one of a chain of black states surrounding South Africa which were committed to the 'liberation' of the last white-ruled state in Africa. Mugabe's assumption of power undoubtedly created new apprehensions in South Africa about Namibia's movement toward independence. At independence in 1990, Namibia joined SADCC instead of the constellation.

Apart from all these factors, the most devastating setback to the establishment of the constellation was the formation of SADCC and its objectives, which were sharply contrary to what South Africa was trying to achieve. It should be noted that when SADCC defined its principal objective as being to bring about a reduction in dependence mainly, but not only, on the Republic of South Africa, it did not do so merely as a response to Pretoria's policy of deepening ties as part of its Constellation strategy. The SADCC perspective was based on a recognition that bringing about the goals of economic liberation and development in the independent states of Southern Africa necessitated the radical restructuring of historically created patterns of regional economic domination and dependency, whatever the policies pursued by South Africa. The SADCC project thus aimed from the start at bringing about a delinking from such relationships of subordination to apartheid capitalism, through promoting cooperation in a number of areas: transport, food, security, energy, industrial development, manpower planning and tourism. It is important to note that the SADCC project represented a challenge not only to the Constellation, but also to one of the more immediate objectives of South Africa's regional policy, that is the maintenance and deepening of economic ties with independent states. The establishment of SADCC and the accession to it of all the key target states of the Constellation project, represented an important defeat for South African strategy.

The fact that apartheid had been seen as a barrier to the realization of both the security (peace) and economic (development) goals of the independent Southern African states, gave the SADCC countries determination to press ahead with their objectives. SADCC's determination was reflected in its repeated policy declarations, that the elimination of apartheid was the essential precondition for lasting peace and development in the region.

However, taking into account the increasingly conflictual circumstances in the region, the constellation concept had no real prospect of success in this respect. Given the coercive manner in which South Africa conducted itself in the region, even the economic objectives of the constellation were bound to have been regarded warily by its neighbours. For instance, its political objectives, which expressly included recognition of the so-called 'independence' of South Africa's homelands, absolutely guaranteed its rejection. Beside this, the independent black states had recognized that political independence had not been accompanied by economic independence, and that considerable responsibility for the absence of the latter rested, both directly and indirectly, with South Africa. There was still deep resentment among at least some of South Africa's neighbours at the poor economic hand which they considered they had been dealt during the colonial era, and of which the iniquitous racial inequalities in living standards and political power had been both cause and consequence. There was also genuine anger and a sense of humiliation at what they felt, and at what the prevailing academic wisdom seemingly confirmed, to be their involuntary manipulation and exploitation by the forces of neocolonialism and its agents. There was the widely espoused desire for 'economic liberation' and for the capacity to exercise self-determination in creating more 'equitable' and 'balanced' economic structures. There was outrage at the violations of political and territorial integrity and at the human and economic costs suffered, both directly and indirectly, on account of South Africa's policies. In addition, perhaps most decisively, there was the political need to stand up and be counted, and if necessary to pay a heavy price, to secure for the black peoples of South Africa the rights and freedoms which they were denied.

It followed that the lack of economic sovereignty could be mitigated only by reducing the dominance. The fact that this economic power was vested in a country with a government which was committed to the maintenance of white minority rule aggravated the neighbours' need to break free from economic relations with South Africa. Against this background, it was difficult to envisage the success of the constellation. Constellation was regarded by the black states as being the key instrument for maintaining both the 'dependence' of the neighbours and the subjugation of the black peoples of South Africa. The failure by the South African government to persuade the neighbouring states to join the constellation was a clear sign of the end of the Total National Strategy and its objectives. The outcome of the constellation indicated a remarkable misreading by South Africa of the political climate of Southern Africa and its inability to anticipate events, specifically those in Zimbabwe.

(b) South Africa's Failure to Constrain Zimbabwe from its Call for International Sanctions

One of the main objectives of South Africa's destabilization of Zimbabwe was to create a buffer against sanctions, by constraining Zimbabwe publicly from supporting international sanctions against South Africa. In seeking to neutralize Zimbabwe, Pretoria supplemented forward defence with economic leverage. The economic component of the neutralization effort was rooted in the special links South Africa had built up with Rhodesia during the UDI period. South Africa had become Rhodesia's main trading partner during the Rhodesian sanctions. Under a special bilateral trade agreement, Rhodesia was allowed access, at reduced duties, to South Africa's protected market, such that by independence South Africa imported three-quarters of Zimbabwe's manufactured exports. South Africa had also become a key supplier of inputs and consumer goods. With these economic advantages on its side, South Africa tried to manipulate these special economic links in order to constrain Zimbabwe from being hostile. As Deon Geldenhuys put it, 'existing economic ties...in the region must be maintained and indeed strengthened'.[2] Mugabe had acknowledged this geographical fact of proximity to South Africa and the historical economic connections that tied the two countries.[3] But on his foreign policy towards South Africa, Mugabe made it clear that he would make efforts to reduce this dependence; he would support the South African liberation movements with moral, political, diplomatic and material means through international organizations, but would allow neither bases in, nor transit facilities through, Zimbabwe. Furthermore, he would support sanctions against South Africa if they were properly agreed to and executed by the international community. On the other hand, the Republic of South Africa did not hide its dislike of Mugabe's government, as was clearly reflected in the Republic's cool response to his election victory. When the Foreign Minister P. Botha commented,

> It would be a lie, it would be deceit for me to claim that I enjoyed the result of the last election in Zimbabwe. I did not at all. I would have preferred Bishop Muzorewa to have won. Let me be very frank about that.[4]

Also, there was the statement issued by P.W. Botha warning Mugabe,

> Any neighbour ... which allows its territory to be used for attacks on or the undermining of South Africa and its security will have to face the full force of the Republic's strength.[5]

From the objectives or policies of the two countries towards each other, one can sense the tension and determination from each country to make sure that these policies were taken seriously. It seems that the Pretoria regime, with its mighty military and economic advantages over Zimbabwe, was determined to win its objectives while in contrast Mugabe, with the support of the OAU, FLS, and the international community, was determined to inflict serious damage upon the Pretoria regime. The new Zimbabwe government wasted no time in demonstrating its implacable opposition to South Africa's domestic policies. It did so by reducing its diplomatic ties with Pretoria. As observed by Zimbabwe's Foreign Minister in 1980: 'We shall not establish diplomatic ties with that country (South Africa) ...'.[6] Mugabe refused to have any formal ministerial contact and diplomatic relations with South Africa. All contact with South African ministers was banned, because it was felt that such contact would imply recognition of the apartheid government. It was this, more than any other single point, that Pretoria tried to reverse and failed. Mugabe also cancelled intelligence cooperation between the CIO and the SAMID which were the principal means of political and security communication between the two countries during the UDI regime.

(i) South Africa's Counter-Strategy
South Africa moved against Zimbabwe on two fronts: economic and military. South Africa put economic pressure on Zimbabwe by imposing economic sanctions. First Pretoria threatened to terminate a trade

agreement that provided significant benefits to the Zimbabwe economy.[7] Then it precipitated a transport[8] crisis and squeezed Zimbabwe's supply of essential goods by withdrawing a large number of locomotives, freight trucks, and tanker cars that were on loan to Zimbabwe's railroad. All of this caused disruption and delay on National Railway of Zimbabwe (NRZ) at a time when the railway was trying to cope with sharply increased traffic due to the economic boom in Zimbabwe. The main purpose for all these actions was to force the Zimbabwe government to make a high-level request which would involve formal diplomatic or ministerial contacts with South Africa, so as to force Zimbabwe to reverse its decision on diplomatic recognition, but Zimbabwe refused. South Africa disrupted Zimbabwean transport and imposed a full embargo. It slowed Zimbabwean cargoes and at times left Zimbabwean goods stranded in South African ports, causing all sorts of confusion and shortages in Zimbabwe. Zimbabwe was losing about $5 million per week due to lost exports.

(ii) Reasons for South Africa's Change of Economic Pressures on Zimbabwe
There were many factors that contributed to South Africa's change in using its economic pressure on Zimbabwe, in order to restrain Zimbabwe from being hostile to the Republic's domestic policy. The major reasons were the intervention by both the Zimbabwean and South African businessmen, and the pressure from the international community, especially from the American government.

Pressure from Zimbabwean and South African Businessmen   The general manager of the Dairy Marketing Board and the President of the Zimbabwe Chamber of Commerce went to South Africa to protest against South Africa's destabilization behaviour. They warned South African businessmen that the South African government's 'deliberate actions' to damage the Zimbabwe economy were not in their interests, and appealed to those businessmen to put pressure on their own government.[9] It became clear that some of the South African businessmen believed that they could do business with Mugabe's government and they did not support South Africa's destabilization tactics against Zimbabwe. Large companies in Zimbabwe, such as Lonrho and Anglo-American, were reported[10] to have been impressed by and satisfied with Mugabe's management of the economy and by the increased level of understanding in government of commercial considerations.

This led to a strong disagreement between the business community in South Africa and the South African government on its method of destabilization policy towards the neighbouring countries. The businessmen's argument was that South Africa's extensive destabilization of Zimbabwe was damaging their business and destroying their market. The head of South African railways also opposed the use of his trains to put the squeeze on Zimbabwe. The pressure from South African businessmen led the then Minister of Transport Hendrick Schoeman to admit in parliament that South Africa was deliberately delaying Zimbabwean cargo. For him the problem could have been solved, if an approach could have been made by Zimbabwe at ministerial level, giving high-level assurances that the ANC would not be allowed to operate in Zimbabwe.[11] Once again the Zimbabwean government refused to be blackmailed by the South African government and did not accept its demands.

Pressure from the International Community   South Africa was put under pressure from the Western embassies, particularly from the Americans, to stop destabilizing Zimbabwe. Chester Crocker, the United States Under-Secretary of State for African Affairs at that time, warned South Africa that its destabilization tactics were only speeding up Zimbabwe's reduction of economic links with South Africa, and it was in South Africa's interest to maintain the trade agreement so as to keep Zimbabwe economically dependent.[12] Under pressure from the United States and from their own business community, the South African government backed down. This led to some sharp divisions, with some in the military and the Nationalist Party who still argued that Robert Mugabe was a 'dangerous communist who represented a serious threat to the apartheid state, while others in the Foreign Ministry and in the business community felt that Mugabe could be worked with, controlled and perhaps even coopted'.[13] As time went by, those in the Foreign Ministry and in business were gaining some ground, simply because the hardliners had failed to break the newly independent state and Zimbabwe had not dissolved into chaos as they would have wished. The departure of whites had not destroyed the new government, and many whites were staying. Destabilization had failed to squeeze Zimbabwe government in the South African direction.

(iii) Other Contributing Factors
South Africa's decision in 1983 to end the transport disruption against Zimbabwe was only partly a response to internal and foreign pressure.

The transport disruption had patently failed, and Zimbabwe had managed to break free of the South African pressure. The transport problem, which had been created by the South African withdrawal of its locomotives and artisans, had been solved by the arrival of 500 Indian and Pakistani artisans and of 60 diesel locomotives which had been ordered from the US and Canada.[14] The situation had returned to normal before South Africa decided to end its transport disruption of Zimbabwe.

Perhaps the most important factor of South Africa's economic pressure on Zimbabwe was the fact that it pushed an important segment of the business community towards supporting the new ZANU government. This in itself was a counter-productive element on the South African part because one of its objectives in disrupting the Zimbabwean economy was to create a division between the white community and the government, so as to block the policy of multi-racial reconciliation. According to Hanlon, the South African government had failed to achieve its special aim of thwarting reconciliation and of creating divisions between the white community and Mugabe's government.[15] The whites began to defend Mugabe's government openly. The economic pressure did force many Zimbabwean whites to opt for majority rule instead of taking South Africa's point of view of destabilization. An important aspect of the cooperation between the business community and the Zimbabwean government was demonstrated by the railway priority committee, which successfully assigned the limited capacity available through Mozambican and South African ports to the highest value cargoes. This minimized the balance of payment problems. Through the recommendations of this committee arrangements were quickly made to shift cargo through Mozambican ports. The Lonrho oil pipeline was repaired and re-opened, so that South Africa had less control over Zimbabwe's fuel. This reduced the impact of South African economic pressure. It is important to note that the South African government ended its economic squeeze on Zimbabwe without Mugabe meeting the conditions which Pretoria had demanded, such as: refraining from campaigning for international sanctions against South Africa; stopping support for the liberation struggle in South Africa; and restoring a full diplomatic mission which Harare had terminated. South Africa's economic squeeze on Zimbabwe damaged its own foreign policy not only with its neighbours but also with the international community. The international community began to be more sympathetic to Zimbabwe's predicament and increased their support in financing Zimbabwe's efforts in delinking its economy from South Africa. South Africa lost a golden opportunity to win Mugabe to its side. Confrontation was a disastrous policy by South Africa because it pushed Mugabe on the defensive, and made him seek support from the international community to fight back. Instead of narrowing the gap between Mugabe and Pretoria, the confrontation policy widened it further. Mugabe gained confidence that his government would not only defend its freedom, but that it would use its power with the help of other states to help liberate Namibia and later fight for majority rule in South Africa itself. To the embarrassment of the South African government, Mugabe became more determined to fight back. He mobilized international opinion[16] to put pressure on the Pretoria government. He also became critical and vocal, and publicly supported calls for sanctions on South Africa. In fairness to South Africa, it had a short period of time (one year)[17] in which economic pressures could have been effective on Zimbabwe. If more time had been given to this economic squeeze, the story could have been different.

South Africa had only limited success in maintaining the ZANU–ZAPU split. Once the split emerged and dissidents were active in the bush, Pretoria moved to use them, as it did with UNITA in Angola, the MNR in Mozambique, and the LLA in Lesotho. With ZIPRA's close ties to the ANC and its strong anti-apartheid tradition, the new dissidents refused to cooperate with the South African military. This created a problem to the South African government in the sense that it could not control ZIPRA and use it as effectively as it would have liked. This anti-apartheid tradition and ZIPRA's close ties with the ANC might be one of the reasons why ZIPRA did not survive long enough, because it did not have a strong ally or base from which to operate and secure supplies of ammunition.

However, South Africa managed to create an entirely new force, known as 'Super-ZAPU'. Super-ZAPU acted in the shadow of, and in the name of, the dissidents. Some Zimbabweans were recruited, particularly from refugee camps in Botswana, trained in South Africa and sent back to Zimbabwe.[18] Super-ZAPU was well supplied with arms, and it carried out assassinations of white farmers and other provocative acts which led to crackdowns by the Zimbabwe government. The response by Zimbabwe's Fifth Brigade as well as the strict curfews in Matabeleland, created more dissidents and more refugees, and kept the pot boiling. The dissidents destroyed a lot of government projects and impeded rural development, to such an extent that the people of

Matabeleland area continued to suffer from the after-effects of the dissidents' activities many years later .

Pretoria's support of the dissidents was a success in the sense that it damaged Zimbabwe's political image abroad and seriously affected the economy's infrastructure in Matabeleland. The dissidents ravaged large areas of Matabeleland, displaced thousands of people, destroyed schools, homes, clinics, roads, rails, buses, government equipment, and other development projects. They also murdered government staff in the health and agricultural department, teaching, adult literacy, white commercial farming, community development and administrative services. Supporters of the ruling party, ZANU(PF), in the rural areas were also killed, together with foreign tourists. All these activities sent a clear message to the rural population in general that the new government was too weak to protect them, and that the only way to peace, prosperity and development was through collaboration rather than confrontation with apartheid. The attack on development and infrastructural projects impeded all post-independence reconstruction and development efforts,[19] so that until the mid-1990s the development of Matabeleland was left behind the rest of Zimbabwe. This has created a lot of unhappiness and angered some politicians from Matabeleland who accused the government of neglecting development in the area. Their complaints were centred on the lack of a water security programme for the semi-arid province, and the lack of a clear development policy.

Mugabe was able to compromise to share power with Nkomo who was then the leader of PF-ZAPU. The dissident activities were related to the political development in the country, particularly the political unity between ZAPU and ZANU. Both leaders realized that peace, stability and their historic commitments to the development of Zimbabwe would only be fulfilled if they were united. Furthermore, there was the issue of security. In order to concentrate the defence forces' efforts on the external enemy, Zimbabwe itself had to be internally united. The reasons for the unity accord is summed up in Mugabe's speech:

> After eight years of experience we have examined the position in the country; the interests of the people, the interests of our parties and the interests of the leadership and we have come to no other conclusion than that unity would enhance our freedom and independence. Unity would demonstrate the oneness of direction for our people. And unity, of course would mean a common allegiance,

common loyalty and a common struggle against both internal and external forces of destabilization.[20]

Without unity it would have been difficult for the Zimbabwe government to stop the dissident activities. The inclusion of political amnesty in the unity package was very important as it eased the tension in the country and the dissidents' overwhelming response to it posed a problem to South Africa because it had nobody to use to destabilize Matabeleland.

(iv) The Signing of Non-aggression Pacts: Failure to Put Pressure on Zimbabwe

One would have expected the South African policy-makers to capitalize on the Nkomati Accord with Mozambique, the Swaziland peace agreement and the Lusaka Cease Fire Agreement with Angola and to use more diplomacy than aggression. South Africa's relations with and policy towards other independent states in the region did not change. In the mid-1980s aggression once again became the main feature of South African regional policy. The fact that two regional states had entered into security agreements with Pretoria was seen by the apartheid regime as creating a precedent for other states in the region to follow. The post-Nkomati period saw a concerted attempt to cajole other states in the region into concluding similar 'non-aggression pacts'. Lesotho and Botswana particularly were singled out, while Zimbabwe came under some pressure as well. One of the notable features of this period was the resistance put up by Zimbabwe to South African pressures. Zimbabwe refused to sign a formal agreement, although it had reiterated that it would not permit liberation movements to operate from its territory. Pretoria failed to use this opportunity to advance some of these objectives, to the extent that it even lost ground on others. This was largely due to the gains made by popular struggle inside South Africa. The other reason is that South Africa failed to abide with the peace terms it had signed with Mozambique. South Africa continued to support MNR and to attack the neighbouring states. The death of Samora Machel in 1986 angered most SADCC states and increased further their mistrust of the Pretoria regime. South Africa failed to reduce its destabilization activities in the region and its support of MNR, UNITA, LLA and Super-ZAPU as a gesture to its commitment to restore peace in the region. It also failed to concentrate on internal policy, especially the reforms of the apartheid system. Instead, credit is given to Zimbabwe for its commitment in rescuing the SADCC organization from collapse.

7.2   ACHIEVEMENTS OF SOUTH AFRICA'S POLICY OF DESTABILIZATION OF ZIMBABWE

(a) Keeping the Zimbabwean Economy Weak and Dependent on South Africa

In military and economic terms, South Africa had some success. In military terms South Africa was successful in dislocating Zimbabwe's military development. In 1983 the South African defence force infiltrated Zimbabwe's best air base in Gweru and destroyed ten planes. This was a devastating blow because much of the AFZ's strike and interception capability was destroyed. The air defence radar system of the AFZ was irretrievably lost and the ZNA lost its air umbrella. It was unlikely that the AFZ would regain the strike capability and operational effectiveness it possessed in 1982. This posed grave problems for ZDF operations in Mozambique.

In late 1980 there were several small actions, including a robbery of arms and ammunition from Cranbourne Barracks, followed in 1984 by the sabotaging of 30 army vechicles at King George VI Barracks. The most spectacular raid was on August 1981, when an ammunition dump at Inkomo Barracks was blown up.[21] All three incidents involved whites in the army who had stayed on after independence, but were by then working as South African agents. Undoubtedly the most important raid took place in Harare, when a South African bomb shattered the ZANU headquarters and killed seven people.[22] The bomb is said to have been targeted for Robert Mugabe, and the rest of the ZANU Central Committee, who were scheduled to meet there; all would probably have been killed had the meeting not been delayed. The above actions were a clear success on the part of South Africa in preventing Zimbabwe from gaining sufficient strength to pose a threat to South Africa. At the same time it shows how successful the South African army was in penetrating Zimbabwean security and thus demonstrating Zimbabwe's vulnerability.

The kidnapping and murder of foreign tourists was politically damaging for Zimbabwe. It portrayed the new state internationally as chronically unstable and therefore dangerous for foreigners. In this way, one of its major foreign exchange earners, tourism, was damaged. In economic terms South Africa was successful in keeping the Zimbabwean economy weak and to a certain degree dependent on South Africa. There was a severe impact on the Zimbabwean economy during the period 1981–83 when South Africa took steps to disrupt transport, suspended the special bilateral trade agreement and cut back on trade. The delay in renegotiating the trade agreement cost tens of millions of dollars in temporarily lost exports. The expulsions of migrant miners probably cost Zimbabwe an extra Z$50 million in foreign exchange earnings. On top of this came the cost of lost exports and disruptions caused by shortages. There was the really serious cash-flow problem caused by delayed exports, which exacerbated the growing balance of payments deficit. This forced Zimbabwe to turn to the IMF, which imposed a series of limitations on the new government.

Zimbabwe's alternative trade route, the Beira–Mutare link, was seriously disrupted by the MNR raids and attacks; it closed from 1983 to 1985. By that time over 90 per cent of external trade had to go through South African ports. South Africa imposed an effective 5 per cent tax, costing Zimbabwe about Z$100 million extra a year.[23] It was only in 1987 that a significant proportion of trade was restored to the Beira corridor by Zimbabwean troops. By 1988 after the completion of the rehabilitation of the Maputo line Zimbabwe's dependence on South Africa began to fall below 50 per cent of trade. This was so, because the attacks on the Beira line were kept down by Zimbabwean soldiers, but the fear of attack prevented the running of trains at night.

South Africa was successful in reversing Zimbabwean transport through Beira in 1981 by forcing Zimbabwe cargo back through its ports and railways. Zimbabwe failed completely to delink itself from South Africa. At the same time South Africa was unable to cut off the Beira–Mutare route completely. However, South Africa was successful in damaging the Zimbabwean economy and it cost a lot of money to keep the transport going through Beira. According to Joseph Hanlon, 'adding together the cost of direct war damage, higher transport costs, lost tourist revenue, it is estimated that Zimbabwe lost about US $1 400 million between 1980 and 1986'.[24] On the assumption that a proportion of these costs would have been invested, this could have helped Zimbabwe tremendously in alleviating some of its problems in the reconstruction of the country, which had just emerged from war. Indeed Zimbabwe could have used some of this money in improving farms, building new industries, providing jobs and incomes, building more houses, schools, hospitals and clinics. Through destabilization Zimbabwe suffered a huge increase in its security bill. The following table shows the money spent on defence since independence.

Table 7.1   Zimbabwean Defence Expenditure: Zimbabwean Defence as % of Total Expenditures (Z$) in 1989

Year	Expenditures	Defence	%
1989	6 150 763 950	760 287 363	12.40
1988	5 206 114 391	671 912 665	12.91
1987	4 675 418 957	631 350 139	13. 50
1986	3 688 475 530	504 644 229	13. 68
1985	3 222 199 423	394 627 874	12.19
1984	2 886 132 701	415 106 915	14.38
1983	2 558 893 750	345 410 713	13.50
1982	1 896 390 456	289 466 753	15.26
1981	1 468 884 060	231 812 011	15.78
1980	1 155 226 965	266 204 668	23.04

Source: Audire Klotz, 'Race and Nationalism in Zimbabwean Foreign Policy,' *The Round Table*, July 1993, 327, pp. 255–79.

7.3   A SUMMARY OF SOUTH AFRICA'S ACHIEVEMENTS

In its attempt to counteract Zimbabwe's threat, South Africa was successful in achieving the following objectives:

• It gravely weakened Zimbabwe's military capabilities and prevented it from being a military threat to South Africa's security.
• It reduced economic growth in Zimbabwe by deepening a state of chronic political instability with its support of the dissidents.
• To some extent it created the impression that the troubles inside South Africa were not caused by apartheid but by Marxist guerrillas supported by communist regimes, infiltrating through the neighbouring states.
• It forced Zimbabwe to pay more attention to her own problems and succeeded in creating a division among the ruling party on Zimbabwe's policies towards South Africa (on, for instance, the imposing of sanctions on South Africa).
• To a great degree it prevented the liberation movement from using Zimbabwe as a base to attack South Africa. To a large extent South

Africa forced the liberation movements to withdraw their bases near South Africa to more distant bastions in the continent's interior.[25]

• To some extent it restrained the Zimbabwean government from its Socialist and Marxist tendencies.

Beside South Africa's contribution, other factors such as the end of the cold war, the fall of Communism in the Eastern bloc,[26] and the lack of political will among the ruling petit-bourgeois elite, weakened the government's idea of implementing Socialism. Apart from these points the most important factors were both economic and political, affecting the implemention of Socialism. Economically, problems had arisen in relation to access to adequate foreign investment inflows. These problems were due to the political instability in the country, and under-utilization of capacity resulting from too great a defence expenditure. All this was a result of destabilization.

In Chapters 5 and 6 we have seen how destabilization slowed economic growth by forcing the government to concentrate most of its resources on security. The economic destruction inflicted upon the Matabeleland area by the dissidents and the discouragement of businessmen by the South African government from investing in a Socialist country severely restricted the government's move towards Socialism.

7.4 WEAKENING ZIMBABWE BY ATTACKING ITS NEIGHBOURS

This section looks at the achievements of South Africa's policy of destabilization at the regional level. The argument is that by weakening the SADCC, South Africa was also weakening the Zimbabwean economy. The question to be answered is: how far did South Africa succeed in doing so? By taking the destabilization policy to its logical extreme, South Africa managed to achieve a series of unexpectedly clear victories in the region. In military and economic terms, it had some success. It managed to create chaos in Mozambique and Angola so that Zimbabwe was landlocked and left with no option but to use South Africa as the sea route for trade. The effects of its destabilization are still haunting people in these countries.

As observed by Robert Rotberg, that weakening of Mozambique was essential for South Africa because it continued to humble states like Zimbabwe.[27] The following activities of destabilization had serious political and economic effect indirectly and directly on Zimbabwe. South Africa, using the MNR, attacked the key bridges linking Beira to Zimbabwe and marker buoys in Beira port, making it difficult for Zimbabwe and other SADCC states to use the sea route. The attack in 1982 on the fuel storage depot in the port of Beira which served Zimbabwe caused $20 million of damage.[28] The attacks were focused on economic targets, particularly transport links. The MNR attacked hospitals, clinics, schools and destroyed important government buildings in the rural areas. There was much killing of peasants, including hospital workers, patients, infants and teachers. The tactics behind this killing of innocent people was to make others afraid to use the facilities. More than two thousand schools were destroyed by the MNR and over five hundred health units were destroyed.[29] Schools and health facilities were targeted because they were seen in rural areas as the main gains of independence. South Africa hoped that if peasants lost these tangible gains they would withdraw their support from FRELIMO. The MNR used terror to disrupt commerce and transport by attacking the commercial network. More than four thousand shops, mostly privately-owned, were destroyed.[30] Trains, buses, lorries and cars were ambushed and their victims slaughtered, sometimes hacked to death with machetes or burned alive in the vehicles. This was intended to make people too fearful to travel. The attacking of the oil pipeline and railway from Beira to Zimbabwe by the MNR led to the closure of the railways from Zimbabwe to Maputo. In practical terms this trade route was extremely important for the operation of SADCC.

This policy of violence was very brutal and apparently mindless, but it was well thought out. As Deon Geldenhuys noted, a key aspect of destabilization was to deny food supplies to local people in an attempt 'to cause serious hardship to the population, who would in turn direct their frustration and fury at the regime'.[31] According to the British charity Oxfam, South Africa had created 'famine as a weapon of war' in Mozambique.[32] As a result of all these activities many Mozambican people ran away to safety in Zimbabwe. That country, with its already strained economy, had to deal with the problem of the Mozambican refugees. Zimbabwe was faced with the problem of providing the refugees with land and security. The government is estimated to have spent a total of about US$8 million for this purpose.[33] The famine of 1983 exacerbated the

Mozambican economic situation and thousands of people died of hunger. At the time, when Mozambique looked very vulnerable, South Africa seized the opportunity, and intensified its attacks and support of the MNR, which intensified its offensive by cutting the means of communication and transport between Zimbabwe and Mozambique. Cargo levels through Mozambican ports and railways dropped tremendously between 1981 and 1984 because of MNR attacks. These activities damaged business confidence in Zimbabwe because of the instability of the Mutare–Beira route. These actions resulted in Zimbabwe sending more forces into Mozambique in order to stabilize the situation.

All these activities of the MNR and the South African raids caused enormous social, political as well as economic damage and Mozambique came under enormous pressure which forced it to sign a public peace treaty with South Africa in 1984. After the signing of the Nkomati Accord, Mozambique expelled nearly all ANC members and guerrilla access ended.[34] It came to be known later that in 1982 Swaziland had signed a similar peace agreement, secretly, with South Africa.[35] Swaziland moved vigorously against the ANC personnel; many of them were expelled and some were arrested and handed over to the South African government. In Lesotho, the South African government managed to use its military and economic muscle to topple Dr Jonathan's government in 1986, and replaced it with a military government. The military government was forced to expel all ANC members and refugees from Lesotho. Once again these actions were a serious setback to the SADCC in the sense that it was not acting as a united force in regard to the regional policy towards South Africa. The Mozambique and Swaziland action of signing a peace agreement with South Africa demoralized other member states. In this respect South Africa had succeeded in reducing covert support for the ANC, forcing the ANC to withdraw from their bases near South Africa to more distant bases. Nevertheless, this did not seem to have hindered ANC activities inside South Africa, nor did it stop outspoken political support for the liberation movement in SADCC states.

South Africa was more successful in her hopes of shaping the international perceptions of the region. Because its destabilization actions in Mozambique, Angola and Zimbabwe were frequently referred to as a 'civil war' or 'rebel attacks', the terror of UNITA, MNR and Super-ZAPU were presented at times by the media as 'black on black violence'.[36] This suited racist assumptions in the

West as well as in South Africa that majority rule meant chaos. To a certain extent, South Africa was successful in weakening SADCC's progress in delinking from South Africa. It manipulated the transport links in such a way that it forced SADCC to temporarily reverse its process of delinking. Between 1982 and 1985, South Africa disrupted the links that were vital for the development of SADCC (see Map 2 on page 77). That is, the railway lines from Nacala to Malawi, Beira to Mutare (Zimbabwe) were all closed. The Beira to Mutare line was reopened again at the end of 1985, after Zimbabwe had sent its troops to guard the line.

(i) Damage Inflicted on the SADCC

Pretoria attempted to use the Nkomati Accord as a springboard to break out of its international isolation, but the deepening domestic crisis undermined the regime's attempt and its early success. The attempt by Pretoria to break out of international isolation had two main aspects. First, in the politico-diplomatic sphere, the regime launched a new offensive seeking *de facto* recognition for itself as the 'regional power' in Southern Africa, that is, as the force with whom all other interested parties in the region would have to come to terms whether they liked it or not. This was clearly one of the principal objectives of P.W. Botha's visit to Western Europe in June 1984, an event which would have been inconceivable before Nkomati. The visit was a success at this level, but it failed to generate any greater support for the regime's apartheid policies among the peoples of the countries visited; the massive demonstrations were testimony to this. However, his visit achieved a significant breakthrough at the level of the state officials and leading figures of Western Europe. The *South African Sunday Express* claimed that 'European leaders have now acknowledged that South Africa is the regional power in the [Southern] African subcontinent.'[37] *The Sunday Times* commented as follows;

> Mr Botha has cast himself in the only role open to him, not as the defender of apartheid nor as hesitant reformer, but as an African statesman, an earnest advocate of the nations which share the subcontinent.... In these post-Nkomati days, however, not even the most hesitant European leader could fail to recognise Mr Botha's claim to the title, or the seriousness of his intentions.[38]

The second aspect was a sustained effort to persuade potential external investors to regard South Africa as the 'natural route' for channelling investments to countries in the region. This too was a major objective of Botha's European tour, which included a number of closed-door seminars with leading Western European capitalists.[39] The objectives here appeared to be threefold: to attract foreign investment to South Africa's own crisis-ridden economy; to ensure that South African firms had a stake in profitable ventures elsewhere in the region; and to undermine SADCC's attempts to reduce the dependence of regional states on South African capitalism. Again some measure of success appeared to have been achieved[40] during the initial post-Nkomati period.

Pretoria's strategists again seemed to be emphasizing diplomacy and economic action in advancing their regional policy objectives. The question is, what change in the balance of forces brought about this shift in Pretoria's stance towards its neighbours in the region? There were several factors that contributed to undermining some of these earlier gains. The main ones were as follows: the growing concern within the international community about South Africa's duplicity over Nkomati, since Pretoria had been shown to be violating its peace agreements with Mozambique and Angola; it had proved to be far from being the region's peacemaker; Pretoria could not control the mass popular uprisings in black residential areas; its economy was in crisis, the rand was collapsing and the world economic recession deepened Pretoria's domestic crisis. The 'stay aways', the Indians' and Coloureds' successful boycott of the elections in August 1984 and the sending in of troops and the imposition of a state of emergency inflamed more violence. The cracks between business and government widened into a yawning chasm. In November the *Rand Daily Mail* reported that

> South Africa's ability to borrow overseas is beginning to be adversely affected by a combination of a deteriorating economy and recurring reports of interest in black townships. London based bankers say South African borrowing costs have now increased....[41]

This was followed by an important new element of the international disinvestment campaign which created perhaps one of the most difficult periods ever for the apartheid regime on the international stage. Some but not all of this was as a result of the shortsightedness of Pretoria's policy of destabilization. The military dominance of South

African foreign policy and its attitude of a military quick-fix solution prevented it from knowing when to stop and apply diplomacy. The regime could not realize that the more it created instability in the region the more it was putting off businessmen from investing in South Africa.

7.5 FACTORS THAT LED TOWARDS THE ABANDONMENT OF REGIONAL DESTABILIZATION AND TO THE END OF APARTHEID

The most important immediate objective which the apartheid regime had hoped to achieve through the non-aggression pacts was to 'spike the guns' of the ANC and thereby dampen down the mass struggle within the country at all levels. Pretoria's refusal to acknowledge the apartheid system as the main cause of the escalation of mass struggle within the country was a serious mistake. Pretoria also made a serious error of judgement in thinking that, once it had deprived the ANC of its bases in Mozambique and in neighbouring countries, it would be able to crush the internal popular struggle. The policy of the regime was proved to be wrong because after the crack-down of the ANC in neighbouring countries, other forms of militant mass struggle continued unabated, and indeed escalated. There were more strikes than in previous years. The United Democratic Front (UDF) led a militant boycott campaign against the elections for the so-called Coloured and Indian chambers of the Botha regime's new tri-cameral parliament. This campaign, plus the inept response of the regime in detaining UDF leaders, largely succeeded in demonstrating to the world at large the total unacceptability of the new constitution to the majority of the people of South Africa. This was followed by an explosion of popular resistance[42] in the black residential areas of Vaal triangle on a scale which even surpassed the 1976 Soweto uprising.

The uprising was seen by the world as an indicator of popular rejection of the Botha regime's constitutional plans. The regime responded by sending in police and troops in an attempt to quell the uprising by force.[43] The regime did not succeed in dampening down the struggle; instead the situation escalated and a two-day 'stay away' strike was called to protest against brutality and in support of the people's demands. Backed by a number of major unions, as well as the UDF, this was described by one academic as 'the most successful stay away since the tactic was first adopted years ago'.[44] These activities had shown that the mass struggle had deepened the crisis in South Africa to the point where it was now becoming clear to all that the Botha regime had failed to impose its restructuring plan on society. It also became clear that the South African government had power but no authority to govern its people. As indicated earlier, the international repercussions were such that the gains made at this level earlier at Nkomati were being visibly eroded. The failure of the Nkomati Accord to produce the expected dampening down of popular struggle inside South Africa caused a number of influential figures in and around the Botha regime tentatively to suggest the initiation of a 'dialogue' with the ANC.

The question now to be examined is: what were the contributing factors that led to Pretoria's abandonment of the regional destabilization policy in 1989, including its attack on Zimbabwe? It would be wrong to attribute the end of regional destabilization completely to P.W. Botha's departure from office. The decisive factors behind Pretoria's apparent change were the setbacks it suffered during the destabilization which made it too costly in military as well as political, economic and diplomatic terms. In the earlier period of destabilization, Pretoria counted on military action in advancing its tactical goals whenever it experienced diplomatic and economic reverses. In the late eighties Pretoria could not always expect to get its own way through military action because of the balance of power in the region.

The most important reverse was that at Cuito Cuanavale in Angola.[45] The Cuban forces had smashed the myth of SADF invincibility and revealed important respects in which it was vulnerable. Firstly, the equipment of the South African Air Force (SAAF) was technologically inadequate. Partly as a result of the cumulative effects of the international arms embargo, the SAAF found itself unable to penetrate Soviet-made Angolan and Cuban radar and missile defences in Cuito Cuanavale, and lost its previous air superiority. Secondly, Cuito Cuanavale revealed a major political constraint on the SADF.[46] Thirdly, Cuito Cuanavale pointed to economic vulnerabilities made greater by financial sanctions.[47]

In addition to Cuito Cuanavale, reverses were also being suffered on the other main fronts of destabilization. In Mozambique, FRE-LIMO government forces, supported by their Tanzanian and Zimbabwean allies, began after late 1987 to achieve some military victories. The security situation on main road and rail links to the capital greatly improved, and a new government offensive in the centre-north succeeded in dislodging bandits from a number of bases

they had occupied since 1986. In addition, the Mozambican government offered an amnesty to bandits surrendering to the authorities.
These developments together provoked considerable disarray within
the ranks of the MNR. By December 1988, around three thousand
former bandits had surrendered and clashes were reported between
different bandit groups in Mozambique.[48] At the same time, Pretoria's known involvement with the MNR threatened to increase its
international isolation.

Pretoria also suffered a setback with its hit-and-run raids. A network of suspected South African agents was uncovered after a bomb
blast outside an alleged ANC residence in Bulawayo, Zimbabwe, in
1988. Three people were later sentenced to death for murder. Two
members of the SADF were captured and convicted of assault after a
bungled raid in Botswana in 1988. The raid reinforced calls in the
United States for South Africa to be declared a 'terrorist state'.[49]

On top of this came a growing concern from the businessmen about
the increasing violence in the country; the view that destabilization
was not working, chaos was being created in the neighbouring states
to no obvious benefit to South Africa. It had become clear to the
businessmen that the government was mismanaging the economy and
had failed to fulfil its two promises as part of the Total National
Strategy package: the Constellation of States and internal reform.
The Constellation of States had failed and the promised changes to
the race laws were not forthcoming. The government was under
pressure from businessmen who saw a regional settlement as one
way to reduce the defence budget and create the necessary room for
the free market reforms. In short, military aggression and destabilization were going awry, were proving costly in terms of money and lives
and were threatening to exacerbate South Africa's international isolation. At the same time, economic and diplomatic objectives were
being perceived as increasingly important. All these factors, combined,
forced South Africa to change its policy of destabilization and begin
the negotiations for the independence of Namibia and the withdrawal
of its troops from Angola. The greater level of cooperation between
the superpowers on 'regional conflicts' since *glasnost, perestroika* and
the 'new thinking' in the Soviet Union, the fall of Communism in
Eastern bloc countries and the increasing pressure on South Africa by
the international community for reforms, also played an important
role in this regard. It was also acknowledged by President De Klerk,
on a number of occasions, that global developments in 1989, in
particular the weakening and later the collapse of the Soviet empire

and along with it the USSR's regional ambition in sub-Saharan Africa, significantly altered the threat perception of South Africa's civil and military elites so that by early 1990 the National Party leadership felt that the time was now opportune to begin the process of regime transformation.[50]

7.6   CONCLUSION

The experience of the destabilization period also shows that the apartheid leviathan was not invincible. While it had tremendous military and economic resources at its disposal, compared to those available to its neighbours, its regional policy efforts have been characterized by contradictions and real limits on its scope for manoeuvre. It was forced to pull back in 1982 from some of the more blatant destabilization tactics, even if in many cases simply to substitute these with more subtle, concealed 'techniques of coercion'. On the one hand, Pretoria evidently desired to maintain regional states in a position of weakness as the basis on which to exercise its domination over them. It certainly did not wish to see economically strong independent states arising in the region, and much of its activities in the 1980s were explicitly designed to undermine the economic viability of other Southern African states. On the other hand, the experience of Nkomati proved that the regime did not hesitate to act deviously even to the point of violating, whether by act of omission or commission, undertakings given in formal treaties.

To a large extent the entire history of Pretoria's acts of destabilization in the region had been an attempt to export the domestic crisis arising from the irreconcilable contradictions of the apartheid system. The failure of destabilization to bring about the hoped for dampening down of the mass struggle inside South Africa was a clear sign of the defeat of its Total National Strategy.

This book has demonstrated that the 1980–89 destabilization of Zimbabwe by South Africa had an extremely adverse economic effect on Zimbabwe, but also helped to shape its internal politics. For example, the move to political unity between the main political parties ZANU and ZAPU; the shift by the ruling party in its political ideology and its idea of a one-party state. It is argued in this book that if Zimbabwe had not been led by Robert Mugabe and ZANU, it might have been spared the destructive consequences of South African destabilization. If Zimbabwe had become subservient to South Africa's self-image and ambition, for instance by denouncing the campaign for sanctions, Marxism-Leninism, the Namibian and South African liberation movements, and by diplomatic recognition of, and singing praise-songs to, South Africa, then it would not have become a target for South African destabilization. However, given the armed struggle and the progressive radicalization of the people of Zimbabwe and the overwhelming wish of the people as indicated in the 1980 general election, Zimbabwe could not accept a role subservient to South Africa.

Commentors like, Robert Davies, Deon Geldenhuys, Dan O'Meara, Joseph Hanlon and Phillip Frankel have all agreed on the following points: the reasons for the South African policy of destabilization, the ideological foundations of South Africa and basic propositions of the Total Strategy and the indices and dimensions of militarization. This book complements the criticisms Geldenhuys made of the policy of destabilization, more specifically of its implementation. He criticized the direction in which South African foreign, and particularly regional policy, had been applied. He substantiates his criticisms by stating that South Africa's lack of emphasis on diplomacy and its excessive use of military force led to the failure of the destabilization policy. For example, given the fact that Mugabe had repeatedly stated that he wanted to maintain normal relations with its neighbour, and taking into account Pretoria's economic and political advantages, South Africa should have used diplomacy and persuasion.

This was an element which was to complement the whole policy of destabilization and cover up its 'apartheid' image from the international community. According to Geldenhuys, the use of military force was supposed to be minimal, so as to pave the way for a strong bargaining position during negotiations. This work agrees with the fundamental criticisms Geldenhuys advocates with regard to the reasons which led to the failure of the South African policy of destabilization.

However, where this book brings forward a new dimension is in assessing the reasons behind the achievements and failures of South Africa's destabilization of Zimbabwe. With reference to the Zimbabwean experience, the scope of destabilization was heavily influenced by the potential political threats Pretoria foresaw in Zimbabwe's independence. In addition, the work identifies and assesses the role played by destabilization in the political development that took place in Zimbabwe, notably the political unity and the diversion of the ruling party from pursuing its Marxist and Socialist goals.

The experience of the destabilization period has clearly demonstrated that the apartheid regime was not prepared to live in 'peaceful coexistence' with its neighbours in Southern Africa, if this is taken to mean leaving these states to determine for themselves their internal social systems and the regional and external relations they wished to develop. Credit has been given to all Frontline States in their cooperation and the courage they have shown in their resistance against a powerful neighbour. Their determination and strong stand against the apartheid regime contributed enormously to the failure of South Africa's policy of destabilization. Credit should go to Robert Mugabe, Kenneth Kaunda, Leabua Jonathan, Samora Machel and Julius Nyerere for their uncompromising attitude towards the evils of apartheid, even in times of hardship. They stood firm together for their objective of seeing apartheid buried.

Appendix: A Chronology of Political Events in Southern Africa, 1975–89

January 1975
MPLA, FNLA and UNITA form a common front to negotiate independence from Portugal.

April 1975
Fighting between the three Nationalist movements in Angola resumes.

June 1975
Mozambique becomes independent.

August 1975
First reports of a SADF presence in Southern Angola are made. Zairean and Cuban troops, Chinese, Soviet and US technical and material support are also deployed.

September 1975
South Africa convenes the Turnhalle Constitutional Conference on Namibia. SWAPO is excluded.

November 1975
Angola becomes independent; the country is divided into an MPLA zone and a FNLA/UNITA zone. FNLA/UNITA forces with support from South Africa and Zaire advance on Luanda which is in MPLA hands. They are beaten off with assistance from Cuban forces.

March 1975
Following an MPLA–Cuban counter-attack, SADF withdraws from Angola. P.W. Botha, South Africa's Defence Minister, announces that South Africa is not prepared to fight alone on behalf of the free world.

June 1976
Soweto uprising. Black school children protest against the introduction of Afrikaans as the medium of instruction.

July 1976
SADF attacks SWAPO targets in Zambia, 22 people are killed. South Africa denies making the attack. The UN Security Council condemns South Africa.

May 1977
MPLA dissidents, supporting the dismissed Interior Minister Nito Alves, attempt to overthrow the government.

June 1977
Commonwealth agree the Gleneagles Agreement against sporting links with South Africa. The UN adopts the International Declaration against apartheid in sport.

May 1978
SADF launches Operation Reindeer against alleged SWAPO targets in Angola. The Cassinga refugee camp, 250 km inside Angola, is attacked; more than 600 people are killed.

September 1978
The National Party elects P.W. Botha Prime Minister.
UN Security Council adopts Resolution 435, setting out a timetable for Namibian independence. SWAPO accepts the plan but South Africa initially rejects it. Later, in October, it says it will accept it subject to certain conditions.

October–November 1978
South African and Angolan forces clash on the Namibian border.

November 1978
Two bombs in Huambo (Angola) explode, killing 24 people. Angola blames South Africa and closes air space to South Africa's civilian flights to Europe, claiming that reconnaissance missions are being flown over its territory.

December 1979
South Africa accepts the idea of a demilitarized zone along the Namibian border but SWAPO refuses the terms South Africa imposes.

February 1980
Following renewed fighting, Lesotho claims that 300 LLA guerrillas have entered the country armed with SADF weapons. In the same month, Lesotho establishes diplomatic relations with Cuba.

April 1980
Zimbabwe becomes independent and SADCC is launched in Lusaka with an economic and political agenda.

May 1980
Mozambique claims publicly that South Africa had inherited the MNR from Rhodesia.

June 1980
Major SADF offensive in Southern Angola with SAAF and artillery support. 400 Angolans and Namibians are reported killed. The invasion lasts three weeks.

July 1980
Mozambican forces attack MNR bases in Manica province and uncover SADF arms and evidence of presence of South African instructors.

August 1980
South Africa scraps plans for a black council as part of proposed constitutional reform.

October 1980
Attempted coup in Zambia. President Kaunda claims South Africa's involvement and that SADF were massing troops across the border in Namibia. South Africa denies involvement.

November 1980
SADCC meeting in Maputo; membership increases to nine states.

January 1981
Reagan is sworn in as President of the US. Dr Chester Crocker, Assistant Secretary of State for African Affairs, embarks upon the 'constructive engagement' with South Africa and begins developing the linkage between Namibian independence and the Cuban withdrawal from Angola.
SADF launch a commando raid on ANC houses in Matola outside Maputo. Twelve people are killed (one commando is killed as well). SADF forces attack an alleged ANC Headquarters in a Maputo suburb. Mozambique describes the target as a refugees' house. Twelve ANC members are reported killed.

February 1981
The South African President's Council is set up, replacing the Senate.

July 1981
The ANC representative in Zimbabwe is killed in Harare. South Africa denies responsibility, claiming that ANC infighting was to blame.

August 1981
SADF launch Operation Protean into Angola, its largest offensive since 1975. This marks the launching of the intensive phase of the Total Strategy. The operation clears a buffer zone of 100–150 km in Angola's Cunene province in which UNITA could operate freely. The UN is prevented by US veto to depart from its customary practice of condemning South Africa over such actions.

September–November 1981
LLA steps up its campaigns in Lesotho with bomb attacks in Maseru. South Africa and LLA deny cooperation between them. But since 1979, LLA activities tended to increase each time Maseru angered Pretoria by not handing over ANC members escaping into Lesotho.

November 1981
South Africa launches Operation Daisy against alleged SWAPO targets in Southern Angola.

December 1981
South Africa denies that its forces are still occupying the buffer zone in Cunene taken during Operation Protean in August.
Swazi police reported that South Africa has threatened to turn Swaziland into an operational zone if it does not take action against the ANC there. Swaziland complies. South Africa offers Swaziland a land deal which would give it access to the coast; the land offer is linked to the ANC issue.

Appendix

February 1982
The Zimbabwe government uncovers huge arms caches on ZAPU-owned farms. Later, reports emerge of plans by ZAPU and Smith's Rhodesian Front to overthrow the ZANU government. The idea was apparently approved by the South Africa. Swaziland signs a secret non-aggression pact with Pretoria. Its existence is revealed only after the Nkomati Accord in 1984.

March 1982
South Africa launches Operation Super in Southern Angola against alleged SWAPO targets. Kaunda accuses South African air and land forces of having made incursions into Zambia in February and in March.
Mozambique releases papers seized in December during the capture of the MNR base. These give further evidence of South Africa's involvement with the MNR.

July 1982
Nine Zimbabwe Air Force planes are blown up at Gweru. Several senior white air force officers are arrested and charged with aiding and abetting South Africa in the mission.

June 1983
The Namibian Council of Ministers resigns and South Africa takes over direct administration of the country.

August 1983
Following a call by Dr Allan Boesak, a prominent Coloured leader and president of the World Alliance of Reformed Churches, the United Democratic Front (UDF) is formed. It is a multi-racial movement with membership comprising civic and sporting bodies, religious organizations, trade unions and student associations.

September 1983
Under pressure from the LLA and South Africa's border checks, Lesotho agrees to expel an undisclosed number of South African refugees from a list of 68 drawn up by South Africa.

November 1983
A whites-only referendum in South Africa approves the proposed tricameral constitution.

December 1983
South African forces, still in Angola since 1981, launch Operation Askari against alleged SWAPO targets 250 km north of the border.

January 1984
Angolan, South African and American delegations meet in Cape Verde. Subsequently, South Africa announces a unilateral ceasefire and its intention to withdraw its troops from Angola, on condition that the areas vacated are not used to mount attacks into Namibia. The following month, the arrangement is formalized into the Lusaka Agreement and troop withdrawals begin. They take over a year.

March 1984
Samora Machel of Mozambique and P.W. Botha sign the Nkomati Accord. Over the following month the MNR steps up its campaigns, hitting the Nampula–Nacala road and rail link for the first time.

October 1984
Despite Mozambican expulsion of 800 ANC members under the terms of the Nkomati Accord, MNR continued its sabotage activities. South Africa hosts talks with the MNR and the Mozambican authorities and announces a planned ceasefire. Negotiations break down in November and the ceasefire does not materialize.

December 1984
Swaziland and South Africa agree to exchange trade missions.

May 1985
SADF members caught attempting to sabotage Angolan oil installations at Cabinda.

June 1985
SADF commandos raid an alleged ANC target in Gaborone. Four houses are demolished, there is no loss of life. Subsequently, 24 ANC members are reportedly obliged to leave Botswana.

July 1985
US Congress repeals the Clark amendment prohibiting US military and financial support to UNITA. The South African government declares a state of emergency in 35 districts. This follows unrest caused by police opening fire on a procession marking the 25th anniversary of the Sharpeville massacre.

August 1985
A combined Zimbabwean and Mozambican force takes the MNR headquarters at Casa Banana in the Gorongoza National Park and brings back diaries showing continued SA support and even ministerial visits after the Nkomati Accord. The base falls back into MNR hands after Zimbabwean troops are withdrawn.

September 1985
SA's Defence Minister, General Magnus Malan, publicly admits that SA supported UNITA over a number of years.

October 1985
Reagan pre-empts Congressional moves towards the imposition of sanctions by issuing an Executive Order banning most loans and nuclear technology and computer exports.
The Congress of South Africa Trade Union (COSATU) is formed.

December 1985
A South African commando force kills nine people, six of whom are ANC members, in Maseru. LLA claims responsibility while SA denies involvement.

January 1986
MNR blows up power lines from SA to Mozambique; it takes three days to restore them. In Lesotho the new year starts with SA's virtual border block-

ade which precipitates the overthrow of Leabua Jonathan on January 20. The coup leader and Chairman of the Military Council Maj. General Justin Lekhanya agrees to deal with SA. Fifty-seven ANC members are expelled to Zambia despite SA application for extradition. In SA, the State of Emergency is partially lifted.

April 1986
Zimbabwean forces retake the MNR's Casa Banana base. On 25 April, Mswati III is sworn in as King of Swaziland.

May 1986
SA launches raids on alleged ANC targets in Zambia, Zimbabwe and Botswana. The raids scupper the efforts of the Commonwealth's Eminent Persons Group to mediate. At the same time, SA steps up its support of UNITA and deploys own troops and hardware in Cunune and Namibe provinces.

June 1986
Seaborne attack against the Angolan port of Namibe. Missiles and limpet mines are used against six oil tankers. Pretoria denies involvement but is widely disbelieved. As the 10th anniversary of the Soweto uprising approaches, Botha declares a nationwide state of emergency.

August 1986
Commonwealth mini-summit in London is convened. Britain is in minority of one against sanctions. Zambia and Zimbabwe strongly favour sanctions.
SA imposes a levy on Zambian and Zimbabwean imports passing through SA. In case of the latter, it is only for a brief period.

September 1986
MNR launches another major offensive in northern Mozambique, allegedly from Malawi. Prior to this offensive and after heavy pressure from Mozambique, Zambia and Zimbabwe put pressure on Malawi to force it to act more decisively against the MNR. It is alleged that Malawi is threatened with a blockade.
Despite presidential veto, the US Congress passes the Comprehensive Anti-Apartheid Act – a package of selective sanctions against SA banning new investment, loans to the government including some aspects of trade and direct airlinks. The EEC broadens its measures of sanctions against SA.

October 1986
MNR declares war on Zimbabwe. SA bans further recruitment of Mozambican workers.

October 19/20, night 1986
President Machel is killed in a plane crash inside SA's border. SA claims to have discovered, in the wreckage of the plane, papers on a joint Zimbabwe–Mozambique plot to overthrow Malawi's Kamuzu Banda. It denies any responsibility for the crash.

December 1986
Six people including a Swiss couple (these are subsequently released) and probably a senior commander of the ANC's Umkhonto we Sizwe, disappear in a South African raid into Swaziland.

February 1987
Bophuthatswana imposes a visa requirement on Botswana and Zimbabwean train drivers. Use of South African drivers gets around the problem.

April 1987
SADF commandos attack Livingstone, a Zambian town.

May 1987
SA resumes operations in southern Angola; some 3000 troops are involved. Withdrawal still not complete by the end of April 1988, despite announcement that it would end in December 1987.

June 1987
MNR attacks against villagers in eastern Zimbabwe are reported to be on the increase.

July 1987
Afrikaner liberals meet the ANC in Dakar. In Mozambique, MNR kill over 40 civilians at Homoine.

September 1987
Angolan forces launch an attack on Mavinga, UNITA's base. The attempt fails because of SADF support for UNITA but heavy casualties are incurred on both sides.

December 1987
Mozambique announces a one-year amnesty to surrendering MNR rebels.
A series of five bombs explode in Gaborone over four days. The government stops short of accusing SA.

December 31 1987
ZANU and ZAPU finally agree to form one party. Mugabe becomes Zimbabwe's first executive president.

January 1988
UNITA and SADF forces lay siege to the Fapla stronghold at Cuito Cuanavale, but fail to take it.
A car bomb explodes outside the house of ANC members in Bulawayo. Chester Crocker meets Angolan and Cuban officials in Luanda. After the meeting he announces a breakthrough on the question of Cuban withdrawal but it is denied by other parties.

March 1988
Mazizi Maqekeza, a member of Umkhonto we Sizwe, is shot dead in a hospital bed in Maseru. Another ANC representative in Paris, Dulcie September, is shot in her office. Four people, with no known connection with the ANC, are killed in a house in Gaborone; SA acknowledges responsibility for the attack describing the four as terrorists.
P.W. Botha announces new proposals for reforming the constitution. Blacks might, for the first time, be allowed representation in central government. Most black leaders reject the ideas.
In Maputo a car bomb seriously injures Albie Sachs, a South African and anti-apartheid campaigner in exile in Mozambique.

May 1988
Following secret US–Soviet talks in April, Angolan, Cuban, South African and US delegations meet in London to discuss foreign troop withdrawals from Angola and Namibia. This event is followed by a meeting between South African and Angolan ministers in Brazzaville, Congo.
Afrikaner liberals meet ANC officials in Frankfurt, West Germany.

13 June 1988
Further SA–Angolan talks take place at a meeting in New York between the four principal countries. They agree on the 'Basic Principles of the Agreement'.

29 July 1988
A fifth round of the SA–Angolan talks takes place in New York.

2 August 1988
Another round of SA–Angolan talks takes place in Geneva. At the same time, a meeting, to take place in Canada, of Commonwealth Ministers on apartheid is announced.

3 August 1988
140 young white men announce in South Africa that they will not be serving in the SADF, because it only serves to prop up a racist system.

7 August 1988
Angolan forces shoot down Botswana President Masire's plane on his way to Luanda for a FLS meeting. They mistake it for an enemy aircraft. He escapes the accident.

8 August 1988
A ceasefire between SA and Angola is announced. SA announces that it would start troop withdrawal on the following Wednesday and expect to finish in September.

13 August 1988
Angolan–SA talks in Brazzaville, Congo, take place. Pik Botha and General Malan head the SA delegation. Botha talks about the Afghanistan style of withdrawal from Angola, with no winners or losers.

15 August 1988
Pik Botha announces in Austria that SA has the capability to manufacture nuclear weapons. Three days later, SA insists it would only sign the Nuclear Non-Proliferation Treaty if it is given unrestricted trading rights of uranium and access to nuclear technology.

24 August 1988
More Angolan–SA peace talks in Brazzaville.

30 August 1988
SA announces final withdrawal from Angola.

12 September 1988
P.W. Botha visits Mozambique to renew the Nkomati Accord on his way back from Malawi.

January 1989
P.W. Botha has a stroke.

April 1989
United Nations Transitional Assistance Group (UNTAG) arrive in Namibia to monitor Namibia's transition to independence, including overseeing the elections.

1 April 1989
SWAPO incursions into Namibia. It seems to have moved 2000 troops across the border from Angola starting from the last week of March in violation of the August 1988 Geneva Accords which both SA and UN considered binding on SWAPO. SA receives intelligence, some reportedly from US intelligence, about SWAPO troop movement. This move by SWAPO proves a costly miscalculation: 300 SWAPO fighters are killed by superior SA firepower.

4 April 1989
In post-mortem, Pérez de Cuéllar, the UN Secretary-General, confirms that SWAPO had sent its fighters into Namibia but that it meant no hostile intent.

5 April 1989
Pik Botha, SA Foreign Minister, warns the UN that unless it can control SWAPO and control the fighting in Northern Namibia, the peace plan will become null and void.

6 April 1989
The FLS offer their troops to UN to help restore peace.

7 April 1989
P.W. Botha announces that he will step down.
On the same day, SA suspends the Namibian Peace Process and says it is re-activating the militia in the areas affected by fighting.

8 April 1989
SWAPO backs down from the confrontation with SA and announces that it will pull its forces back into Angola within 72 hours under UNTAG supervision.

25 May 1989
ANC is disarmed in Zambia. This follows a spate of killings of Zambians by ANC cadres; the ANC High Command in Zambia takes the decision.

14 June 1989
ANC in Zambia publicly disagree with President Kaunda about his call to meet with SA's new leader F.W. De Klerk. ANC argues that neither Botha nor De Klerk has done anything to suggest new thinking in Pretoria.

22 June 1989
Oliver Tambo, President of ANC, makes it known that he does not think that De Klerk has anything to offer.

23 June 1989
Reports in Zambia suggest that SA is about to test a new ballistic missile developed with Israeli assistance.

24 June 1989
Angolan ceasefire between UNITA and the Angolan government comes into effect. Suggestions are made that Savimbi has accepted to go into self-exile; he later denies the report.

5 July 1989
Nelson Mandela is invited to meet P.W. Botha. Pik Botha later says the gesture will go down well in Western capitals.

9 July 1989
The Mandela family issues a statement through Rev. Frank Chikani that the meeting was not significant and was merely a ploy to hoodwink the world.

15 August 1989
F.W. De Klerk is sworn in as Acting President.

21 August 1989
De Klerk and Kaunda meet at Livingstone, a border Zambian town.

6 September 1989
SA's white parliamentary elections take place amid widespread unrest and protests from the black population. The NP is returned to power with reduced majority.

30 September/1 October 1989
ANC and the Afrikaner Broederbond make history by meeting in London to discuss the future of SA. De Klerk is part of the Broederbond's delegation.

28 November 1989
De Klerk dismantles the National Security Management System. This not only allows him to distance himself from the old regime and the Total Strategy, but it also breaks the security grip on the government.

Notes

1 THE BACKGROUND OF DESTABILIZATION: SOUTH AFRICA'S REGIONAL POLICY, 1977–89

1. Patel, H. H., 'South Africa's Destabilisation Policy', *The Round Table*, July 1987, Issue No. 303, p. 306.
2. O'Meara, D., 'Destabilisation in Southern Africa: Total Strategy in Total Disarray', *Monthly Review*, April 1986, pp. 52–3.
3. Patel, H. H., 'Zimbabwe', *Survival*, January/February, 1988, Vol. XXX, No. 1, p. 42, 'Total Strategy involved the mobilization of all possible South African resources, especially the four "power-bases", i.e., political/diplomatic, economic, social/psychological and security'.
4. Davies, R. and O'Meara, D., 'Total Strategy in Southern Africa: An Analysis of South African Regional Strategy since 1978', *Journal of Southern African Studies*, 11, 2, April 1985, p. 185.
5. Tanzania is included here because of the formidable political role it has played in the past 28 years in the liberation struggle of Southern Africa.
6. See Blumenfeld, J., *Economic Interdependence in Southern Africa: From Conflict to Cooperation*, London, The Royal Institute of International Affairs, 1991, pp. 20–5; and see Shaun Johnson (ed.), *South Africa: No Turning Back*, London, Macmillan, 1988, pp. 206–7.
7. See Mandaza, I., *Southern Africa in the 1990s: Towards a Research Agenda*, Harare, Southern Africa Political Economy Series, Occasional Paper Series, No. 1, 1991, p. 4.
8. Ibid., p. 4.
9. Such as Blumenfeld, J., *Economic Interdependence*.
10. Wilson, F., *Labour in the South African Gold Mines*, London, Cambridge University Press, 1972; also see Blumenfeld, 1991, op. cit., pp. 32–3.
11. Davies, R., 'Some Implications of Competing Post-Apartheid Scenarios for the Southern African Region' (unpublished), a paper prepared for joint seminar with Fernand Braudel Centre for the Study of Economies, Historical Systems and Civilizations, State University of New York at Binghamton, November 1989, p. 22. The number of the migrant labourers had reduced in great number because after the independence of Zimbabwe, most of the Zimbabwean miners working in South Africa were sent back and South Africa stopped recruiting from Zimbabwe.
12. See Stoneman, C. and Cliffe, L., *Zimbabwe: Politics, Economics and Society*, London, Pinter, 1989, pp. 50 and 147.
13. See Blumenfeld, J., 1991, pp. 50–4 and 118–121.
14. See Davies, R., O'Meara, D. and Dlamini, S., *The Struggle for South Africa*, London, Zed Books, 1984, pp. 51–93.
15. Here I refer to the British government and its European partners, who had huge investment interests in the region. For more information on

the Western foreign policy to Southern Africa, See Legum, C., *The Western Crisis over Southern Africa*, New York, African Publishing Company, 1979, pp. 3–30.

16.		See Ncube, M. M., 'The U.S., South Africa and Destabilisation in Southern Africa', *Journal of African Marxists*, No. 6, October 1984, pp. 15–25; and also see Legum, C., 1979, pp. 3–30.

17.		Johnson, P. and Martin, D. (eds), *Destructive Engagement: Southern Africa at War*, Zimbabwe Publishing House for Southern Africa Research and Documentation Centre, Harare, 1986, pp. 271–2.

18.		Jenkins observes that when South Africa invaded Angola it was done 'with the encouragement of the American Secretary of State Henry Kissinger' who later on could not back up the South African government with assistance when the Luanda government appealed for more help from Cuba, who responded by sending more troops and forced the South African army to withdraw. The main reason why the US did not assist South Africa in its invasion of Angola is that there was disagreement within Congress as to whether the US should be involved in the war. See Jenkins, S., 'Destabilisation in Southern Africa', *The Economist*, 16 July 1983, p. 17; and also see Cock, J. and Nathan, L. *War and Society: The Militarisation of South Africa*, Johannesburg, David Philip, 1989, p. 93.

19.		Price, R. M., 'Pretoria's Southern African Strategy', *African Affairs*, Vol. 83, No. 330, January, 1984, p. 18.

20.		See Ncube M. M., 'The U.S., South Africa and Destabilisation', p. 18.

21.		Patel, H. H., 1987, pp. 302–10.

22.		Wheeler, D.C., 'Portuguese Withdrawal from Africa', in Seiler, J., ed., *Southern Africa since the Portuguese Coup*, Boulder, Colorado: Westview Press, 1980, Chapter 1.

23.		Jaster, R. S., 'South Africa's Narrowing Security Options', Adelphi Papers, No. 159, London: International Institute for Strategic Studies, 1980, pp. 22–3.

24.		Geldenhuys, D., *The Diplomacy of Isolation: South African Foreign Policy Making*, Cape Town: Macmillan, 1984, pp. 19–21.

25.		*The Root of Armed Banditry*, Mozambique Briefing, No. 5, Ministry of Information, 1987.

26.		During UDI and following the UN mandatory sanctions, South Africa became Rhodesia's lifeline as it battled for economic survival. See Hill, C. R. 'UDI and South African Foreign Policy', *Journal of Commonwealth Political Studies*, Vol. 8, No. 2, July 1969, pp. 96–103. In addition, South Africa sent a police contingent to assist Rhodesia in countering the growing threat from nationalist forces. The reason given, not believed by the international community, was that they were meant to intercept ANC insurgents *en route* to South Africa.

27.		See Nolutshungu, S. C., *South Africa in Africa: A Study in Ideology and Foreign Policy*, Manchester, Manchester University Press, 1975, pp. 173 and 263.

28.		Vale, P., 'The Botha Doctrine: Apartheid, Southern Africa and the West', in Chan, S. *Exporting Apartheid: Foreign Policies in Southern Africa 1978–88*; London, Macmillan, 1990, pp. 170–1.

29. Chan, 1990, pp. 267–78.
30. Ibid., p. 173.
31. Halpern, J., *South Africa's Hostages*, London: Penguin, 1965, pp. 52–3.
32. Ibid., p. 55.
33. Davies, R. and O'Meara, D., 'Total Strategy in Southern Africa: An Analysis of South African Regional Strategy since 1978', *Journal of Southern African Studies*, 11, 2, April 1985, p. 186.
34. See Johnson, S. (ed.), *South Africa: No Turning Back*, London, Macmillan, 1988, p. 216. The Broederbond became a secret society in 1922 in order to function more effectively. Membership was by invitation only and invitations were restricted to Afrikaans-speaking Protestant males, financially sound, of approved behaviour and who were prepared to be active members.
35. Grundy, K. W., *Confrontation and Accommodation in Southern Africa*, London and Berkeley: University of California Press, 1973, p. 244.
36. This strong and uncompromising anti-communist stance resulted from what Grundy calls irrational and highly institutionalized fear of communism. In particular, South Africa feared (i) communist ideology taking root in Africa; (ii) Russian naval power in the Indian Ocean; (iii) Russian and Chinese aid to nationalist groups; (iv) Chinese domination, which according to them, was already evident in Tanzania and Zambia; and (v) Chinese migration to Africa; they called this the 'Yellow peril'. See Grundy, 1973, p. 244.
37. Geldenhuys, 1984, p. 23.
38. Ibid., p. 34.
39. Hanlon, J., *Beggar Your Neighbours: Apartheid Power in Southern Africa*, James Currey for Catholic Institute for International Relations, London, 1986, pp. 81–90.
40. Hanlon, 1986, pp. 81–90.
41. See Grundy, 1973, pp. 243–6.
42. Ibid.
43. Ibid., p. 243.
44. See Geldenhuys, D., 'South Africa's Regional Policy', in Michael Clough (ed.), *Changing Realities in Southern Africa: Implications for American Policy*, Research Series, Berkeley, University of California, No. 47, 1982, pp. 125ff.
45. Davidson, B., *Southern Africa: The New Politics of Revolution*, London: Penguin, 1977, pp. 204–331.
46. The move was partially successful. In January 1967 Vorster and Leabua Jonathan, then Prime Minister of Lesotho, met. Later in September of the same year, Dr Banda of Malawi agreed to establish full diplomatic links with Pretoria on a reciprocal basis.
47. Ibid., p. 99.
48. Johnson, R. W., *How Long will South Africa Survive?*, London, Macmillan, pp. 115–28.
49. Davies, R., *South African Strategy Towards Mozambique in the Post-Nkomati Period: A Critical Analysis of Effects and Implications*, Scandinavian Institute of African Studies, Uppsala, 1985, Report No. 73.

50. See Hanlon, J., 1986, pp. 114 and 142.
51. See Davies, R., 1985, p. 5.
52. Davies. R. and O'Meara, P., 'Conclusion: Total Strategy in South Africa: An Analysis of South African Regional Policy since 1978', in Shaw, T. M. (ed.), *Confrontation and Liberation in Southern Africa: Regional Directions after the Nkomati Accord*, Colorado, Westview, Boulder, 1987, p. 245.
53. Geldenhuys, D., *The Diplomacy of Isolation: South African Foreign Policy Making*, Cape Town: Macmillan, 1984, p. 39.
54. Concerned by the developments in Mozambique and Angola, South Africa did not want to see Namibia dominated by another hostile communist group like SWAPO. As it turned out, the Lisbon *coup d'état* precipitated a watershed in the history of the region and South Africa's foreign relations with its neighbours. The South African government entered the constitutional talks on Namibia with great reluctance and did so only because it feared that it would lose Western support (US, UK and France) in the UN Security Council on resolutions calling for international sanctions unless it could demonstrate that there was a South African initiative on the table. Seiler, J. (ed.), *Southern Africa Since the Portuguese Coup*, Boulder: Westview, 1980, pp. 87–97.
55. Martin, D. and Johnson, P., *The Struggle for Zimbabwe: The Chimurenga War*, London: Faber & Faber, 1981, pp. 129ff.
56. Ibid.
57. Refer to O'Meara, P. 'Rhodesia: From White Rule to Independence Zimbabwe', in Carter, G. M. and O'Meara, P. (eds), *Southern Africa in Crisis*, Bloomington and London: Indiana University Press, 1977, pp. 33–47; see also Manganyi, N.C., 'The Baptism of Fire: South Africa's Black Majority Rule after the Portuguese Coup', in Seiler, op. cit., pp. 169–79.
58. Sesay, A., 'The Role of the Frontline States in Southern Africa', in Aluko, A. and Shaw, T. M. (eds), *Southern Africa in the 1980s*, London: George Allen and Unwin, 1985, p. 21.
59. See Fact Paper on Southern Africa No. 8, *The Apartheid War Machine: The Strength and Deployment of the South African Armed Forces*, International Defence and Aid Fund, London, April, 1980, p. 68.
60. Ibid., p. 68.
61. Sesay, A., 1985, p. 21.
62. Sesay, A. in Aluko, A. and Shaw, T. M. ibid., Chapter 2. See also Ajala, A., 'The OAU and Southern Africa', in Aluko and Shaw, ibid., Chapter 1.
63. The Bureau of State Security (BOSS) was formally constituted in 1969. It replaced the Republican Intelligence, which had functioned as a division of the security police since the early 1960s and which established its reputation by infiltration of the ANC and CP (Communist Party) underground. Under Vorster's government (1966–78) Boss became the 'elite' security apparatus of the state with a major influence on all aspects of security policy. It was involved in planting agents in a number of progressive and liberal organizations and engaged in bribery and 'dirty tricks' campaigns in South Africa, other African countries

and abroad. For more information about BOSS, see Davies, R., O'Meara, D. and Dlamini, S., 1984, p. 193.

64. See D. Geldenhuys, 'Some Strategic Implications of Regional Economic Relationships for the Republic of South Africa', *ISSUP Strategic Review*, University of Pretoria, January 1981.

65. *The Root of Armed Banditry*, Mozambique Briefing, No. 5, Ministry of Information, 1987, pp. 1–13.

66. See D. Geldenhuys, 'Some Strategic Implications of Regional Economic Relationships for the Republic of South Africa,' *ISSUP Strategic Review*, University of Pretoria, January 1981. Deon Geldenhuys became professor of political science at Rand Afrikaans University in 1982, and he was a major analyser of destabilization, who explained the concept and showed how it could be done.

67. See Martin, R. 'Regional Security in Southern Africa: More Angolas, Mozambiques or Neutrals?', *Survival*, September/October 1987, Vol. XXIX, No. 5, p. 389.

68. Davies, O'Meara and Dlamini, op. cit., pp. 29–34.

69. See Hallett, R., 'The South African Intervention in Angola 1975–76', *African Affairs*, vol. 77, no. 303, July 1978, pp. 356–7.

70. Detente was a new diplomatic political initiative orchestrated by Vorster and supported by BOSS. Its objective was a search for influential allies within the OAU. Bribery, secret diplomatic contacts (often arranged through BOSS's contacts in Western intelligence services), a visit by Vorster to a number of West African countries and a meeting with President Kaunda of Zambia were all used to achieve this end. At the same time some minor internal changes, such as the scrapping of some forms of 'petty apartheid' sought to give credence to 'dialogue' as a viable alternative to confrontation.

71. Grundy, K. W., *The Militarisation of South African Politics*, Oxford: Oxford University Press, 1987, p. 89.

72. See Davies, R. and O'Meara, P., 1985, pp. 188–9.

73. Grundy, 1987, p. 91; Geldenhuys notes that the reason 'for the strained relations that are widely known to have existed between PW Botha... and Van den Bergh... may have been Van den Bergh's position as Vorster's close confidant and adviser... thus further enhancing (his) standing with Vorster and the Boss's willingness to take issue openly with Cabinet members, notably PW Botha. Van den Bergh, rather than Vorster or any other Cabinet member, it was said, was prepared to stand up to the headstrong, often impetuous Minister of Defence.' See Geldenhuys, D., *The Diplomacy of Isolation; South African Foreign Policy Making*, Cape Town, Macmillan, 1984, p. 147.

74. Ibid.

75. Holnes, M., *Apartheid's War against Angola*, UN: New York, February 1983, pp. 8–9.

76. Davies, R. and O'Meara, D., 'Total Strategy in Southern Africa: An analysis of South African Regional Strategy since 1978', *Journal of Southern African Studies*, 11, 2, April 1985, p. 188. Article reprinted in T. M. Shaw (ed.) *Confrontation and Liberation* (1987).

77. Cawthra, G., *Brutal Force: The Apartheid War Machine*, London:
     International Defence and Aid Fund for Southern Africa 1986, pp.
     24–5.
78. Grundy, 1987, Chapter 6, pp. 88–92.
79. See Davies, O'Meara and Dlamini, 1984, p. 182.
80. See Johnson, P. and Martin, D., *Destructive Engagement: Southern
     Africa at War*, Harare, Zimbabwe Publishing House, 1986, pp. 174–5.
81. Ibid., p. 175.
82. Jaster, R. *Southern Africa: Regional Security Problems and Prospects*,
     Gower, The International Institute for Strategic Studies, 1985, p. 107.
83. Davies and O'Meara, 'The State of Analysis of the Southern African
     Region: Issues Raised by South African Strategy', *Review of African
     Political Economy*, No. 29, 1983–84, p. 68.
84. Since the 1940s, large Afrikaner capital had emerged as a major force in
     the South African economy. Starting from nothing, the Afrikaners
     could, by the 1970s, boast of Sanlam, second only to the Anglo-Amer-
     ican Corporation, Rembrandt and Volkskas, which are among the eight
     leading conglomerates in the South African economy. Refer to Davies
     and O'Meara, 1983–84, op. cit., pp. 68–9.
85. See Davies, O'Meara and Dlamini, 1987.
86. The Soweto uprising emerged particularly from the students and
     sections of the petty bourgeoisie, whose dominant ideological form
     was that of Black consciousness. The uprisings began in Soweto and
     spread throughout the country. The immediate causes were the pres-
     sure being put on black school students by a 'Bantu education'
     system, itself increasingly in crisis. The breaking point was a decree
     by the department of Bantu Education that Afrikaans should be the
     medium of instruction for half the subjects taught in all African
     secondary schools. When the students of Soweto responded with a
     peaceful mass demonstration on 16 June 1976, they were met with a
     hail of bullets. For more on this topic see Davies, O'Meara & Dla-
     mini, 1987, pp. 32–5.
87. Most of the students who went out seeking military training joined the
     ANC military wing, Umkhonto we Sizwe. This, plus the changed
     situation in the region after 1975, permitted a resurgence of armed
     struggle within the country on a much greater scale than before. Since
     the new wave of armed action was launched in 1977, the armed struggle
     of the ANC had advanced steadily and eleven incidents were reported
     by South African media by 1977, this rose to 15 in 1978 and by mid
     1981 the total number of incidents in the previous four and half years
     had reached 62. Davies, O'Meara and Dlamini, 1987, p. 34.
88. For the reasons that had hampered progress, refer to Legum, C.,
     'Southern Africa: The Year of the Whirlwind', in Legum, *Africa Con-
     temporary Record*, London, Rex Coolings, 1977, pp. 3–55.
89. See Legum, C., *The Western Crisis Over Southern Africa*, New York,
     Africana Publishing Company, 1979, pp. 201–13; and see Patel, 'Zim-
     babwe', *Survival*, January/February 1988, Vol. XXX, No. 1, pp. 38–59.
90. Gordon, L. (ed.), *Survey of Race Relations in South Africa 1980*,
     SAIRR, Johannesburg, pp. 635–8.

91. Gutteridge, W., *South Africa Strategy for Survival? Conflict Studies*, London Institute for the Study of Conflict, No. 131, June 1981, pp. 21–4.
92. Davies and O'Meara, 1983–84, p. 68.
93. Cawthra, G., 1986, pp. 24–5.
94. See Davies, O'Meara and Dlamini, 1987.
95. 1977 Defence White Paper, p. 5, quoted from Davies and O'Meara, 1983–84.
96. Ibid. Refer to Grundy, 1987, Chapter 3.
97. See Beaufre, A., *Deterrence and Strategy*, London, Faber, 1965. (He was a French counter-insurgency and psychological warfare strategist, a product of the Algerian war.)
98. Frankel, P. H., *Pretoria's Praetorians: Civil-military Relations in South Africa*, London, Cambridge University Press, 1984, p. 46.
99. Price, R. M. 1984, p. 11.
100. Ibid.
101. Refer to 'South Africa: States vs Churches' (special report), *West Africa*, 21 March 1988, pp. 495–6; See also Price, 1984, op. cit, pp. 19–25.
102. Grundy, 1987, pp. 19–25.
103. Nigeria was also considered as a potential source of danger if it became stable politically. Apart from Nigeria, it was less concerned with the OAU which, despite its rhetoric, was considered to be too divided to devise any serious military package against the Pretoria government. See Matatu, G., 'Southern Africa: An Uneasy Peace,' *Africa*, no. 153, May 1984, pp. 8–10, 15.
104. Sakwa, R. 'Gorbachev and the new Soviet Foreign Policy', *Paradigms: The Kent Journal of International Relations*, vol. 2, no. 1, June 1988, pp. 18–27.
105. Price, R. M., 1984, p. 13.
106. By 1980, however, the effects of these partial sanctions were effectively countered by political changes that took place in the US, the UK and West Germany, three of the leading allies of the South African regime. As Conservative governments came to power, they not only reversed the policies of the previous administrations, but also blocked any further attempts to impose further sanctions. Partly too, the rapid increases of the price of gold and other precious minerals helped to cushion the economy against the impact of the sanctions.
107. See *The Commonwealth Sanctions Report, South Africa: The Sanctions Report*, London: Penguin, 1989, Chapters 16, 21 and 6 [see particularly pp. 47–50 and 104–7].
108. To appreciate the extent of potential threat, as South Africa saw it, see Landgren, S., *Embargo Disimplemented: South Africa's Military Industry*, Oxford: Oxford University Press, 1989, p. 177; and see Chingambo, L. and Chan, S., 'Sanctions and South Africa: Strategies, Strangleholds and Self-Consciousness', *The Kent Journal of International Relations*, vol. 2, no. 2, winter 1988–89, pp. 112–28.
109. Adam, H. and Moodley, K., *South Africa without Apartheid: Dismantling Racial Domination*, London and Berkeley: University of California Press, 1986, pp. 197–203.

110. See Boesak, *A Black and Reformed*, Johannesburg: Skotaville, 1983, pp. 1 ff.
111. *West Africa*, 'South Africa: State vs the Churches', op. cit., p. 495.
112. Meli, F. A, *History of the ANC: South Africa Belongs to Us*, London: James Curry, 1988, pp. 187–8.
113. Quoted by Adam and Moodley, op. cit, p. 280.
114. See Hornsby, M., 'What Hope for Pulpit Power?', *The Times*, London, 2 March 1988, p. 10.
115. See 'Tutu arrested in Clergy march on Parliament', *The Times*, London, 1 March 1988, p. 1.
116. Davies, O'Meara and Dlamini, 1984, pp. 38–40.
117. Johannesburg, *Financial Mail*, March, 1979.
118. Details on the other issues are found in Jaster, R. S., 'South Africa's Narrowing Options', *Adelphi Papers*, no. 159, 1980.
119. This was manifested when Botha appointed the former defence force chief and architect of the Total Strategy, Magnus Malan, as Minister of Defence, the first time in South African history that a serving officer had been appointed to the cabinet. For more detail on the military, see Grundy, 1987, op. cit.
120. Davies, R., *South African Strategy towards Mozambique in the Post-Nkomati Period: A Critical Analysis of Effects and Implications*, Scandinavian Institute of African Studies, Uppsala, 1985, Report No. 73.
121. Jenkins, S. 'Destabilisation in Southern Africa', *Economist*, 16 July 1983, pp. 15–28; and Jone, J.D.F., 'Botha's Point of No Return,' *Financial Times*, 6 August 1982.
122. Munck, R., 'The Constellation of Southern African States: A New Strategic Offensive by South Africa', *Review of African Political Economy*, May/August 1980, no. 18, pp. 102–3.
123. Jenkins, 1983, pp. 20–1.
124. Davies, R., 1985.
125. Price, 1984, p. 15.
126. Davies and O'Meara, 1987, p. 257.
127. Widner, J. and Foltz, W. J., *The OAU after Twenty Years*, New York: Praeger, 1984, pp. 249–69.
128. Geldenhuys, D. and Gutteridge, W., *Instability and Conflict in Southern Africa: South Africa's Role in Regional Security. Conflict Studies*, London: The Institute for the Study of Conflict, No. 148, 1983, pp. 3–9.
129. For a critique of Pretoria's regional policy, See E. Njal Tjonneland, *Pax Pretoriana. The Fall of Apartheid and the Politics of Regional Destabilisation*, Sweden, Scandinavian Institute of African Studies, 1989.
130. See D. Geldenhuys, 'Some Strategic Implications of Regional Economic Relationships for the Republic of South Africa', *ISSUP Strategic Review*, University of Pretoria, January 1981.
131. For detailed information on the methodology of destabilization, see D. Geldenhuys, 'Destabilisation Controversy in Southern Africa', *SA Forum Position Paper*, Johnnesburg, September 1982. In this paper Professor Geldenhuys explains the concept of destabilization and shows how it could be done.

132. Davies, R. and O'Meara, D., 'Total Strategy in Southern Africa: An Analysis of South African Regional Strategy since 1978', *Journal of Southern African Studies*, 11, 2, April 1985, p. 185.
133. See D. Geldenhuys, 1981.
134. This option was to be implemented as a last resort, and only after a serious considerations of the consequence of such an option because it would involve high costs for South Africa, as observed by Nolutshungu; '...if it could possibly be implemented, would involve high costs for South Africa. Among other things, a "Lebanon" situation might ensue in the form of a counter-counter-revolutionary struggle. This could be valuable to the ANC.' See Nolutshungu, S. C., 'Strategy and Power: South Africa and Its Neighbours', in Johnson, S. (ed.), *South Africa: No Turning Back*, London, Macmillan, 1988, p. 346.
135. Hanlon, J., *Beggar Your Neighbours: Apartheid Power in Southern Africa*, London, James Currey for Catholic Institute for International Relations, 1986.
136. Davies, R. and O'Meara, D., 1985, p. 199.
137. Patel, H. H., 1987, pp. 302–10.
138. Hanlon, 1986, pp. 30–1.

2 DESTABILIZATION: THE ZIMBABWE EXPERIENCE

1. *Rand Daily Mail*, Johannesburg, 3 March 1979.
2. Patel, H.H., 'Zimbabwe,' *Survival*, Jan/Feb., 1988, Vol. XXX, No. 1, p. 43.
3. See for example, Hanlon, J., *Apartheid's Second Front: South Africa's War against its Neighbours*, London, Penguin, 1986, pp. 1–12; Hanlon, J., *Beggar Your Neighbours: Apartheid Power in Southern Africa*, London, James Currey for Catholic Institute for International Relations, 1986, p. 4 and S. C. Nolutshungu, 'The South African State and Africa', *Africa Journal of Political Economy*, No. 1, 1986, pp. 60–74.
4. Hanlon, *Beggar Your Neighbours: Apartheid Power in Southern Africa*, pp. 199–218 and D.G. Clarke, *Foreign Companies and International Investment in Zimbabwe*, Gweru, Mambo Press, 1980, p. 10.
5. Jaster, R., *Southern Africa: Regional Security Problems and Prospects*, International Institute for Strategic Studies, IISS, Gower, 1985, p. 70.
6. Hanlon, *Apartheid's Second Front: South Africa's War against its Neighbours*, p. 55.
7. Gregory, M., 'The Zimbabwe Election: The Political and Military Implications', *Journal of Southern African Studies*, Vol. 7, No. 1, October 1980, p. 24. This was the first time that South Africa had made clear that the defence of the laager recognized no frontiers, that if necessary she would be prepared to extend the fight beyond her borders whether invited to do so or not.
8. See Jaster, R. *Southern Africa: Regional Security Problems and Prospects*, p. 142.
9. *The Guardian* (London), 19 February 1980.

10.   *The Times* (London), 21 February 1980.

11.   *The Guardian*, 24 February 1980.

12.   Banana, C., *Turmoil and Tenacity: Zimbabwe 1890–1990*, Harare, College Press, 1989.

13.   Rhoodie, E., 'The Real Information Scandal', *Orbis* (South Africa) 1983. One of South Africa's many secret projects was code-named 'Operation Chicken'. This involved funding some Zimbabwean 'nationalists' such as Muzorewa, Sithole and James Chikerema. Approximately US$1 million was committed to the 1979 Muzorewa campaign, and some 450 motor vehicles worth $2.5 million were supplied for the same purpose. Quoted in Johnson, P. and Martin, D. (eds), *Destructive Engagement: Southern Africa at War*, Harare, Zimbabwe Publishing House, 1986, p. 351.

14.   Johnson, P. and Martin, D. (eds), *Destructive Engagement*, p. 45.

15.   Gregory M., 'The Zimbabwe Election: The Political and Military Implications', *Journal of Southern African Studies*, Vol. 7, No. 1, October 1980, p. 27.

16.   *The Herald*, Harare, 18 April 1980, quoted from De Waal, V., *The Politics of Reconciliation*, London, Hurst, 1990, pp. 48–9.

17.   *Herald*, Harare, 9 May 1981. The care with which South African leaders orchestrate their counter-measures is indicated by the statement of a South African official (in private) that the relatively junior Minister of Police was selected to issue the warning to Zimbabwe, since South Africa did not want to make a major issue of it at that particular time.

18.   *Sunday Mail*, Harare, 10 May, 1981. Once again the fact that Hove, rather than the Defence Minister or Mugabe himself, responded to South African accusations reflected the leadership's interests in keeping the war of words at a relatively low pitch.

19.   *The Sunday Times*, London, 30 November 1980.

20.   *The Observer*, London, 1 February 1981.

21.   See Serfontein, H., 'The Collapse of Botha's Constellation Strategy', *African Affairs*, No. 111, November 1980, p. 48.

22.   See *Africa*, No. 104, April 1981.

23.   Ronald Weittzer, 'In Search of Regime Security: Zimbabwe since Independence', *Journal of Modern African Studies*, 22, 4 1984, pp. 529–57.

24.   South Africa Institute of Race Relations, *Survey of Race Relations*, 1980, p. 207.

25.   See Hoare, M., *The Seychelles Affair*, London, Bantam Press, 1986, pp. 46, 62.

26.   Johnson and Martin (eds), *Destructive Engagement*, p. 44.

27.   *The Herald*, 27 October 1989.

28.   Government of Zimbabwe, Central Statistical Office, *Quarterly Statistical Bulletin*, Second Quarter 1980, p. 26, Table 19, and Economist Intelligence Unit, *Quarterly Economic Review*, Third Quarter, October 1980.

29.   Hanlon, *Apartheid's Second Front*, p. 61. and see Patel, H.H., 'Zimbabwe', *Survival*, Jan/Feb. 1988, Vol. XXX, No. 1, p. 48.

30.   Johnson and Martin, *Destructive Engagement*, p. 47.

31.   Ibid., p. 49.

32. Ibid., p. 48.
33. *The Herald*, 25 July 1982. See also Hanlon, J. 'Destabilisation and the Battle to Reduce Dependence', in Stoneman, C. (ed.), *Zimbabwe's Prospects*, p. 39.
34. Johnson and Martin, *Destructive Engagement*, p. 48; and see Patel, H.H., 'Zimbabwe', p. 48.
35. *The Herald*, Harare, 29 January 1982.
36. Ibid., 11 June 1988; *The Star* (International Airmail Weekly, Johannesburg), 23 February 1988.
37. *The Herald*, Harare, 22 June 1989.
38. Ibid.
39. *The Herald*, 23 August 1982; and Economist Intelligence Unit, *Quarterly Economic Report*, Fourth Quarter, October 1982, p. 8.
40. *Africa News*, 13 September 1983.
41. For a detailed discussion see Johnson and Martin *Destructive Engagement*; Hanlon, *Apartheid: Second Front* and Thompson, C.B., *Challenge to Imperialism: The Frontline States in the Liberation of Zimbabwe*, Harare, Zimbabwe Publishing House, 1985.
42. See Hanlon, 'Destabilisation and the Battle to Reduce Dependence'.
43. Ibid.
44. *The Herald*, 6 January 1986.
45. Economist Intelligence Unit, *Country Report*, No. 2. 1986, p. 10.
46. Ibid., *Quarterly Economic Report*, No. 4, 1985. In mid-1986 the CIO's regular liaison meetings with the South African Military Intelligence were stopped.
47. Economist Intelligence Unit, *Country Report*, No. 3, 1986, p. 13.
48. *The Herald*, 16 October 1987; 16 November 1987.
49. See Dan O'Meara, 'Destabilization of the Frontline States of Southern Africa, 1980–1987', Background Paper, Canadian Institute for International Peace and Security, June 1988, No. 20. p. 6.
50. Commonwealth Committee of Foreign Ministers on Southern Africa, *South Africa and Its Neighbours*, Harare, August 1989. (The study was compiled by David Martin and Phyllis Johnson under the auspices of the Southern African Research and Documentation Centre) See section on Zimbabwe, p. 2.
51. Ibid., p. 12.
52. Ibid.
53. Ibid.
54. Ibid.
55. The MNR was formed and largely sponsored by the Smith regime to counteract ZANLA incursion from Mozambique. See Johnson and Martin, *Destructive Engagement*.
56. *The Herald*, 14 May 1985. The substation, i.e. Chimaura substation, carries hydroelectricity from the Cabora Bassa Dam to the central and northern provinces of Mozambique.
57. ZIFA does not seem to have been effective on paper. Part of its strategy was to infiltrate ZANU(PF). For instance, in October 1987, seven Sithole supporters were apprehended and charged with recruiting potential dissidents for Ndabaningi Sithole's ZIFA. About 48 people were alleg-

edly recruited for military training in South Africa. The seven men, who also held leadership positions with the ZANU(PF), were members of a committee responsible for recruiting volunteers who could receive military training in South Africa. Of the 48 men recruited between 1985 and 1987 only six have been brought to court.

58. *The Sunday Mail* (Harare), 8 November 1987; Parliament of Zimbabwe, Parliamentary Debates, 24 January 1989.
59. See Africa Watch, Zimbabwe, *A Break with the Past? Human Rights and Political Unity* (London), October 1989, pp. 79–81; Parliament of Zimbabwe, *Parliamentary Debates*, 24 January 1989.
60. Africa Watch (see note 59).
61. See *The Herald*, 11 May, 27 July 1987; *The Times* (London), 28 November 1987.

3 ZIMBABWEAN DEFENCE AND SECURITY POLICY IN THE CONTEXT OF THE SOUTH AFRICAN THREAT

1. 'Total onslaught' was a belief by the South African policymakers that there was a conspiracy between Moscow and its allies to overthrow its government and replace it with a Marxist-orientated form of government. A crucial element in the argument was that the ANC was the Soviet Trojan horse. This formulation of the problem had two important advantages for white South Africa. On the one hand, all criticisms of apartheid could be dismissed as communist-inspired. On the other hand, it allowed South Africa to demand that the West support it as a bastion against communism, despite any distaste for apartheid; when the West attacks apartheid it only aids Moscow. The concept 'Total Onslaught' shaped South Africa's ideological and political atmosphere in which the state policy was formulated. As observed by General Magnus Malan, 'Total onslaught is an ideologically motivated struggle and the aim is the implacable and unconditional imposition of the aggressor's will on the target state .... South Africa is today ... involved in total war. The war is not only an area for the soldier. Everyone is involved and has a role to play.' See Kenneth Grundy, *The Militarisation of South African Politics*, Bloomington, Indiana University Press, 1986, p. 11.
2. Zimbabwe's socialism was mere rhetoric because since independence the government's programme was more of a capitalist development rather than of transition to socialism.
3. Johnson, P. and Martin, D. (eds), *Destructive Engagement: Southern Africa at War*, Harare: Zimbabwe Publishing House, 1986, p. 46.
4. Extract from an address by the Zimbabwean Foreign Minister, The Hon. Witness Magwende, to the 37th session of the UN General Assembly, in New York, on 11 October 1982. See *Southern Africa Record*, No. 30, February 1983, p. 5.
5. Interview with Prime Minister Robert Mugabe by Robert MacNeil and Jim Lehrer, broadcast on Voice of America, transcript published in *The Star*, Johannesburg, 12 April, 1980.

6. Gann, L. H. and Duignan, P., *Africa South of the Sahara: The Challenge to Western Security*, Stanford Hoover Institution Press, 1981, p. 20.

7. *The Star*, Johannesburg, 12 April, 1980.

8. Although Mugabe might have favoured such policies the point is that South Africa's threat made them more necessary.

9. See William, R. H., 'Political Scenarios and their Economic Implication', *Journal of Commonwealth and Comparative Politics*, Vol. 18, 1980, p. 5.

10. The inquiry was about the distribution of motor vehicles from the Willowvale car plant in which the state has a stake in terms of ownership. Vehicles were bought from this place by some politicians, civil servants and business figures who then sold them at much higher prices. This came to be known as the 'Willowgate' car scandal.

11. See Lloyd, S., 'The Context of the Democracy Debate', in Mandaza, I. and Sachikonye, L. (eds), *The One-Party State and Democracy: The Zimbabwe Debate*, Harare, Southern Africa Political Economy Series Trust, 1991, p. 45.

12. Dumiso Dabengwa and Lookout Masuku were the key ZAPU leaders. Dabengwa was a former ZIPRA intelligence chief, and Masuku was a ZIPRA commander. Dabengwa and Masuku were charged with organizing the arms caching. They were acquitted after a trial which ran from 2 February to 27 April 1983. Masuku died later in 1986.

13. AFP, Harare, 9 June, 9 Aug. and 11 Oct. 1982.

14. Banana, C. S., *Turmoil and Tenacity: Zimbabwe 1890–1990*, Harare, College Press, p. 241.

15. See Evans, M., *The Front line States, South Africa and Southern African Security: Military Prospects and Perspectives*, Harare, University of Zimbabwe, 1986, p. 10.

16. See R. Weitzer, 'Responding to South African Hegemony: The Case of Zimbabwe', paper presented at the annual meeting of the African Studies Association, November 23–6, 1985, pp. 2–7; See also *Herald*, Harare, 29 January 1981.

17. Johnson and Martin, *Destructive Engagement: Southern Africa at War*, p. 49. In one stroke Pretoria destroyed the only serious air force in the region ranged against South African air supremacy.

18. Zimbabwe Ministry of Information Press Statement 19/81/SFS 'Defence Agreement Signed', 12 January 1981.

19. The link with Mozambique goes back to Zimbabwe's guerrilla war for independence when Mozambique provided bases for the fighters of Mugabe's ZANLA.

20. Zambia, Mozambique and Tanzania contributed substantially to the liberation of Zimbabwe. They assisted Zimbabwe in training their freedom fighters, allowed Zimbabwe to use their countries as a base to attack Rhodesia, they looked after Zimbabwean refugees, and provided them with some education. All these programmes cost the individual countries money which could have been spent on developing their own national projects. Zambia and Mozambique suffered a great deal from Rhodesian attacks.

21. Zimbabwe has been outspoken in three major forums; the United Nations Security Council, the Non-Aligned Movement, and the OAU. In the United Nations Security Council, Zimbabwe in 1989 did not compromise in its condemnation of the United States in its intervention in Grenada and Panama. Likewise Zimbabwe condemned the Soviet Union in its intervention in Afghanistan and in 1990 Zimbabwe condemned a fellow non-aligned state, Iraq, in its invasion of Kuwait.

22. *The Herald*, Harare, 9 August, 1986.

23. *Financial Gazette*, Harare, 18 July 1986.

24. For Mugabe's comments see the *Herald* (Harare), 8 August, 1985.

25. *The Herald* (Harare), 12 November 1985.

26. *The Herald* (Harare), 12 November 1986.

27. See Patel, H., 'South Africa's Destabilisation Policy', *The Round Table*, July 1987, Issue 303, p. 308.

28. Ibid.

29. *The Times* (London), 11 March 1987.

30. *Chronicle* (Bulawayo), 2 February 1987.

31. *The Herald* (Harare), 1 August 1986. See also *The Times* (London), 17 October, 1986.

32. The ZPM was a special army formed in 1982 for internal security against ZAPU and South Africa. This army was trained by the North Koreans. It is also known as the fifth brigade.

33. The recruiting of more soldiers was going to create a big problem for the Zimbabwean economy, and the government was not going to be able to finance that arm. For a view of the ZPM, see *The Zimbabwe National Army* Magazine (July 1986), p. 12.

34. *The Times* (London), 30 October 1986.

35. This was announced at a wings ceremony at Thornhill air base where 25 pilots received wings, 20 of whom were trained in China. For Mugabe's speech, see *The Sunday Mail* (Harare), 25 May 1986.

36. *The Times* (London), 13 April 1987.

37. Banana, C. S., *Turmoil and Tenacity: Zimbabwe 1890–1990*, p. 296.

38. Report of the Rapporteur, OAU Defence Commission, ninth ordinary session (Harare, Def/Rapt (IX), 27–30 May 1986. See also *The Herald* (Harare), 11 June 1986.

39. The Karanga is a tribe found within Masvingo and the Midlands province on the south-west of Harare.

40. See generally *Statement by the Catholic Commission for Justice: Peace on the Renewal of the State of Emergency*, 25 July 1989, and see *Zimbabwe: A Break with the Past? Human Rights and Political Unity*, an Africa Watch Report, London, 1989, note 18.

4 ECONOMIC SABOTAGE

1. Economist Intelligent Unit, *Quarterly Economic Review*, Third Quarter 1980 p. 12.

2. ODI (Overseas Development Institute) Briefing Paper, 'Sanction and South Africa's neighbours' (London 1987), p. 14.

3. Hanlon, J. *Beggar Your Neighbours: Apartheid Power in Southern Africa*, London, Indiana University Press, Catholic Institute of International Relations, 1986, p. 188. This delay caused many shortages of essential goods like oil supplies and fertilizer, which resulted in hitting Zimbabwe badly over the Christmas of 1981. Travel was impossible, cars were abandoned, factories closed, power cuts became frequent and Harare appealed to the world for help.

4. Hanlon, *Beggar Your Neighbours*, p. 189.

5. Reprinted in *South Africa Digest*, 9 September 1981, p. 23.

6. *The Times* (London), 5 January 1981.

7. During the first half of 1981 diesel supplies fell to 80 per cent of normal national requirements. *The Herald*, 26 July 1981.

8. *African Business*, May 1982, p. 23.

9. *Financial Gazette*, Harare, 10 May 1982. In the end, most of the delayed exports were moved. The delay to sugar proved expensive because sugar prices were falling rapidly during 1981 and 1982. There were other costs, too, particularly in agriculture, industry and transport due to the fuel storages but these are impossible to quantify.

10. The Zimbabwean financial year runs from January to December.

11. *African Business*, May 1982, p. 22.

12. Zimbabwe's industrial and manufacturing sector produces an amazing range of 6200 different products, one of the most advanced by African standards.

13. Standard Chartered Bank, *Africa Quarterly Review*, December 1981, p. 10.

14. Economist Intelligence Unit, *Quarterly Economic Review*, Third Quarter, October 1982, p. 15.

15. *Quarterly Digest of Statistics*, Central Statistical Office, Harare, 1980, p. 22.

16. *The Financial Gazette* (Harare), 22 September 1989.

17. Ibid.

18. Ibid.

19. Ibid.

20. See Johnson, P. and Martin, D., *Apartheid Terrorism: The Destabilisation Report*, London, The Commonwealth Secretariat, 1989, p. 57. As a result of the destruction of Zimbabwean-owned vehicles and the overall foreign currency constraints resulting from destabilization, many haulage contracts have gone to non-Zimbabwean companies in the region which were subsidiaries of South African-owned companies. Zimbabwean operators had been forced to hire equipment from South Africa and this involved foreign currency loss to Zimbabwe and gain for South Africa.

21. *Business Herald* (Harare), 26 October 1989.

22. *The Herald*, 30 October 1981.

23. *African Business*, January 1982, p. 18.

24. South African Broadcasting Corporation, *Home Service News*, 3 November 1981. Reprinted in *African Business*, January 1982, p. 18.

25. South Africa ultimately expelled about 20 000 Zimbabwean migrant workers in 1982. *African Business*, January 1982, p. 20.

26. See Anders Nilsson, *Unmasking the Bandits: The True Face of the MNR*, London, 1990.
27. *African Research Bulletin, Economic Technical and Scientific Series*, 15 January–14 February 1983; *The Herald*, 10 December 1982.
28. The purchase was funded by the Kuwait Fund for Arab Development. *African Business*, January 1983, p. 10.
29. *The Herald*, 16 July 1981. The decision to pump fuel directly from Beira was necessitated by the fact that the Feruka Oil Refinery, owned by the CAPREV Group of oil companies could not be quickly rehabilitated. After years of neglect, the cost of re-opening the refinery was too high.
30. Zimbabwe Ministry of Transport, November 1982.
31. Commonwealth Committee of Foreign Ministers on Southern Africa, *South Africa and Its Neighbours*, London, Commonwealth Secretariat, p. 28.
32. *The Herald*, 10 December 1982; *Africa Research Bulletin, Economic, Technical and Scientific Series*, 15 January–14 February 1983. In June 1983, the Zimbabwe National Army captured saboteurs who had South African manufactured equipment and were on a mission to blow up the Maputo–Harare railway line. See *Africa Confidential*, 30 March 1983.
33. Jenkins, S., 'Destabilisation in Southern Africa', *The Economist*, July, 1983, p. 24.
34. Commonwealth Committee of Foreign Ministers on Southern Africa, *South Africa and Its Neighbours*, p. 28.
35. Hanlon, *Beggar Your Neighbours*, p. 195.
36. In January 1987, two senior customs officials were charged with passing sensitive customs information to South Africa since 1983. *The Herald*, Harare, 10 January 1987.
37. *Africa Research Bulletin, Political, Social and Cultural Series*, 1–31 July 1987, p. 15.
38. Davies, R., 'Sanctions and Zimbabwe', *Southern Africa Political and Economic Monthly*, October 1985, p. 16.
39. Government of the Republic of Zimbabwe, *Budget Speeches* of 1986.
40. *African Business*, March, 1983, p. 16.
41. *Africa Research Bulletin, Economic, Technical and Scientific Series*, July 1986, p. 20.
42. Ibid.
43. *The Herald*, 11 July 1986.
44. *The Financial Gazette* (Harare), 6 November 1987.

5 DESTABILIZATION AND ECONOMIC SANCTIONS: THE IMPACT ON ZIMBABWE

1. *The Herald*, Harare, 20 October 1987.
2. Ibid.
3. See United Nations Programme of Action for Africa, *South African Destabilization. The Economic Cost of Frontline Resistance to Apartheid*, October 1989.

4. *The Herald*, 20 October 1989. The killing of the railway personnel was all part of the strategy, to create fear, dissatisfaction and a sense of hopelessness among the railway workers, so that they could direct their frustration and fury at their government.
5. *The Herald*, 20 October 1988.
6. Zimbabwe Broadcasting Corporation (ZBC) *News Bulletin*, 15 October, 1985. Mugabe was quite clear about the economic consequences of sanctions, but he considered the cost of such policies as economic sanctions against South Africa to be short-term necessities in the face of a fundamental threat to the stability of the new Zimbabwe.
7. Martin Roger, 'Southern Africa: A New Approach', *The Round Table* (1987), 303, p. 325. Thus, while the the debates in the mid-1980s revolved around the costs of damaging economic ties with the country's most important economic partner, South Africa, anti-apartheid sanctions were representative of more abstract debates over fundamental ideological issues. The cost of economic warfare had become an important issue over all other more abstract principles and most fundamental interests, essential for national survival.
8. The pan-Africanists were those committed to racial equality and the promotion of comprehensive international sanctions against South Africa, military defence of neighbouring Mozambique in the face of South African sponsored insurgency and the promotion of Southern African regional cooperation through SADCC. The strengthening of their cooperation and solidarity with other black-ruled states was more important.
9. The distinction being drawn here is primarily that between national and transnational class interests; dependency approaches emphasize the predominance of transnational rather than national capital. Throughout the sanctions controversy, Zimbabwean business attempted to distance itself from association with South African business by articulating its position in terms of national economic interests. In addition, dependency analyses tend to assume that South African capital's regional interests were identical with those of the South African state, an assumption which is problematic, but beyond the scope of this thesis.
10. *Africa Confidential*, Vol. 27, No. 25, 1986, p. 8.
11. A Parliamentary Commission of Inquiry later found Minister Ushewokunze to be incompetent rather than corrupt.
12. *The Herald*, Harare, 23 May 1986.
13. *The Herald*, Harare, 4 July 1986. An editorial on 6 July 1986 in *The Sunday Mail*, Harare, the Sunday edition of the *Herald*, however, expressed some doubt about the sincerity of this CZI declaration. Rumours also circulated that, privately, none of the members supported sanctions. In addition, *The Financial Gazette*, 11 July 1986 reported objections from CZI members over the procedures used in the vote on the proposal. Nevertheless, public support for government policy eliminated one important avenue for influencing policy, regardless of the (in)sincerity of the declaration.
14. *The Herald*, 9 August 1986. It resulted in causing a lot of shortages of domestic goods in Zimbabwe.

15. The mini-summit was held in London in August 1986 and was attended by all members of the Commonwealth. Estimated costs of various measures were still being debated, but the principle of sanctions had been accepted. This shift in opinion coincided with wide-ranging international support for sanctions. With the exception of Britain, Commonwealth countries agreed to partial sanctions, the European Community passed similar measures in September 1986, and the United States adopted more stringent sanctions in October 1986.

16. *Africa Research Bulletin, Economic and Technical Series*, August 31, 1986, p. 10.

17. Ibid. Imports rose by 18 per cent (compared to 1985) to Z$162 million while exports were worth Z$105 million.

18. *The Herald*, Harare, 6 August 1986.

19. *The Herald*, Harare, 25 September 1986.

20. Information supplied by a senior civil servant in Harare, 10 August 1992.

21. Southern African Transport and Communications Commission (SATCC) *Annual Report*, 1987, p. 8.

22. Ibid., p. 10.

23. The Tazara line provides an option for Zimbabwe traders from traditional Mozambican and South African ports. It runs across 1860 kilometres of rugged, often sparsely populated terrain from Kapiri Mposhi junction near the Zambian copper mines to the Tanzanian port of Dar-es-Salaam.

24. These conferences were designed to sustain attention on apartheid, to strengthen sanctions, and to counter South African propaganda and media censorship. They also oversee the development of the rehabilitation of the Beira port and the railway route along the Limpopo linking Zimbabwe with the Mozambican port of Maputo. The conference liaised with the SADCC countries.

25. *African Business*, April 1988, p. 14.

26. SATCC *Annual Report*, 1988, p. 6.

27. It also became apparent that there was a necessity for an extended service to East Africa to meet the region's shipping requirements to and from the USA. This was accomplished by Bankline East Africa (BLEA) exercising their conference rights on the East Africa–USA route and coming to a slot charter agreement with the Safbank line. BLEA subsequently provided shippers with a coastal feeder service for containerized cargo between Beira and Mombasa. This latter development provided the Central African region not only with scheduled services to and from East Africa but also with trans–shipment opportunities on the deep-seas services to those SADCC shippers wishing to exploit import and export markets in the Indian sub-continent and the Middle East.

28. SATCC *Annual Report*, 1988, p. 14.

29. *The Herald*, 28 February 1989.

30. Ibid., 21 February 1989.

31. Ibid.

32. SATCC *Annual Report*, 1988, p. 15.

33. *The Herald*, 12 August 1988.
34. Ibid., 29 June 1989.
35. In May 1989, the Mozambique government established a commission of inquiry chaired by the Interior Minister to investigate theft in the country's ports and railways.
36. *The Herald*, 14 September 1989.
37. SATCC *Annual Report*, 1988, p. 15.
38. *The Herald*, 10 August 1989. On average there was about one attack a week on the railway track, but only one on a train.
39. With Zimbabwe maintaining up to 12 000 troops in the corridor it cost about Z$1 million per day.
40. *The Financial Gazette*, 13 October 1989.
41. Ibid.
42. In 1989, the BCG restructured itself into BCG Limited with the previous debentures converted into shares and most members subscribing to an additional US$2500 share. Malawian members were setting up a separate sister company.
43. The political changes were marked by the release of Mandela and other political prisoners, the unbanning of all political parties and the willingness of President de Klerk to negotiate.
44. An interview I had with South African economists, Harare, 6 August, 1992.
45. *The Financial Gazette*, 12 October 1988.
46. *African Business*, October 1989, p. 10.
47. Ibid.
48. Ibid.
49. Hanlon J., 'On the Front Line: Destabilisation, the SADCC states and sanctions', in Mark Orkin (ed.), *Sanctions Against Apartheid*, London, CIIR, 1989, p. 174.
50. Ibid., p. 197.
51. 'Zimbabwe National Chamber of Commerce, (ZNCC)', *Commerce*, May 1989, p. 19.
52. See Hayes, J.P., *Economic Effects of Sanctions on South Africa*, London, Gower, 1987, p. 12.
53. *The Herald*, 23 June 1988.
54. See Silavecky, Z., *An Assessment of the Likely Effects of South African Economic Sanctions Upon (A) Countries of the Region; (B) Zimbabwe* (mimeo), Standard Chartered Limited, Harare, 1986.
55. 'Budget Speech', Harare, July 1988.
56. *Business Herald*, 2 November 1989.
57. KLM had suspended flights to Harare in 1989 and Air Zimbabwe flights to Holland were also stopped following a dispute which had remained unresolved from 1987.
58. See Hayes, *Economic Effects of Sanctions*.
59. Ibid.
60. See 'Zimbabwe National Chambers of Commerce', May 1989, p. 21.
61. See Silavecky, *An Assessment of the Likely Effects*.
62. SATCC *Annual Report*, 1988, p. 15.
63. See Hayes, *Economic Effects of Sanctions*.

64.   See Silavecky, *An Assessment of the Likely Effects.*
65.   Ibid., p. 10.
66.   *African Business*, October 1989, p. 22. South Africa would not have been pleased with this at all because it would have worked to its disadvantage.

6   OVERALL ECONOMIC AND SOCIAL IMPACT OF DESTABILIZATION

1.   See Johnson, P. and Martin, D., *Apartheid Terrorism: The Destabilisation Report*, London, The Commonwealth Secretariat in Association with James Currey, 1989. p. 67.
2.   See Hanlon J., 'Destabilisation and the Battle to Reduce Dependence', in Stoneman, Colin (ed.), *Zimbabwe's Prospects*, London, Macmillan, 1988, p. 42.
3.   Geldenhuys D., *The Diplomacy of Isolation: South African Foreign Policy Making*, Johannesburg, Macmillan, 1984, p. 145.
4.   ZIMCORD is an acronym for the Zimbabwe Conference on Reconstruction and Development. This was a major fund-raising conference held in Harare in 1981. Zimbabwe was able to raise about US$52 billion to finance various projects during the following three years.
5.   See Thompson, Carol B., 'Toward Economic Liberation: Zimbabwe in Southern African Regional Development' *Contemporary Marxism*, No. 7, 1983, p. 12.
6.   Three central provinces were Manica, Sofala and Tete, where MNR had camps.
7.   UN Economic Commission for Africa, *South African Destabilization: The Economic Cost of Frontline to Apartheid*, Addis Abbaba, October 1989, pp. 1–5. According to Roger Martin this cost conceals a vast disparity between the Lusophone and Anglophone countries. See Roger Martin 'Regional Security in Southern Africa: More Angolas, Mozambiques or Neutrals?', *Survival*, September/October 1987, Vol. XXIX, No. 5, p. 389.
8.   See *The Military Balance 1986/87*, London: International Institute for Strategic Studies, 1986, p. 139.
9.   Ibid., p. 139.
10.   *Africa Research Bulletin, Economic Scientific and Technical Series*, 15 July–14 August 1983, p. 22.
11.   *The Herald*, Harare, 10 July 1988.
12.   *The Financial Gazette*, 20 January 1989.
13.   *The Herald*, Harare, 12 October, 1989.
14.   Johnson and Martin, *Apartheid Terrorism: The Destabilisation Report*, p. 73.
15.   *The Financial Gazette*, 20 January 1989
16.   Ibid.
17.   *Africa Economic Digest*, 'Special Report on Zimbabwe', April, 1986, p. 4.

18. Ibid., p. 3.
19. Ibid., p. 3
20. Central Statistical Office, Harare, 1987, p. 6.
21. For further information see Ranger, Terence, 'Matebeleland since the Amnesty', *African Affairs*, Vol. 88, No. 351, 1989, pp. 161–73.
22. *African Business*, August 1987.
23. *The Financial Gazette*, 5 May 1989; RAL Merchant Bank Limited, *Zimbabwe Quarterly Guide to the Economy*, 5 March 1989, p. 4.
24. Ibid.
25. RAL Merchant Bank Limited, *Zimbabwe Quarterly Guide to the Economy*, 5 March 1982, p. 12.
26. Computed from various Quarterly Statistical Reports, Central Statistical Office, Harare 1980, 1982, 1984. The increment in the debt service ratio on the export earnings was caused by the disruption of transport.
27. *African Economic Digest*, 'Special Report on Zimbabwe', April 1988.
28. RAL Merchant Bank Limited, *Zimbabwe Quarterly Guide to the Economy*, 5 March 1982, p. 20.
29. See Stoneman C., and Cliffe, L., *Zimbabwe: Politics, Economics and Society*, London, Frances Pinter, 1989, p. 153.
30. *The Herald*, Harare, 2 June 1984, This was echoed by Mr John Laurie, who was the President of the Commercial Farmers' Union.
31. *African Business*, October, 1986, p. 13.
32. *The Sunday Mail*, Harare, 22 September 1989. At independence, all the large-scale commercial farmers were white. Since 1980, there has been a substantial purchase of land by senior government officials and the growing black elite.
33. Stoneman, C., 'The Economy: Recognising the Reality', in Stoneman, C. (ed.), *Zimbabwe's Prospects*, London, Macmillan, 1988, p. 55.
34. Government of the Republic of Zimbabwe Transitional National Development Plan, Harare 1983 p. 26.
35. A survey conducted by the Confederation of Zimbabwe Industries (CZI) in late 1988 to early 1989 showed a continuation of the trend towards localization of the economy that started during the period of the Smith regime. Less comprehensive studies carried out between 1985 and 1987 indicated that foreign ownership of the manufacturing sector stood at between 48.1 and 52.3 per cent. See CZI, *Survey of Manufacturing Enterprises*, Harare 1984, p. 3.
36. CZI, Survey of Manufacturing Enterprises. Harare, 1989. See also *The Herald*, 13 April 1989; Standard Chartered Africa, *Quarterly Review*, October 1989, p. 15.
37. *African Business*, August 1984.
38. *African Economic Digest*, 'Special Report on Zimbabwe', April 1987, p. 25.
39. Ibid.
40. Ibid.
41. *The Financial Gazette*, 27 January 1989.
42. The major supplier, the Iron and Steel Corporation (ISCOR) of South Africa, accounts for 70 per cent of Zimbabwe's flat steel and profile

products; it alleged that it could not meet the country's orders because of increased demand in South Africa.

43. *The Herald*, 14 October 1989.
44. Ibid., 2 March 1989.
45. See Government of the Republic of Zimbabwe, The Promotion of Investment Policy and Regulations, Harare, April 1989.
46. The conference, said to be the largest organized by the CBI, attracted 350 delegates, double the number who attended similar conferences on Kenya and Saudi Arabia.
47. Government of the Republic of Zimbabwe, *The Promotion of Investment Policy and Regulations*, Harare, April 1989.
48. Ibid.

7 SOUTH AFRICA'S DESTABILIZATION OF ZIMBABWE: SUCCESS OR FAILURE?

1. For a joint statement issued by the governments of South Africa and Zimbabwe on 3 September 1980 on trade representation, see *Southern Africa Record*, no. 21, October 1980, pp. 47–8.
2. Geldenhuys, D., 'Some Foreign Policy Implications of South Africa's Total National Strategy', Johannesburg, *South Africa Institute of International Affairs*, 1981, p. 20.
3. Johnson P. and Martin, D., *Destructive Engagement: Southern Africa at War*, Harare, Zimbabwe Publishing House, 1986, p. 46.
4. See Geldenhuys, D., 'South Africa's Regional Policy', in Michael Clough (ed.), *Changing Realities in Southern Africa: Implications for American Policy*, Berkeley, University of California, Institute of International Studies, Research Series No. 47, 1982, p. 157.
5. See *The Star*, Johannesburg, 4 March 1980.
6. See Nkiwane, S. M., 'Development of Zimbabwe's Foreign Relations 1980–1990,' *The Round Table*, April, 1993, 326, pp. 199–216.
7. The trade agreement covered the preferential customs duties for Zimbabwe's exports to South Africa, as well as guaranteed quotas for some products. This agreement dated from the UDI period, and in 1980 had allowed $54 million of Zimbabwean radios, clothing, and steel rod and wire into South Africa. Up to 7000 jobs were affected. See Hanlon, J., *Beggar Your Neighbours*, London, James Currey Publishers, 1986, p. 186.
8. During the Rhodesian period the South African Railways had seconded its technicians to Rhodesian Railways, to assist in the running of the railway. These were called back to South Africa at the time when white Rhodesian technicians were going to South Africa, while some of the remaining whites were used to sabotage the operation. This created a problem because there were only few black trained artisans by that time.

9.   Klotz Audie, 'Race and Nationalism in Zimbabwe Foreign Policy', *The Round Table*, July 1993, 327, pp. 255–79.

10. This report came from an official of a large US Bank. See Hanlon, J., 'Destabilisation and the Battle to Reduce Dependence', in Colin Stoneman (ed.), *Zimbabwe's Prospects*, London, Macmillan, 1988, p. 35.

11. Hanlon, *Beggar Your Neighbours*, p. 189.

12. Ibid., pp. 32–3.

13. Hanlon, J., 'Destabilisation and the Battle to Reduce Dependence', in Colin Stoneman (ed.), *Zimbabwe's Prospects*, p. 36.

14. Hanlon, *Beggar Your Neighbours*, p. 189. The arrival of the Indian and Pakistani artisans lessened Zimbabwe's transport problem. Zimbabwe was able to train its own people with their help.

15. Hanlon, *Beggar Your Neighbours*, pp. 190–1.

16. During South Africa's disruption of Zimbabwean transport Mugabe complained and the US intervened. Mugabe campaigned for sanctions against South Africa in the following organizations; the Commonwealth, the UN, the Non-Aligned Movement and the OAU.

17. The economic blockade by South Africa on Zimbabwe went on only for a year because of the intervention by the international community who put some pressure on the Pretoria government to stop disrupting the Zimbabwean economy.

18. See *The Herald*, October, 1983. In his report to the journalists about the Matabeleland security problem, Mugabe told them that Botswana was not cooperating in eradicating dissidents because South Africa was recruiting dissidents from Dukwe Camp in Botswana and was infiltrating them back into the country through Botswana. See Also Richard Hodder Williams, 'Conflict in Zimbabwe: The Matabeleland Problem', London, Conflict Studies, No. 151, The Institute for the Study of Conflict, 1983, p. 13. Richard Williams offers that Malcolm 'Matt' Calloway, a former Rhodesian Special Branch member and CIO head at Hwange and Beitbridge in Zimbabwe, was later found to be a South African agent who recruited Super-ZAPU from Botswana into South Africa and assisted ex-ZIPRA elements. The Phalaborwa camp in Northern Transvaal was the training base for both Super-ZAPU and MNR and the headquarters of the 5th Reconnaissance Regiment which included white ex-Rhodesian soldiers.

19. See *Horizon*, Harare, February, 1994. See the report on 'The Tribal row Jongwe', where the Matabeleland North governor, W. Mabhena, voiced his views about the practice of tribalism by 'certain individuals' within state institutions. His major complaint was that there was little development in Matabeleland, and the government needed to do more.

20. *The Herald*, 22 December 1987. Mugabe at the signing of the Unity Accord.

21. Inkomo was one of the new army's main arsenals, it contained much of the arms and ammunition which ZIPRA and ZANLA guerrilla forces had brought back to Zimbabwe. According to Hanlon all these arms were destroyed and they were worth Z$50 million. See Hanlon, *Beggar Your Neighbours*, p. 175.

22. *The Herald*, 19 December, 1981. One hundred and twenty four people were injured; these were Christmas shoppers who were packed outside on the street. The dead were workers and customers of a neighbouring bakery which was also destroyed.

23. See Stoneman, and Cliffe, L., *Zimbabwe: Politics, Economics and Society*, London, Pinter, 1989, p. 147.

24. Hanlon J. 'Destabilisation and the Battle to Reduce Dependence', in Stoneman, C. (ed.), *Zimbabwe's Prospects*, London, Macmillan 1988, p. 42.

25. After the toppling of Dr. Jonathan's government in 1986 South Africa ordered all ANC refugees to be removed from Lesotho. Swaziland also signed a secret security pact with South Africa in 1982 and then two years later Mozambique signed the Nkomati Accord.

26. Although no explicit reference was made to Eastern Europe in order to justify the installation of the one-party state in Africa, it was assumed that the durability of the one-party state model in Eastern Europe demonstrated its feasibility and applicability to Africa. Its collapse in Eastern Europe severely undermined whatever case was still being argued by the advocates of Socialism.

27. See Rotberg, R. 'South Africa in its Region: Hegemony and Vulnerability', in (ed.), Rotberg, R., *South Africa and its Neighbors: Regional Security and Self-Interest*, Toronto, Lexington Books, 1985, p. 9.

28. Hanlon, *Beggar Your Neighbours*, p. 28.

29. Mozambique Briefing No. 3 and No. 2, Maputo, 1987.

30. *Mozambique Information Office News Review*, London, 10 September 1987 and see Hanlon, *Beggar Your Neighbours*, p. 141.

31. Geldenhuys, 'Destabilisation Controversy in Southern Africa', Southern African Forum Position Paper, vol. 5, No. 18, Johannesburg 1982.

32. Quan, J., 'Mozambique, A Cry for Peace', Oxfam, Oxford 1987.

33. Johnson, P. and Martin, D., *Apartheid Terrorism: The Destabilisation Report*, London, The Commonwealth Secretariat in Association with James Currey, 1989, p. 70.

34. The ANC was allowed to maintain a ten-member diplomatic mission; also ANC members actually employed by the government remained. Others were allowed to stay if they accepted a non-political refugee status under the United Nations Commission for Refugees (UNHCR); few did, as this implied giving up their positions as ANC militants, and more than 200 people, including women and children, left Mozambique.

35. Hanlon, J., *Beggar Your Neighbours*, p. 94. There were in fact a number of significant differences in the pact signed by Swaziland and the Nkomati Accord. The agreement with Swaziland committed both states to 'combat terrorism, insurgency and subversion individually and collectively' and to 'call upon each other wherever possible for such assistance and steps as may be deemed necessary'. Each state was also obliged to inform the other about any foreign military personnel in their territory. No such clauses were included in the Nkomati Accord.

36. *The Star*, Johannesburg, 18 April 1983.

37. *Sunday Express*, Johannesburg, 10 June 1984.
38. *Sunday Times*, London, 10 June 1984.
39. *The Sunday Times*, London, 6 June 1984, described one such seminar held in Rome as the 'high point' of the Botha European visit.
40. It was reported that there was great interest in Portugal in participating in tripartite ventures in Southern Africa, and in particular in Mozambique. These would have involved the use of Portuguese technicians in projects financed by Western European or North American concerns, and organized in association with South African firms or the South African subsidiaries of multinationals. It also appeared that some interest was expressed by certain West German and American potential investors in Mozambique in routing their activities through South Africa. *Sunday Times*, London, 3 June 1984.
41. *Rand Daily Mail*, 19 November, 1984.
42. The cause of this was the imposition of rent increases by the regime to finance puppet local administrative authorities.
43. According to the South African Institute of Race Relations, 134 people were killed by the army and police on that day. *The Star*, 28 October, 1984.
44. *Rand Daily Mail*, 8 November 1984.
45. It was at Cuito Cuanavale in Angola that the South African Defence Force suffered a major setback at the hands of the Cuban forces.
46. A plan to take the town by infantry invasion was rejected because it was estimated that it would cost many white conscript lives.
47. It had been estimated that the war in Angola was already costing R4bn a year by mid-1988 and any escalation would have put 'an intolerable strain on an economy, already running out of steam.' *The Sunday Star*, 4 July, 1988.
48. *Weekly Mail*, 8–14 December, 1988.
49. *Weekly Mail*, 24–30 June 1988.
50. See Ottaway, Marina *South Africa: The Struggle for a New Order*, Washington, DC, The Brookings Institution, 1993, p. 207. Further evidence of this is the conjunction of events provided by M. Christie, 'Isolation in South Africa', *South Africa International*, Vol., 2, No. 3, January 1992, p. 143, where he asserts that 'the beginning of formal negotiations aimed at regime change occurred within a week of the Soviet Union ceasing to exist'.

Bibliography

1. BOOKS AND BOOK CHAPTERS

Adam, H. & Moodley, K.   *South Africa Without Apartheid: Dismantling Racial Domination*, London and Berkeley: University of California Press, 1986.

Astrow, A.   *Zimbabwe: A Revolution That Lost Its Way?*, London, Zed Press, 1983.

Banana, C.S.   *Turmoil and Tenacity: Zimbabwe 1890–1990*, Harare, College, 1989.

Bailey, M.   *Oilgate: The Sanctions Scandal*, Hodder and Stoughton, London, 1979.

Barber, J.   *South Africa's Foreign Policy 1945–1970*, Oxford University Press, London, 1973.

Beaufre, A.   *Deterrence and Strategy*, London, Faber, 1965.

Blumenfeld, J.   *Economic Interdependence in Southern Africa: from Conflict to Cooperation*, London, The Royal Institute of International Affairs, 1991.

Boesak, A.   *Black and Reformed*, Johannesburg: Skotaville, 1983.

Brotz, H.   *The Politics of South Africa: Democracy and Racial Diversity*, Oxford University Press, Oxford, 1977.

Cawthra, G.   *Brutal Force: The Apartheid War Machine*, London: International Defence and Aid Fund for Southern Africa, 1986.

Carter, G.M. and O'Meara, P. (eds),   *Southern Africa in Crisis*, Bloomington and London: Indiana University Press, 1977.

Cervenka, Z.   *Land-locked Countries of Africa*, The Scandinavian Institute of African Studies, Uppsala, 1973.

Chan, S.   *Exporting Apartheid: Foreign Policies in Southern Africa 1978–88*, London, Macmillan, 1990.

——   *Kaunda and Southern Africa: Image and Reality in Foreign Policy*, Lynn Reinner, Boulder, 1991.

——   *Issues in International Relations: A View from Africa*, Macmillan, London, 1987.

——   *The Commonwealth in World Politics: A Study of International Action 1965–1985*, Lester Crook, London, 1988.

Chung, F. and Ngara, E.   *Socialism, Education and Development: A Challenge to Zimbabwe*, Harare, Zimbabwe Publishing House, 1985.

Cock, J. and Nathan, L.   *War and Society: The Militarisation of South Africa*, Johannesburg, David Philip, 1989.

Cockram, G.M.   *Vorster's Foreign Policy*, Pretoria; Academia, 1970

Davidson, B.   *The Southern Africa: The New Politics of Revolution*, London: Penguin, 1977.

Davies, R., O'Meara, D. and Dlamini, S.   *The Struggle for South Africa*, London, Zed Books, 1984.

Davies, R.   *South African Strategy Towards Mozambique in the Post-Nkomati Period: A Critical Analysis of Effects and Implications*, Scandinavian Institute of African Studies, Uppsala, 1985, Report No. 73.

Davis, J.   *South Africa, Destabilizing the Region*, New York, Praeger, 1983.

Deutsch, K.W.   *Political Community and the North Atlantic Area*, Princeton University Press, Princeton, 1957.

Doxey, M., *Economic Sanctions and International Enforcement*, Oxford University Press, New York, 1980.

Fauvet, P., *South Africa's War against Mozambique: International Hearing on South African Aggression against Neighbouring States*, Oslo, 1984

Flower, K. *Serving Secretly – Rhodesia into Zimbabwe 1964–1981*, John Murray, London, 1987.

Frankel, P.H. *Pretoria's Praetorians: Civil–Military Relations in South Africa*, London, Cambridge University Press, 1984.

Frederikse, Julie. *None But Ourselves; Masses vs Media in the Making of Zimbabwe*, Harare, Zimbabwe Publishing House, 1982.

Gann, L. and Henriksen, T. *The Struggle for Zimbabwe*. New York Praeger, 1981.

Gann, L.H. and Duignan, P. *Africa South of the Sahara: The Challenge to Western Security*, Stanford, Hoover Institution Press, 1981.

Geldenhuys, D. *The Diplomacy of Isolation: South African Foreign Policy Making*, Cape Town: Macmillan, 1984.

Geldenhuys, D. and Gutteridge, *Instability and Conflict in Southern Africa: South Africa's Role in Regional Security. Conflict Studies*, The Institute for the Study of Conflict, No. 148, London: 1983.

Gordon, L. (ed.), *Survey of Race Relations in South Africa 1980*, Johannesburg, SAIRR.

Grundy, K.W. *Confrontation and Accommodation in Southern Africa*, London and Berkeley: University of California Press, 1973.

Grundy, K.W. *The Militarisation of South African Politics*, Oxford: Oxford University Press, 1987.

Gutteridge, W. *South Africa Strategy for Survival?* London, Institute for the Study of Conflict, No. 131, June 1981.

Halpern, J. *South Africa's Hostages*, London: Penguin, 1965.

Hanlon, J. *Beggar Your Neighbours: Apartheid Power in Southern Africa*. London: CIIR and James Currey 1986.

Herbst, J. *State Politics in Zimbabwe*, Harare: University of Zimbabwe Publications, 1990.

Holnes, M. *Apartheid's War against Angola*, UN: New York, February, 1983.

Jansen, D.J. *Zimbabwe: Government Policy and the Manufacturing Sector*, Larkspur, California. 1986.

Jaster, R. *Southern Africa: Regional Security Problems and Prospects*, International Institute for Strategic Studies and Gower, 1985.

Jaster, R.S. *South Africa's Narrowing Security Options*, Adelphi Papers, No. 159, London, International Institute for Strategic Studies, 1980.

Jensen, L. *Explaining Foreign Policy*, Englewood Cliffs, Prentice Hall, 1982.

Johnson, P. and Martin, D. *The Struggle for Zimbabwe: the Chimurenga War*, Harare: Zimbabwe Publishing House, 1981.

—— *Destructive Engagement: Southern Africa at War*, Harare: Zimbabwe Publishing House, 1986.

—— *Apartheid Terrorism: The Destabilization Report*, London: James Currey, 1989.

Johnson, R.W. *How Long Will South Africa Survive?* London: Macmillan, 1988.

Johnson, S. (ed.), *South Africa: No Turning Back*, London: Macmillan, 1988.

Landgren, S. *Embargo Disimplemented: South Africa's Military Industry*, Oxford: Oxford University Press, 1989.

Legum, C. *The Western Crisis over Southern Africa*, New York, Africana Publishing Company, 1979.

—— *Africa Contemporary Record*, London, Rex Collings, 1977.

Lionel, C. *Zimbabwe's Political Inheritance*, New York: St. Martin's Press, 1981.

—— *Zimbabwe: Politics, Economics and Society*, London: Pinter, 1989.

Mandaza, I. *Zimbabwe: The Political Economy of Transition*, Dakar: Codesria, 1986.

—— *Southern Africa in the 1990s: Towards a Research Agenda*, Harare, Southern Africa Political Economy Series, Occasional Paper Series, No. 1. 1991.

Meli, F.A. *History of the ANC: South Africa Belongs To Us*, London: James Currey, 1988.

Nolutshungu, S.C. *South Africa in Africa: A Study in Ideology and Foreign Policy*, Manchester: Manchester University Press, 1975.

Orkin, M. *Sanctions Against Apartheid.* Johannesburg, David Philip, 1989.

Ranger, T. *Peasant Consciousness and Guerrilla War in Zimbabwe*, London, James Currey, 1985.

Rotberg, R. *South Africa and its Neighbors: Regional Security and Self-Interest*, Toronto, Lexington Books, 1985.

Roussos, P. *Zimbabwe: An Introduction to the Economics of Transformation*, Baobab Books, Harare, 1988.

Shaw, T.M. (ed.) *Confrontation and Liberation in Southern Africa: Regional Directions after the Nkomati Accord*, Boulder, Colorado: Westview, 1987.

—— (ed.) *Southern Africa in the 1980s*, London: George Allen and Unwin, 1985.

Seiler, J. (ed.) *Southern Africa since the Portuguese Coup*, Boulder, Colorado: Westview Press, 1980.

Stoneman, C. *Zimbabwe's Prospects*, London: Macmillan, 1988.

Stoneman, C. and Cliffe, L. *Zimbabwe: Politics, Economics and Society*, London, Pinter Publishers, 1989.

Schatzberg, M.G. *The Political Economy of Zimbabwe*, New York, Praeger, 1984.

Thompson, C.B. *Challenge to imperialism: The Frontline States in the Liberation of Zimbabwe*, Harare, Zimbabwe Publishing House, 1985.

Turok, B. *Witness from the Frontline: Aggression and Resistance in Southern Africa*, London: Institute for African Alternatives, 1990.

Whitside, A.W. *Industrialization and Investment Incentives in Southern Africa: Natal*, Press; James Currey Publishers 1989.

Widner, J. and Foltz, W.J. *The OAU after Twenty Years*, New York, Praeger, 1984.

Wilson, F. *Labour in the South African Gold Mines*, London: Cambridge University Press, 1972.

2. JOURNAL ARTICLES

Anglin, Douglas, G. 'SADCC After Nkomati', *African Affairs*, Vol. 84, No. 335, April, 1985.

Adam, H. 'Outside Influence on South Africa: Afrikanerdom in Disarray', *Journal of Modern African Studies*, Vol. 21, No. 2, 1983.

Aluko, O. 'African Response to External Intervention in Africa since Angola', *African Affairs*, Vol. 80, No. 319, April, 1981

Anglin, D. 'SADCC after Nkomati', *African Affairs*, Vol. 84 No. 335, April 1985.

Bowman, L.W. 'The Strategic Importance of South Africa to the United States: An Appraisal and Policy Analysis', *African Affairs*, Vol. 81, No. 323, April 1982.

Burgess, J. 'Stranglehold in Southern Africa', *African Business*, No. 38, October 1981.

Chingambo L.J. and Chan, S. 'Sanctions and South Africa: Strategies, Strangleholds and Self-Consciousness', *The Kent Journal of International Relations*, Vol. 2, no. 2, winter 1988–89.

Chingambo, L,J. 'SADCC and South Africa: Limits and Realities of Economic Integration under Destabilisation', *The Round Table*, No. 308, October 1988.

Christopher, R. 'Regional Cooperation in Southern Africa', *African Affairs*, Vol. 82, No. 327, April 1983.

Coker, C. 'The Western Alliance and Africa, 1949–81', *African Affairs*, Vol. 81, No. 324, July 1982.

Davies, R. and O'Meara, D. 'Total Strategy in Southern Africa: An analysis of South African Regional Strategy since 1978', *Journal of Southern African Studies*, 11, 2, April 1985.

Davies, R. and O'Meara, D. 'The state of analysis of the Southern African region: Issues raised by South African strategy', *Review of African Political Economy*, No. 29, 1983–84.

Dale, R. 'The Armed Forces as an Instrument of South African Policy in Namibia', *Journal of Modern African Studies*, Vol. 17, No. 1, 1980.

Frankel, P. 'Race and Counter-Revolution: South Africa's Total Strategy', *Journal of Commonwealth and Comparative Politics*, Vol. 28, No. 3, October 1980.

Geldenhuys, D. 'Some Strategic Implications of Regional Economic Relationships for the Republic of South Africa', *ISSUP Strategic Review*, University of Pretoria, January, 1981.

—— 'Destabilisation Controversy in Southern Africa', *SA Forum Position Paper*, Johannesburg, Sept 1982.

—— 'The Destabilisation Controversy – an Analysis of a High Risk Foreign Policy Option for South Africa', *Politikon*, No. 9, December 1982.

—— 'The Constellation of Southern African States and the Southern Development Coordination Council: Towards a New Regional Statemate?', *South African Institute of International Affairs*, Johannesburg, 1981.

Greenberg, S.B. 'Economic Growth and Political Change: The South African Case', *Journal of Modern African Studies*, Vol. 17, No. 4, 1981.

Hallett, R. 'The South African Intervention in Angola 1975–76', *African Affairs*, Vol. 77, No. 303, July 1978.

Hill, C.R. 'UDI and South African Foreign Policy', *Journal of Commonwealth Political Studies*, Vol. 8, No. 2, July 1969.

—— 'Regional Cooperation in Southern Africa', *African Affairs*, Vol. 82, No. 326, January 1983.

Klotz, A. 'Race and Nationalism in Zimbabwean Foreign Policy', *The Round Table*, July 1993.

Legassick, M.   'South Africa in Crisis: What Route To Democracy?' *African Affairs*, Vol. 84, No. 337, October 1985.

Lines, T.   'Investment Sanctions and Zimbabwe: Breaking the Rod', *Third World Quarterly*, Vol. 10, No. 3, July 1988.

Mafeje, A.   'One-Party State in Africa: Reflections and Prospects for Southern Africa', *Southern Africa Political and Economic Monthly (SAPEM)*, September 1989.

Mandaza, I.   'The One-Party State in Africa: Out of Step with Reality?' *SAPEM*, September 1989.

—— 'Democracy in the African Reality', *SAPEM*, February 1990.

—— 'Zimbabwe's First Decade: What of the Next?', *SAPEM*, April 1990.

Matatu, G.   'Southern Africa: An uneasy peace', *Africa*, No. 153, May 1984.

Martin, R.   'Regional Security in Southern Africa: More Angolas, Mozambiques or Neutrals?', *Survival*, September/October 1987, Vol., XXIX, No. 5.

Martin, W.G.   'The Future of Southern Africa: What Prospects after Majority Rule?, *Review of African Political Economy*, No. 50, 1991.

Mkandawire, T.   'Comments on Democracy and Political Instability', *Africa Development*, Vol. 13, No. 3, 1988.

Munslow, B.   'Prospects for the Socialist Transition of Agriculture in Zimbabwe', *World Development*, Vol. 13, No. 1, 1985.

Morris, M.   'South Africa: Political Violence, Reform and Reconstruction', *Review of African Political Economy*, No. 53, 1992.

Moyo, J.   'Democracy in Zimbabwe: A Critical Review', *SAPEM*, February 1989.

—— 'Zimbabwe: A Critical Appraisal of the ZUM Challenge', *SAPEM*, August, 1989.

—— 'Delegates Opposing One-Party State Need Ideological Training, says Party Presidency', *Financial Gazette*, 5 January, 1990.

Moyo, S.   'The Promised Land', *SAPEM*, April 1990.

Moyo, S. and Skalnes, T.   'Zimbabwe's Land Reform and Development Strategy: State Autonomy, Class Bias and Economic Rationality', Zimbabwe Institute of Development Studies (ZIDS) Research Paper, No. 3, 1986.

Munck, R.   'The Constellation of Southern African States: A New Strategic Offensive by South Africa', *Review of African Political Economy*, May/August 1980, no. 18.

Ncube, M.M.   'The U.S., South Africa and Destabilisation in Southern Africa', *Journal of African Marxists*, No. 6. October 1984.

Nkiwane S. M.   'Development of Zimbabwe's Foreign Relations 1980–1990', *The Round Table*, April, 1993.

—— *Self-Interest*, Toronto, Lexington Books, 1985.

O'Meara, D.   Destabilisation in Southern Africa: Total Strategy in Total Disarray', *Monthly Review*, April 1986.

O'Neill, K.   'Ending the Cold War in Southern Africa', *Third World Quarterly*, Vol. 12, Nos 3–4, 1990/91.

Patel, H.H.   'South Africa's Destabilisation Policy', *The Round Table*, July 1987, No. 303.

Palmer, R.   'Land Reform in Zimbabwe, 1980–1990', *African Affairs*, 1989.

Riddell, R.C. 'Zimbabwe: The Economy Four Years after Independence', *African Affairs*, Vol. 83, No. 333, October 1984.

Sakwa, R. 'Gorbachev and the New Soviet Foreign Policy: Paradigms' *Kent Journal of International Relations*, Vol. 2, No. 1, June 1988.

Saul, J.S. 'From Thaw to Flood: The End of the Cold War in Southern Africa', *Review of African Political Economy*, No. 50, 1991.

Sachikonye, L.M. 'The Debate on Democracy in Contemporary Zimbabwe', *Review of African Political Economy*, No. 45/46, 1989.

Sylvester, C. 'Zimbabwe's 1985 Elections: a Search for National Mythology', *Journal of Modern African Studies*, Vol. 24, No. 1, 1986.

Szeftel, M. 'Debate: Manoeuvres of War in South Africa', *Review of African Political Economy*, No. 51, 1991.

Thompson, C.B. 'Regional Economic Policy under Crisis Conditions: The Case of Agriculture within SADCC', *Journal of Southern African Studies*, Vol. 13, No. 1, October, 1986.

Tjonneland, E.N. 'Pax Pretoriana: The Fall of Apartheid and the Politics of Regional Destabilisation', Discussion Paper 2, *Scandinavian Institute of African Studies*, October 1988.

Tostensen, A. 'Regional Cooperation in Southern Africa: the Southern African Development Coordination Conference', *Review of African Political Economy*, No. 23, 1982.

William, R.H. 'Political Scenarios and their Economic Implications', *Journal of Commonwealth and Comparative Politics*, Vol. 18, 1980.

Yates, P. 'The Prospects for Socialist Transition in Zimbabwe', *Review of African Political Economy*, No. 18, 1980.

3. NEWSPAPER ARTICLES

Chung, F. 'Socialism is the Only Answer to the Country's Problems', *The Sunday Mail*, 14 January 1990.

Hornsby, M. 'What Hope for Pulpit Power?', *The Times*, London, 2 March 1988.

Jenkins, S. 'Destabilisation in Southern Africa', *The Economist*, July 16, 1983.

Jone, J.D.F. 'Botha's Point of No Return', *The Financial Times*, 6 August 1982.

Kabweza, M. 'One Party State: What Support?', *Moto*, June 1990.

Makamure, K. 'One-Party State: A Way for Leaders to Secure Permanent Tenure of Office', *Financial Gazette*, 6 April 1990.

Mathema, C. 'Marxism-Leninism and the State: Only Socialism Can Meet the Wishes of the People', *The Herald*, 12 January 1990.

—— Editorial in *Moto*, 'The One-Party State Debate', *Moto*, May 1984.

—— Editorial, 'Zvobgo Opposed to One-Party State', *Moto*, October, 1989.

Ncube, W. 'The Challenge to Build a Better Democracy', *Parade*, September 1990.

Rake, A. 'Africa Demands Democracy', *New African*, May 1990.

Raftopoulos, A. 'The One-Party State Debate', *Moto*, No. 26 August 1984.

Rukobo, A. 'Concept of Democracy in Current Debate is Very Narrow', *Financial Gazette*, 4 May 1990.
—— 'The Way Forward is via the Socialist Path', *The Herald*, 18 July 1990.
Samupindi, T. 'The One-Party System has Failed in Africa' *The Herald*, 26 June 1990.
—— 'The One-Party State and Some Economic Effects', *The Herald*, 27 June 1990.
Sithole, M. 'Consequences of a One-Party State: Political Degeneracy and Decay?' *Financial Gazette*, 13 January 1990.
—— 'No Democracy in a One Party State', *Parade*, August 1990.

4. OTHER DOCUMENTS

Ehrenreich, F. 'National Security in Zimbabwe: A Country Study', (ed.) H. Nelson, Washington DC US Government Printing Office, 1983.
Ministry of Information 'The Root of Armed Banditry', *Mozambique Briefing*, No. 5, 1987.
Weitzer R, 'Responding to South African Hegemony: The Case of Zimbabwe', paper presented at the annual meeting of the African Studies Association, 23–6 November, 1985.
World Bank 'Zimbabwe: Country Economic Memorandum: Performance, Policies and Prospects', 28 October 1985.
—— 'Zimbabwe: Industrial Sector Memorandum' (Belli Report), 22 May 1987.
ZANU (PF) 'Zimbabwe at Five Years of Independence: Achievements, Problems and Prospects', Harare: ZANU(PF), Department of the Commissariat and Culture, 1985.

Index